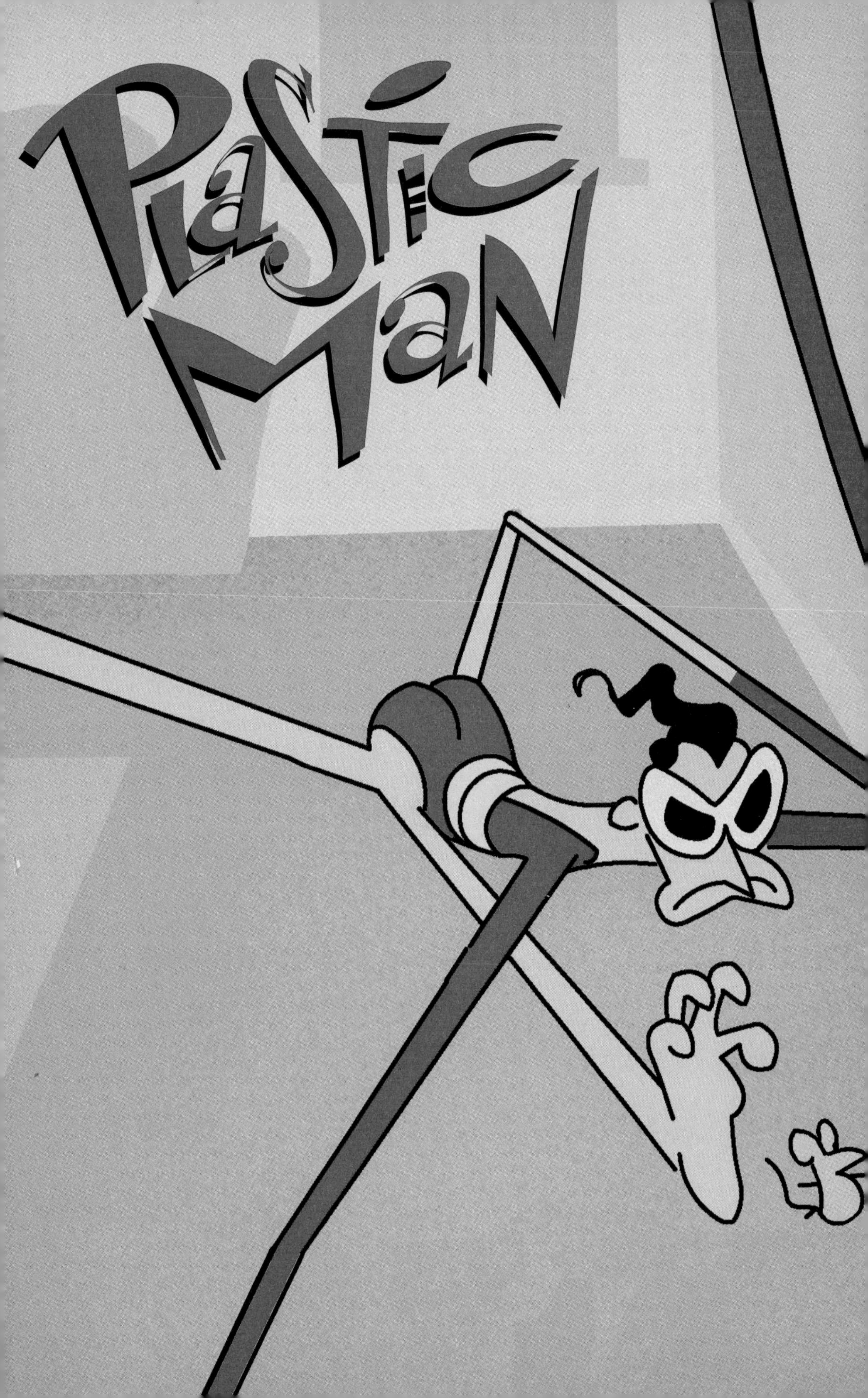
Plastic Man

PLASTIC MAN

RUBBER BANDITS

Written and illustrated by

Kyle Baker

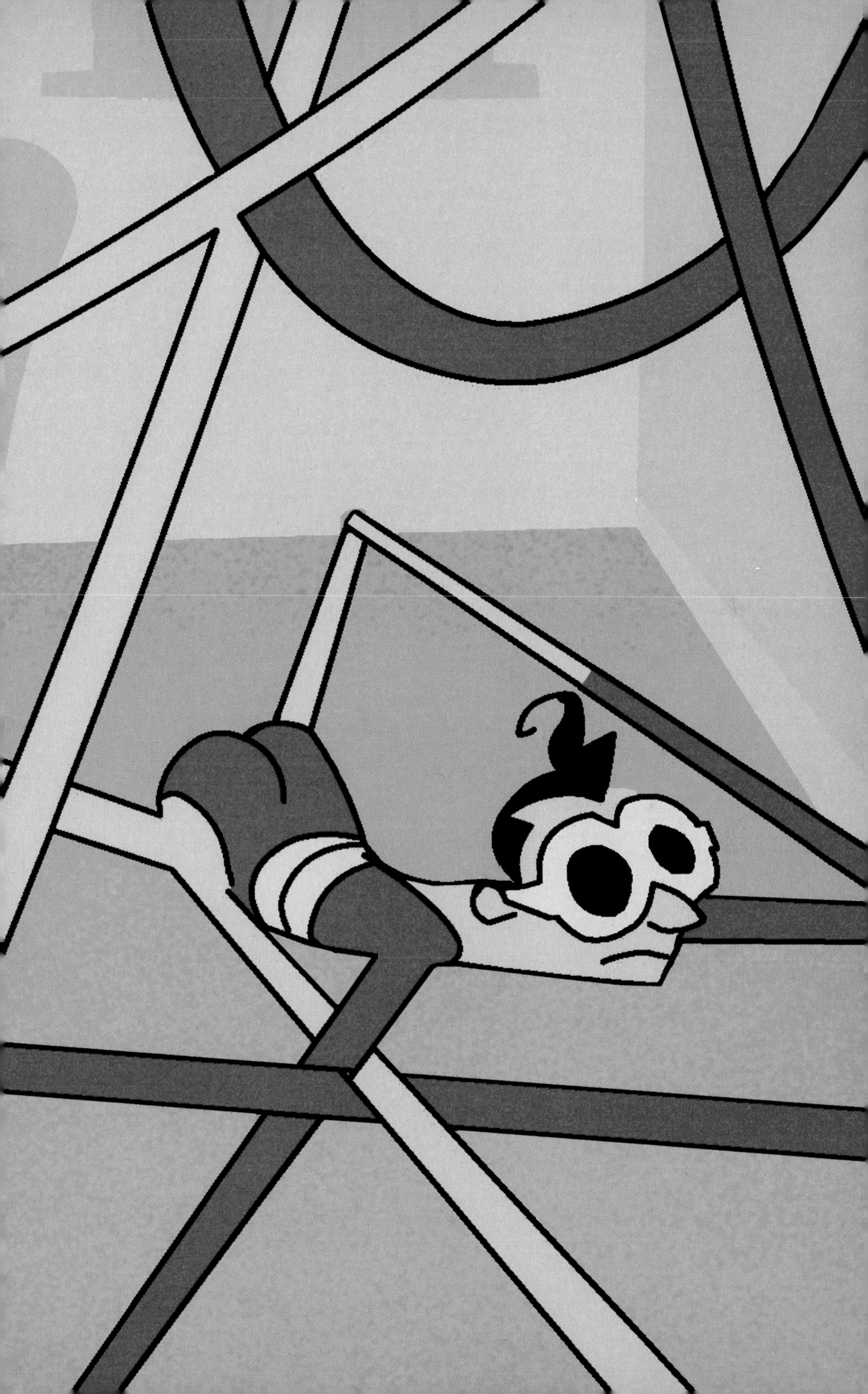

PLASTIC MAN: RUBBER BANDITS.
Published by DC Comics. Cover and compilation copyright
© 2005 DC Comics. All Rights Reserved. Originally published
in single magazine form in PLASTIC MAN #8-11, 13, 14.
Copyright © 2004, 2005 DC Comics. All Rights Reserved.
All characters, their distinctive likenesses and related elements
featured in this publication are trademarks of DC Comics.
The stories, characters and incidents featured in this publication
are entirely fictional. DC Comics does not read or accept
unsolicited submissions of ideas, stories or artwork.

DC Comics,
1700 Broadway, New York, NY 10019.
A Warner Bros. Entertainment Company.

Printed in Canada. First Printing.
ISBN: 1-4012-0729-4.
Cover by Kyle Baker.
Publication design by Peter Hamboussi.

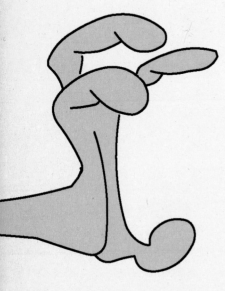

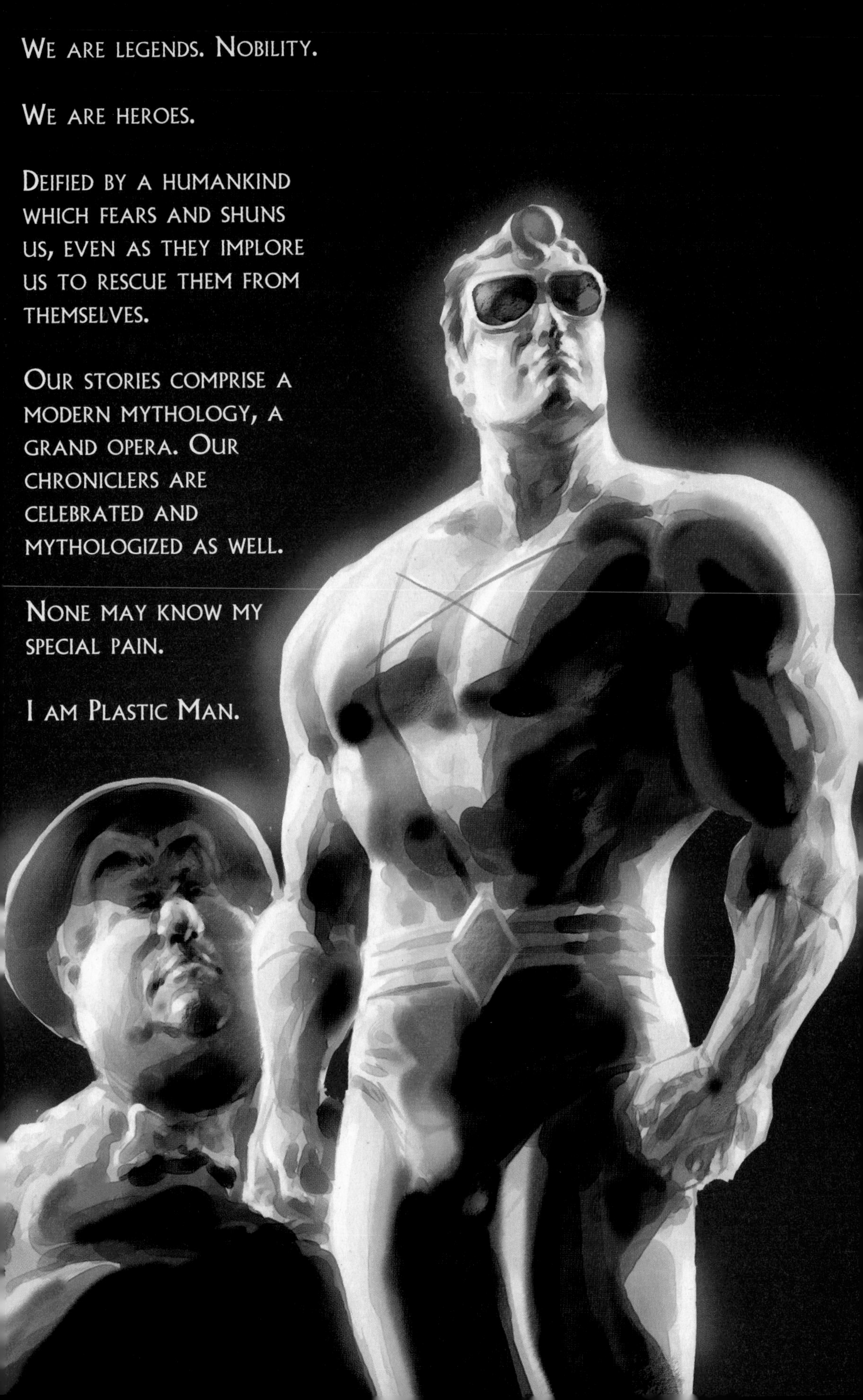
We are legends. Nobility.
We are heroes.
Deified by a humankind which fears and shuns us, even as they implore us to rescue them from themselves.
Our stories comprise a modern mythology, a grand opera. Our chroniclers are celebrated and mythologized as well.
None may know my special pain.
I am Plastic Man.

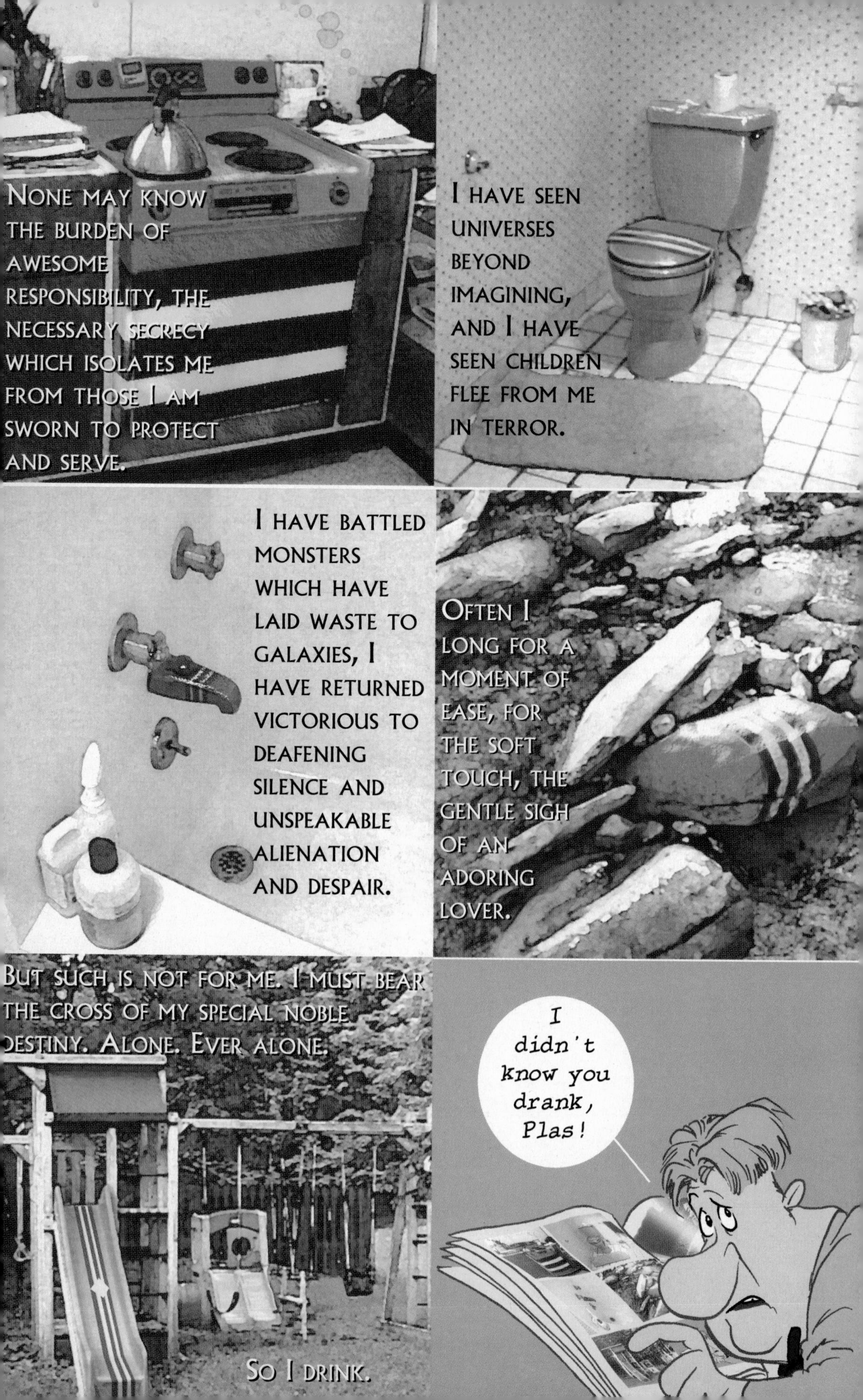
None may know the burden of awesome responsibility, the necessary secrecy which isolates me from those I am sworn to protect and serve.
I have seen universes beyond imagining, and I have seen children flee from me in terror.
I have battled monsters which have laid waste to galaxies, I have returned victorious to deafening silence and unspeakable alienation and despair.
Often I long for a moment of ease, for the soft touch, the gentle sigh of an adoring lover.
But such is not for me. I must bear the cross of my special noble destiny. Alone. Ever alone.
So I drink.
I didn't know you drank, Plas!

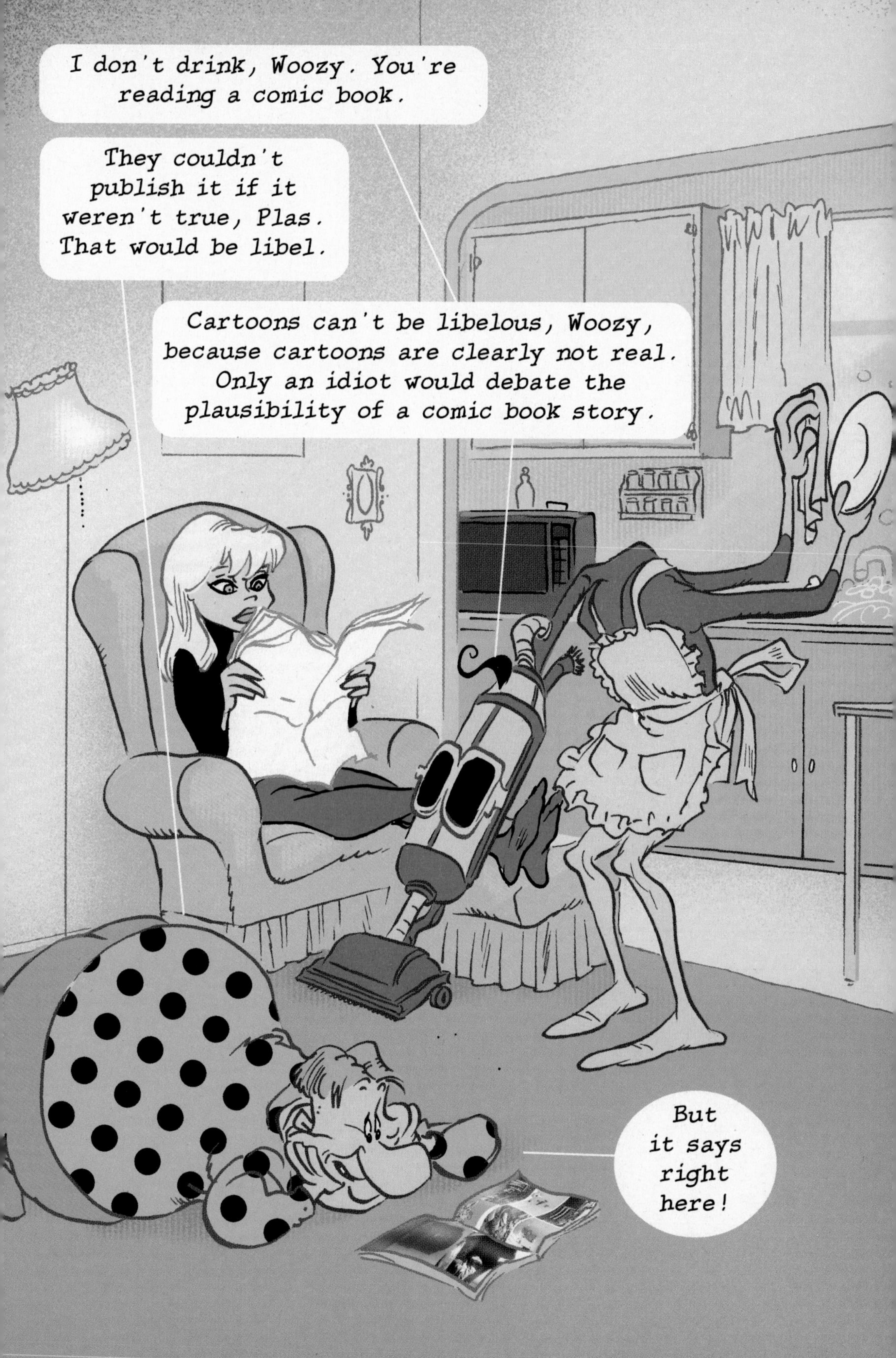
I don't drink, Woozy. You're reading a comic book.
They couldn't publish it if it weren't true, Plas. That would be libel.
Cartoons can't be libelous, Woozy, because cartoons are clearly not real. Only an idiot would debate the plausibility of a comic book story.
But it says right here!

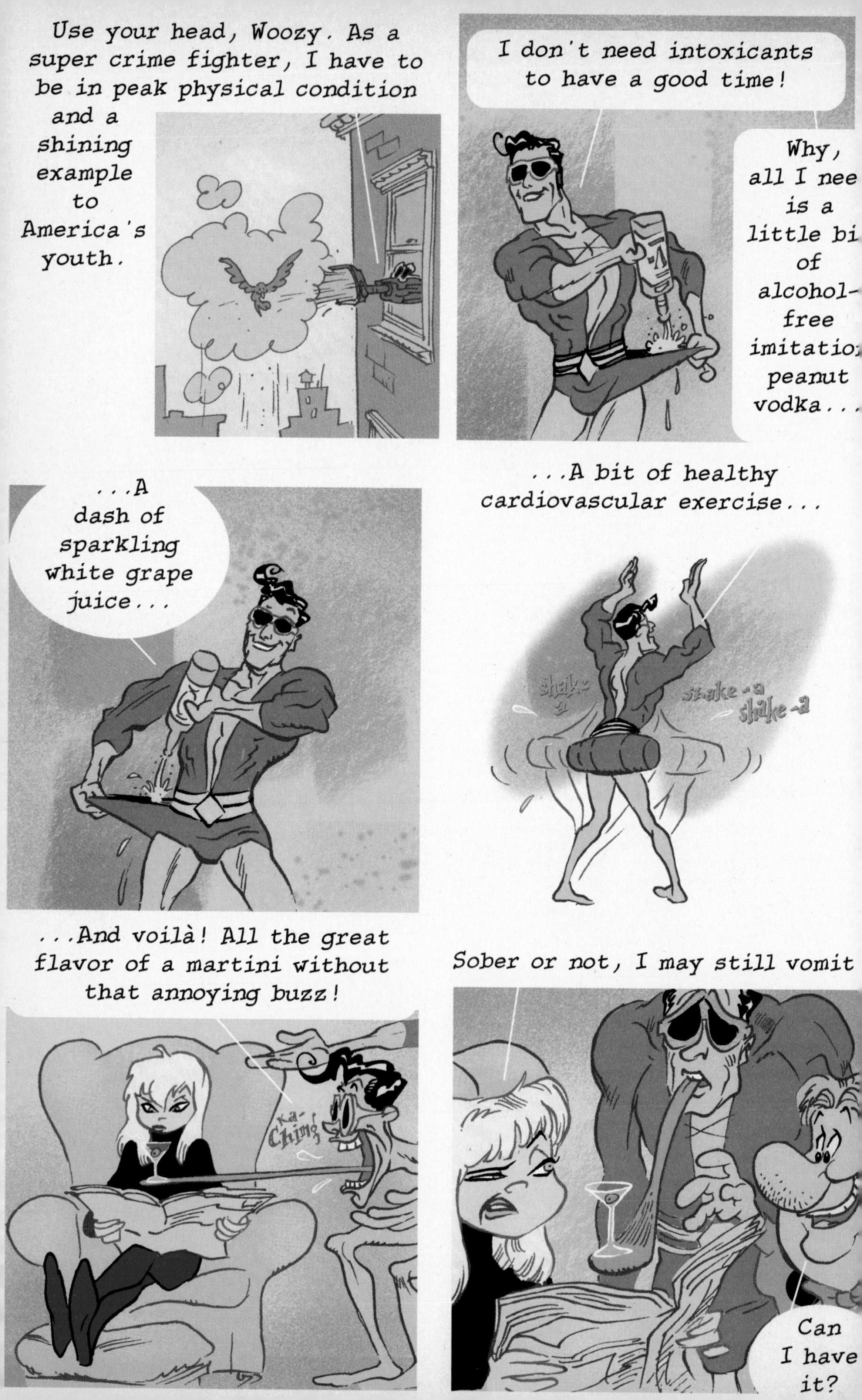
Use your head, Woozy. As a super crime fighter, I have to be in peak physical condition and a shining example to America's youth.
I don't need intoxicants to have a good time!
Why, all I nee is a little bi of alcohol-free imitatio peanut vodka...
...A dash of sparkling white grape juice...
...A bit of healthy cardiovascular exercise...
shake-a
shake-a shake-a
...And voilà! All the great flavor of a martini without that annoying buzz!
Ka-Ching
Sober or not, I may still vomit
Can I have it?

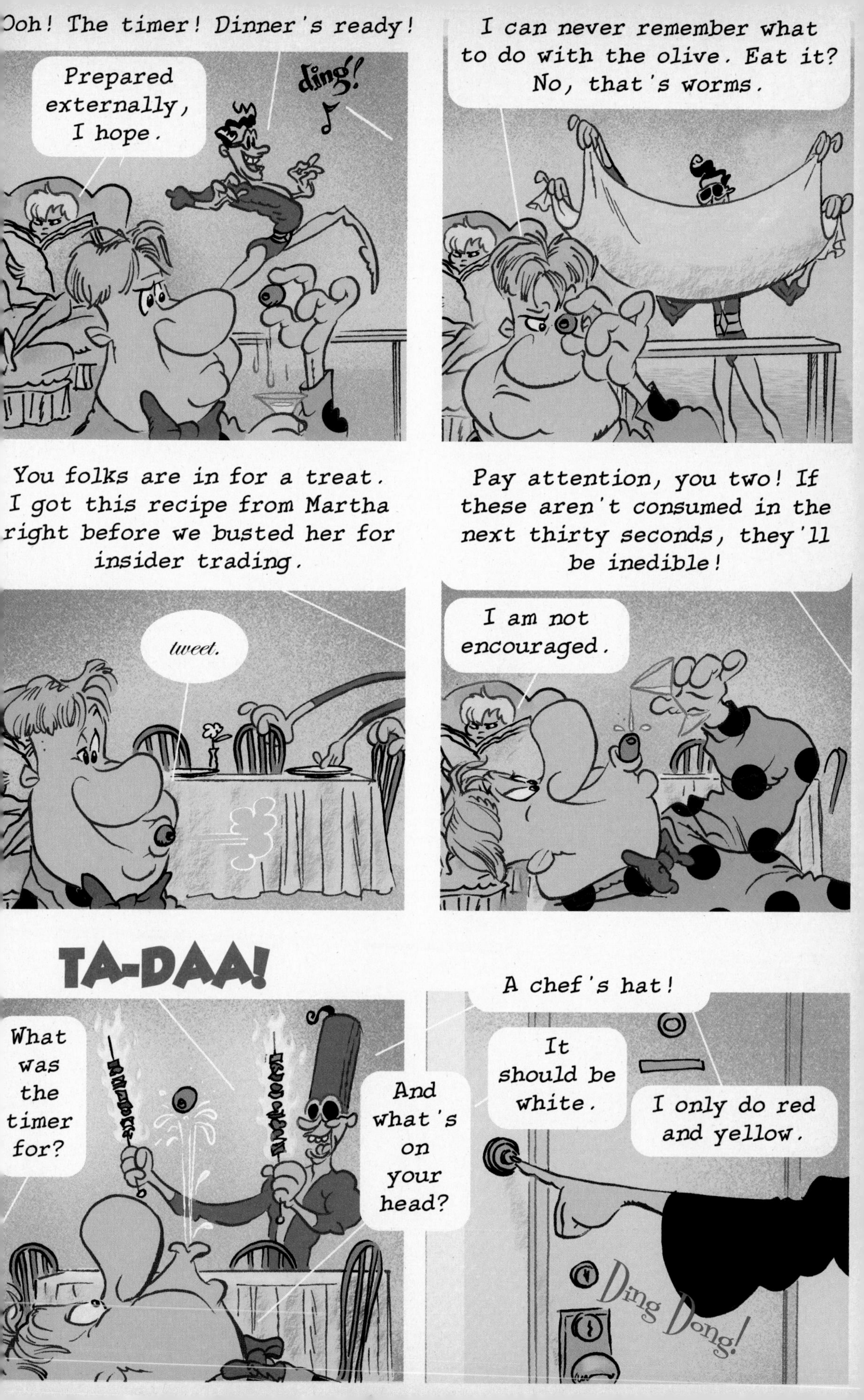
Ooh! The timer! Dinner's ready!
ding!
Prepared externally, I hope.
I can never remember what to do with the olive. Eat it? No, that's worms.
You folks are in for a treat. I got this recipe from Martha right before we busted her for insider trading.
tweet.
Pay attention, you two! If these aren't consumed in the next thirty seconds, they'll be inedible!
I am not encouraged.
TA-DAA!
What was the timer for?
And what's on your head?
A chef's hat!
It should be white.
I only do red and yellow.
Ding Dong!

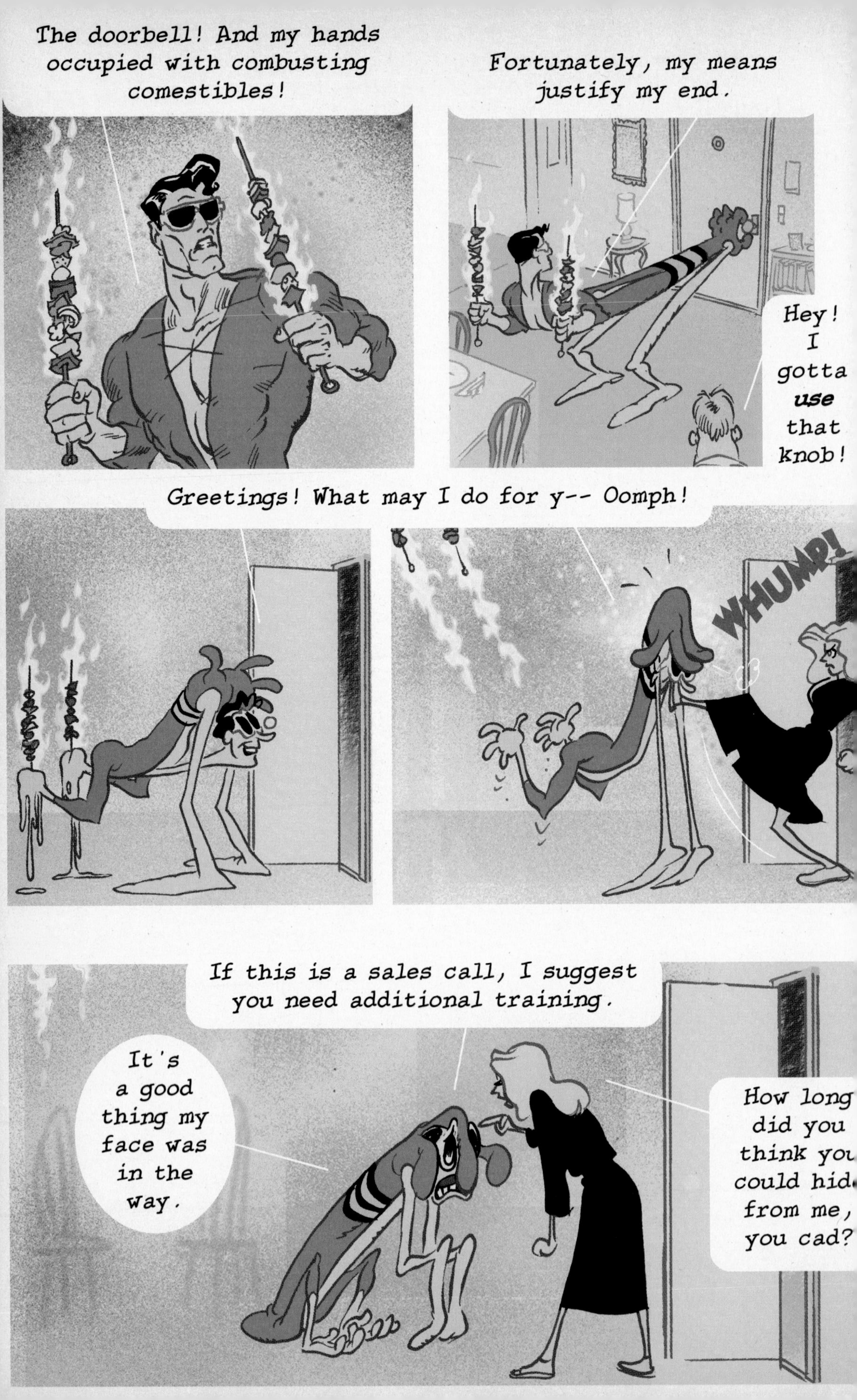

The doorbell! And my hands occupied with combusting comestibles!
Fortunately, my means justify my end.
Hey! I gotta *use* that knob!
Greetings! What may I do for y-- Oomph!
WHUMP!
If this is a sales call, I suggest you need additional training.
It's a good thing my face was in the way.
How long did you think you could hid from me, you cad?

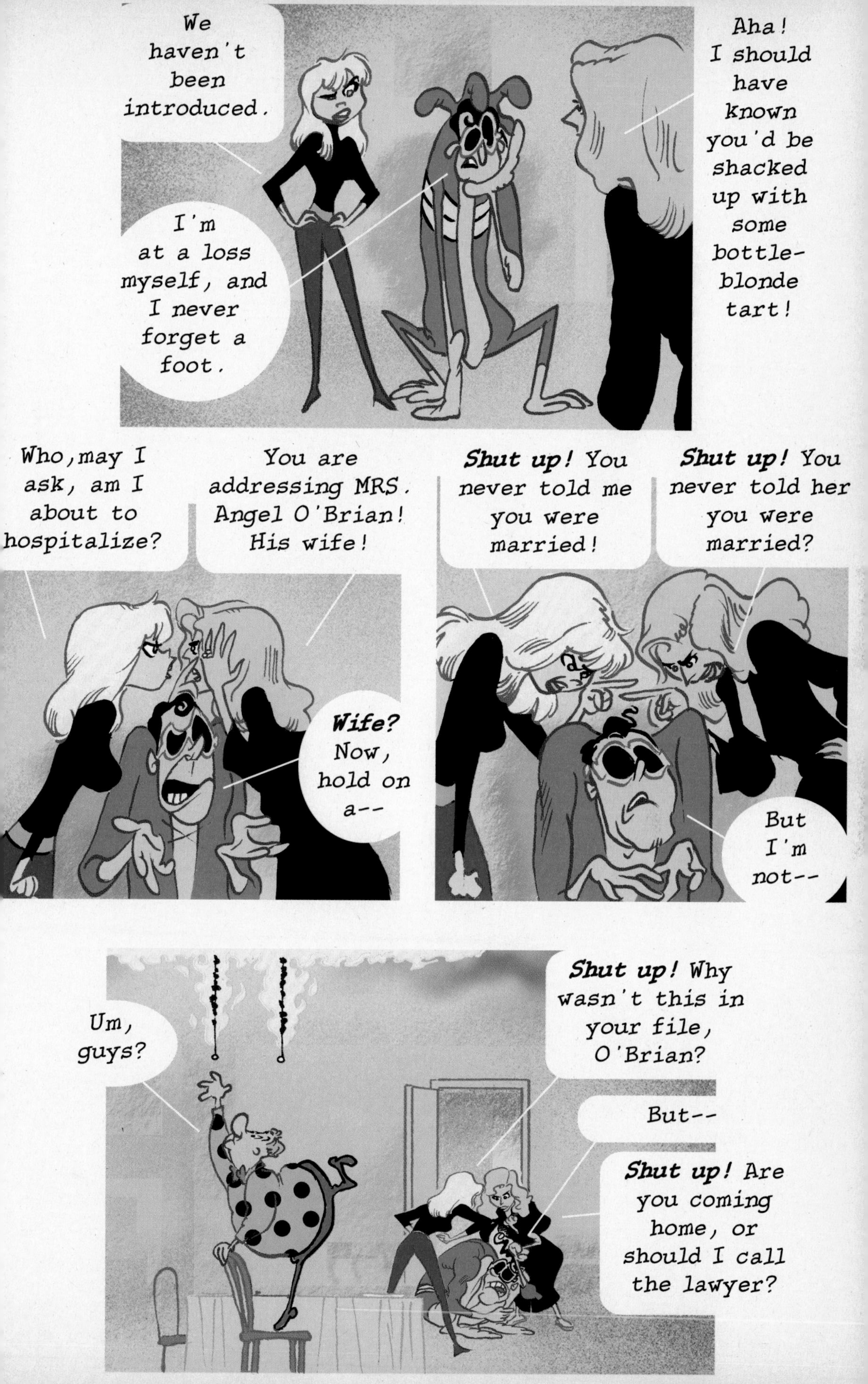
We haven't been introduced.
I'm at a loss myself, and I never forget a foot.
Aha! I should have known you'd be shacked up with some bottle-blonde tart!
Who, may I ask, am I about to hospitalize?
You are addressing MRS. Angel O'Brian! His wife!
Wife? Now, hold on a--
Shut up! You never told me you were married!
Shut up! You never told her you were married?
But I'm not--
Um, guys?
Shut up! Why wasn't this in your file, O'Brian?
But--
Shut up! Are you coming home, or should I call the lawyer?

DADDY! COME HOME!

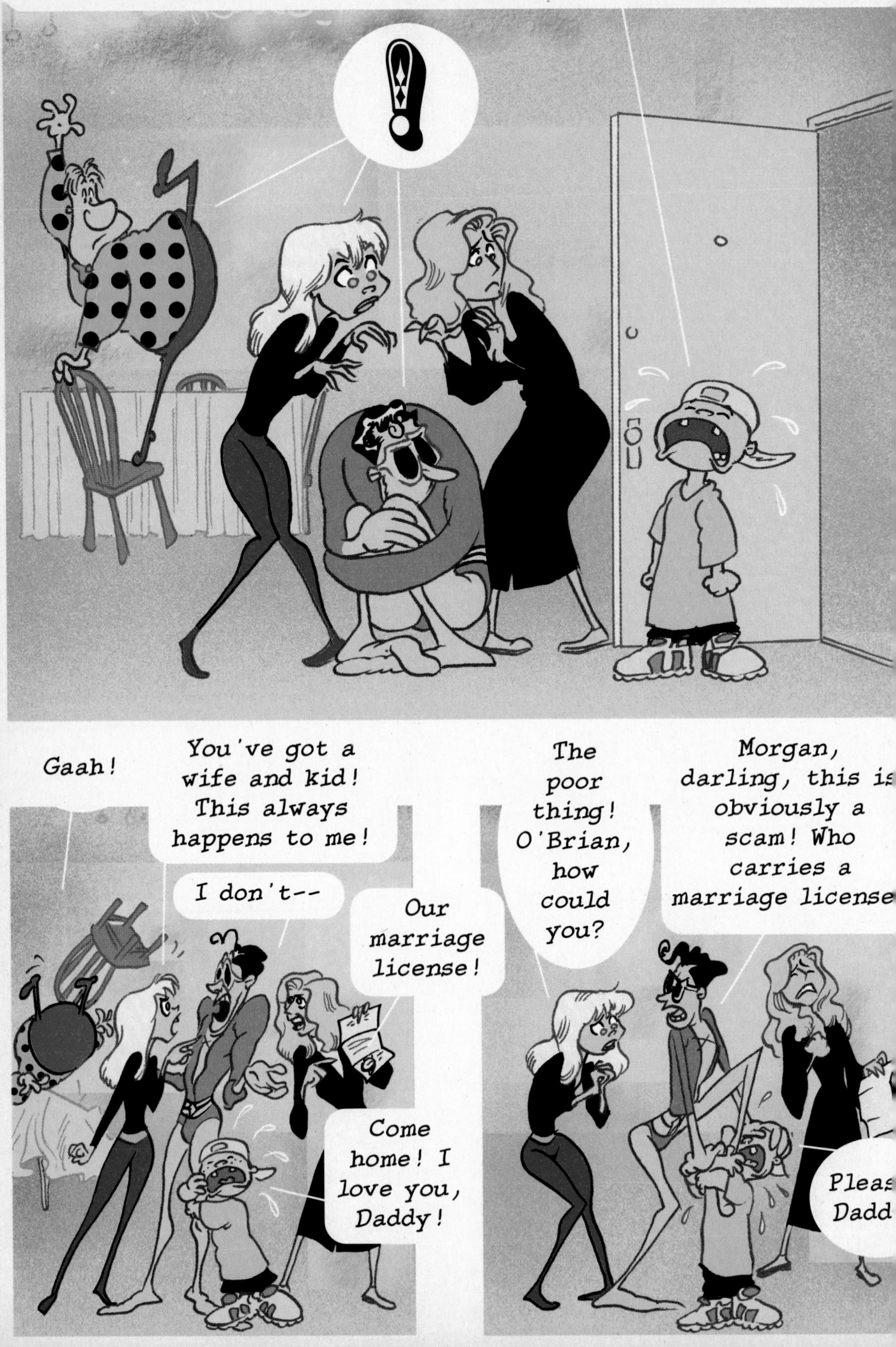
!
Gaah!
You've got a wife and kid! This always happens to me!
I don't--
Our marriage license!
Come home! I love you, Daddy!
The poor thing! O'Brian, how could you?
Morgan, darling, this is obviously a scam! Who carries a marriage license
Pleas
Dadd

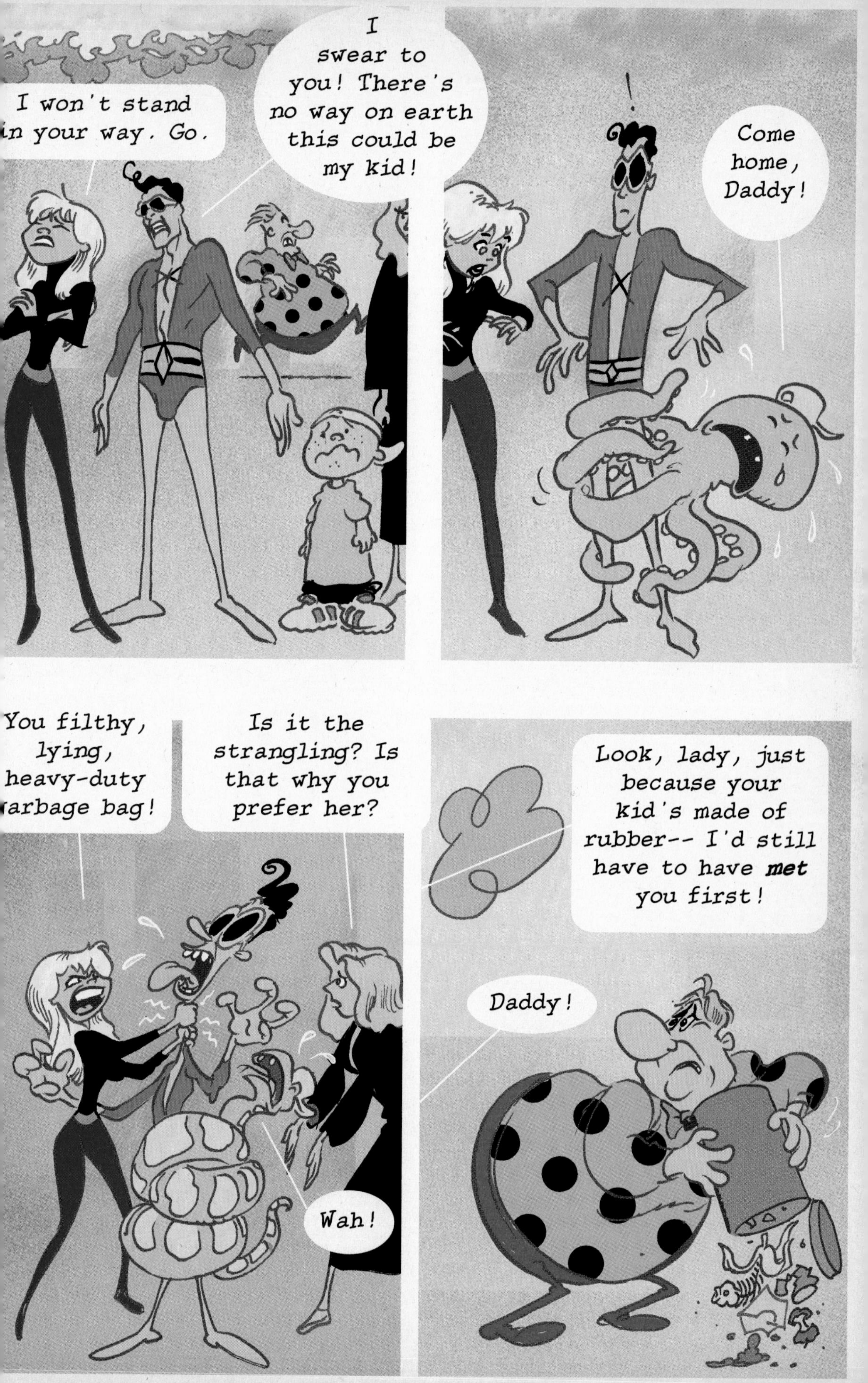

I won't stand in your way. Go.
I swear to you! There's no way on earth this could be my kid!
!
Come home, Daddy!
You filthy, lying, heavy-duty garbage bag!
Is it the strangling? Is that why you prefer her?
Wah!
Look, lady, just because your kid's made of rubber-- I'd still have to have **met** you first!
Daddy!

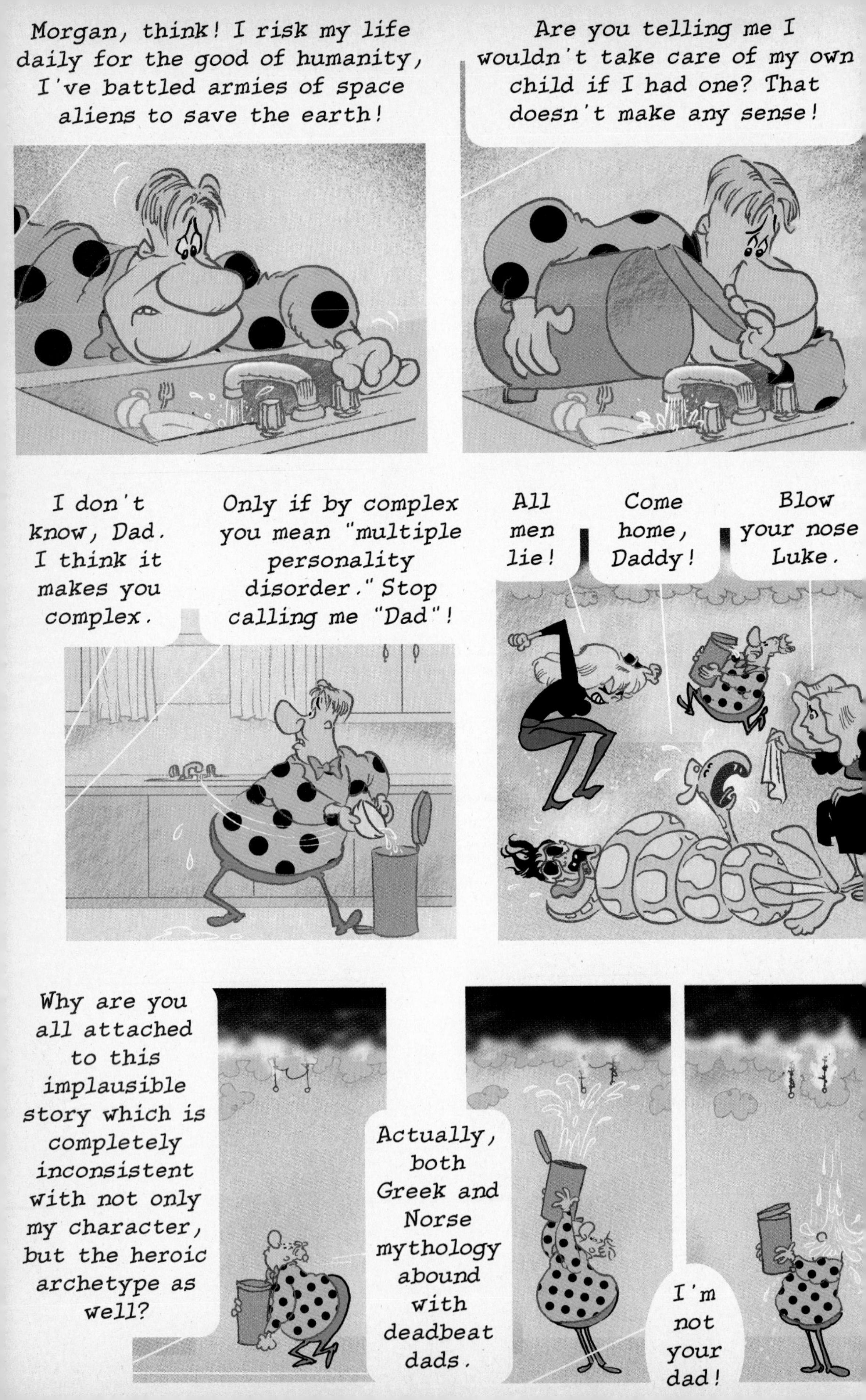
Morgan, think! I risk my life daily for the good of humanity, I've battled armies of space aliens to save the earth!
Are you telling me I wouldn't take care of my own child if I had one? That doesn't make any sense!
I don't know, Dad. I think it makes you complex.
Only if by complex you mean "multiple personality disorder." Stop calling me "Dad"!
All men lie!
Come home, Daddy!
Blow your nose Luke.
Why are you all attached to this implausible story which is completely inconsistent with not only my character, but the heroic archetype as well?
Actually, both Greek and Norse mythology abound with deadbeat dads.
I'm not your dad!

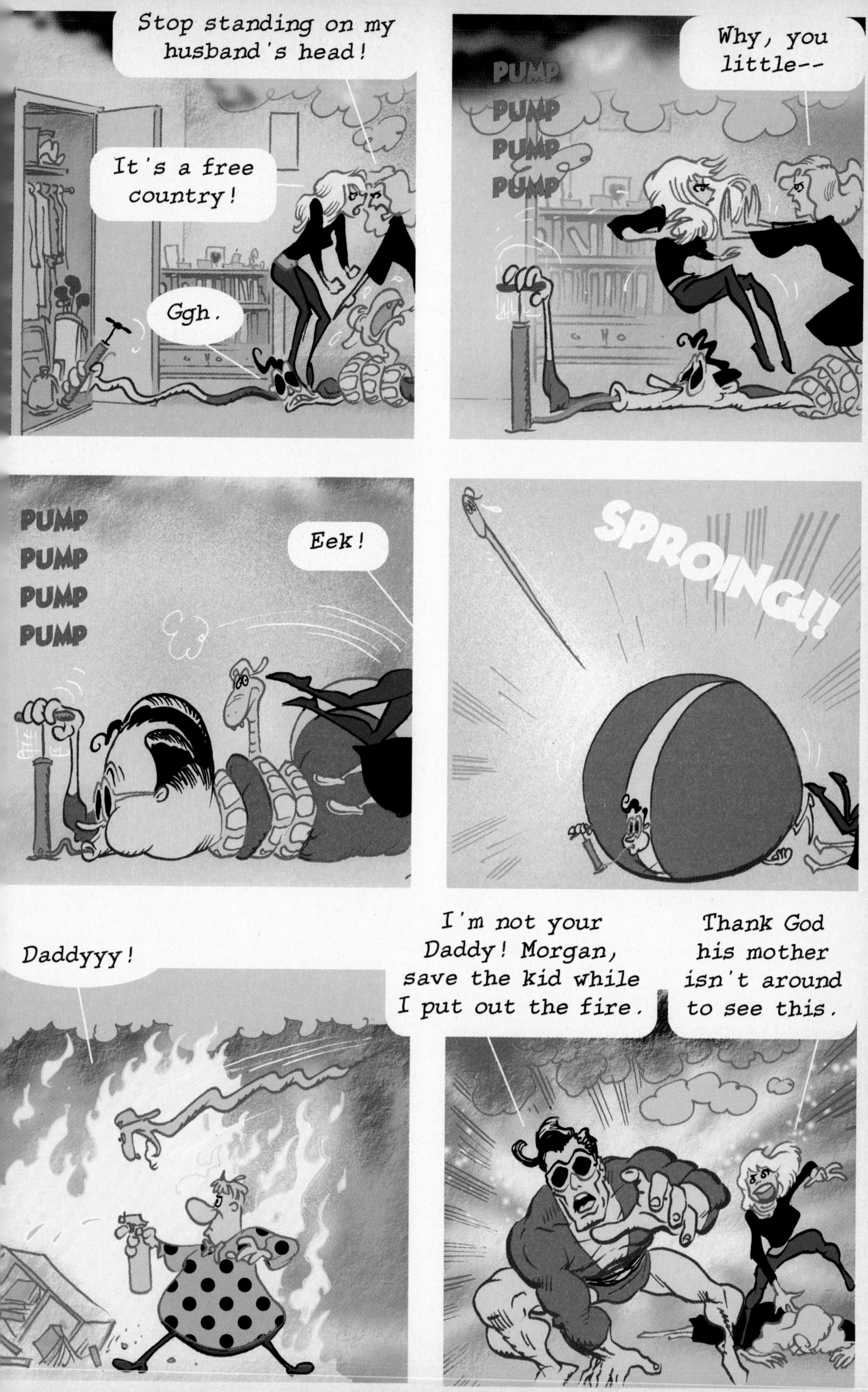
Stop standing on my husband's head!
It's a free country!
Ggh.
PUMP
PUMP
PUMP
PUMP
Why, you little--
PUMP
PUMP
PUMP
PUMP
Eek!
SPROING!!
Daddyyy!
I'm not your Daddy! Morgan, save the kid while I put out the fire.
Thank God his mother isn't around to see this.

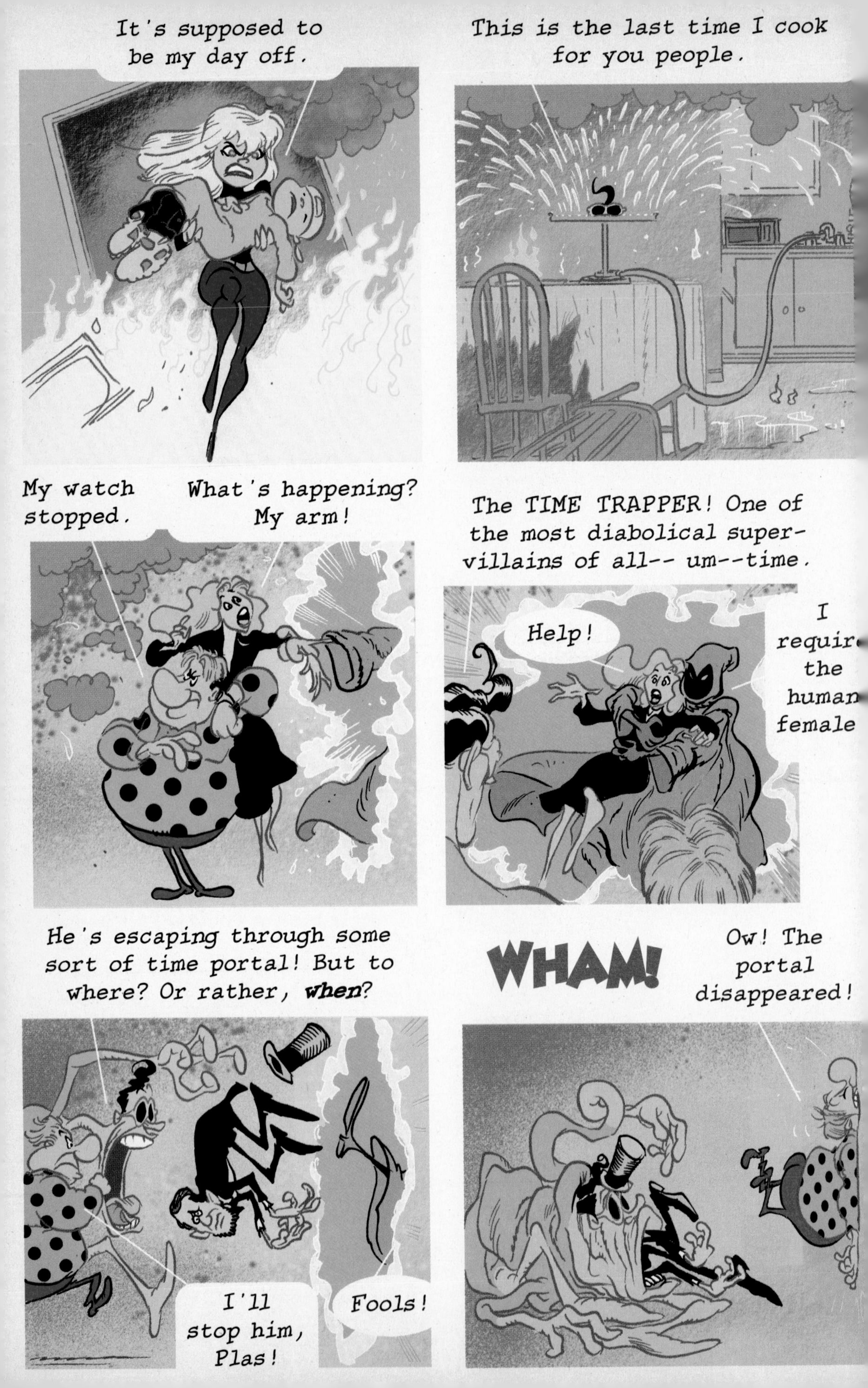
It's supposed to be my day off.
This is the last time I cook for you people.
My watch stopped.
What's happening? My arm!
The TIME TRAPPER! One of the most diabolical super-villains of all-- um--time.
Help!
He's escaping through some sort of time portal! But to where? Or rather, *when*?
I'll stop him, Plas!
Fools!
WHAM!
Ow! The portal disappeared!

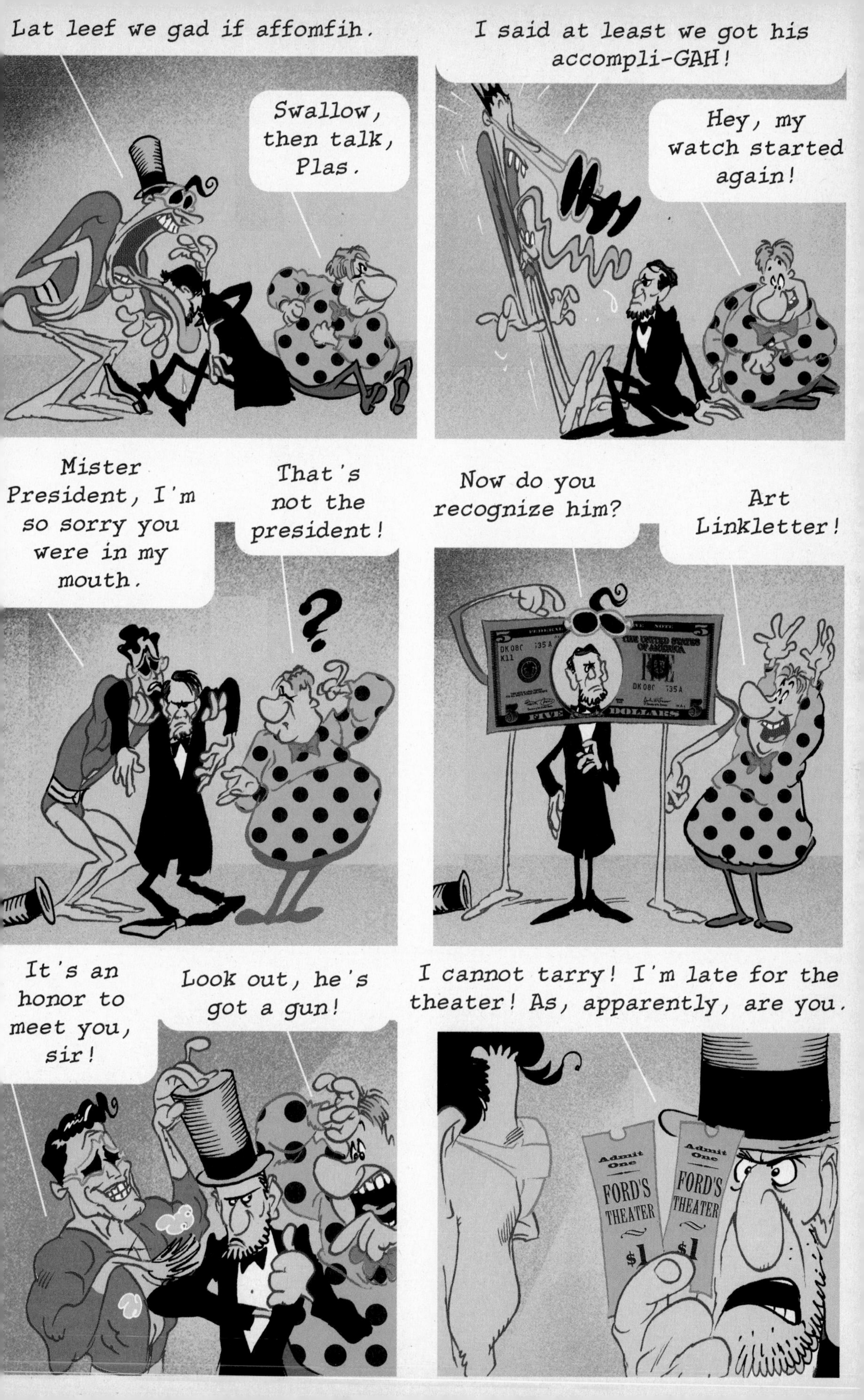
Lat leef we gad if affomfih.
Swallow, then talk, Plas.
I said at least we got his accompli-GAH!
Hey, my watch started again!
Mister President, I'm so sorry you were in my mouth.
That's not the president!
Now do you recognize him?
Art Linkletter!
It's an honor to meet you, sir!
Look out, he's got a gun!
I cannot tarry! I'm late for the theater! As, apparently, are you.
Admit One
FORD'S THEATER
$1
Admit One
FORD'S THEATER
$1

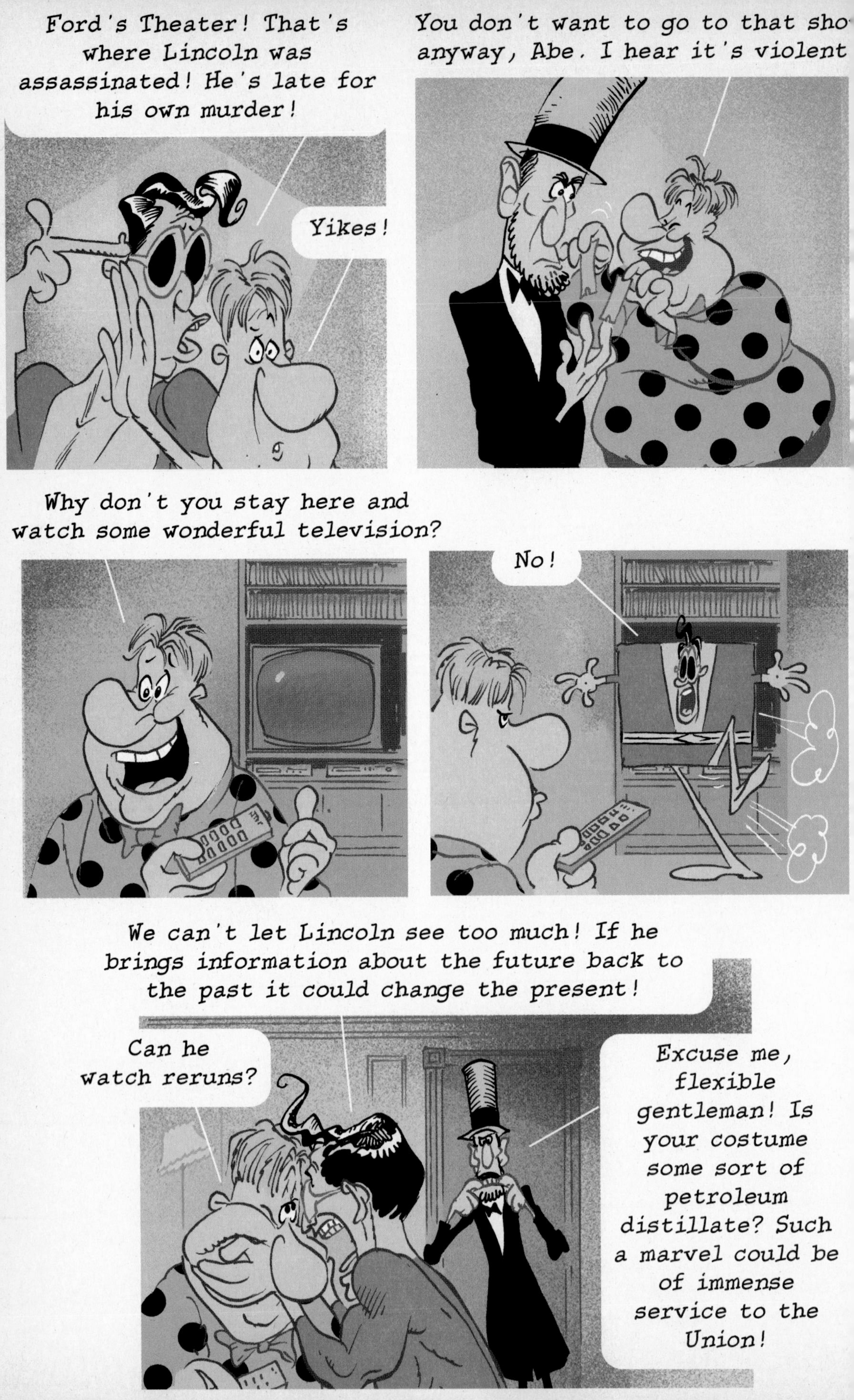
Ford's Theater! That's where Lincoln was assassinated! He's late for his own murder!
Yikes!
You don't want to go to that show anyway, Abe. I hear it's violent
Why don't you stay here and watch some wonderful television?
No!
We can't let Lincoln see too much! If he brings information about the future back to the past it could change the present!
Can he watch reruns?
Excuse me, flexible gentleman! Is your costume some sort of petroleum distillate? Such a marvel could be of immense service to the Union!

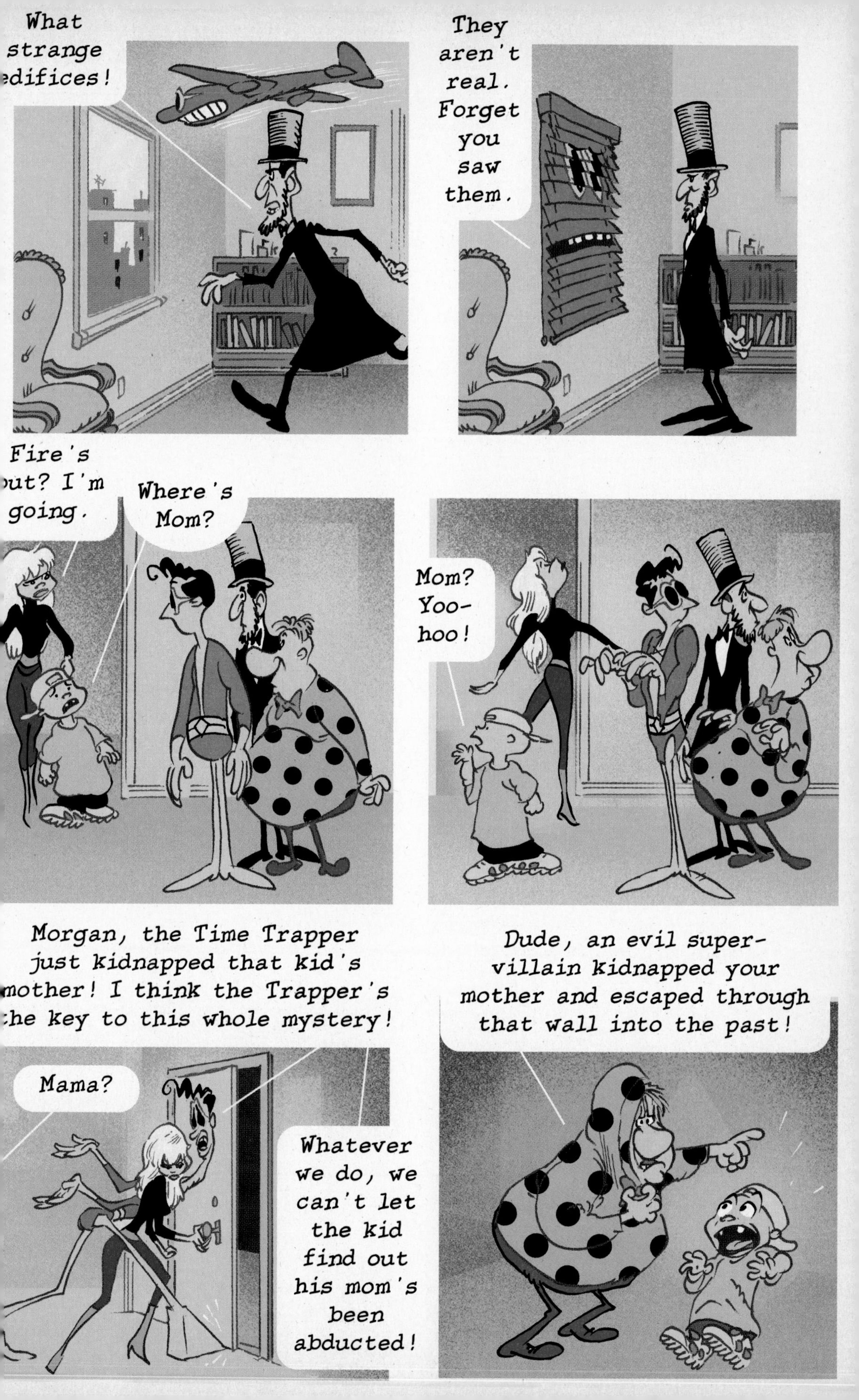
What strange edifices!
They aren't real. Forget you saw them.
Fire's out? I'm going.
Where's Mom?
Mom? Yoo-hoo!
Morgan, the Time Trapper just kidnapped that kid's mother! I think the Trapper's the key to this whole mystery!
Mama?
Whatever we do, we can't let the kid find out his mom's been abducted!
Dude, an evil super-villain kidnapped your mother and escaped through that wall into the past!

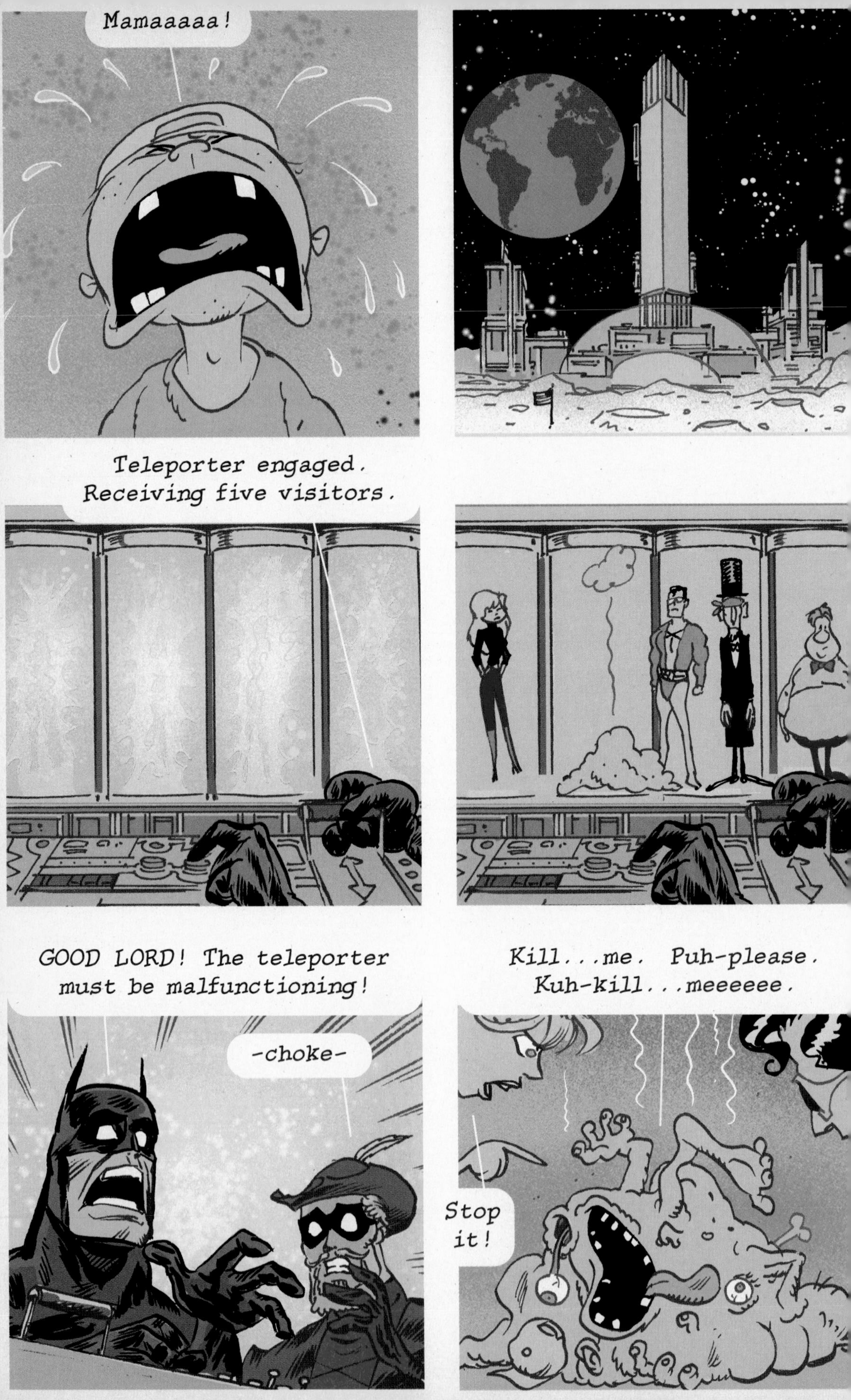
Mamaaaaa!
Teleporter engaged. Receiving five visitors.
GOOD LORD! The teleporter must be malfunctioning!
-choke-
Kill...me. Puh-please. Kuh-kill...meeeeee.
Stop it!

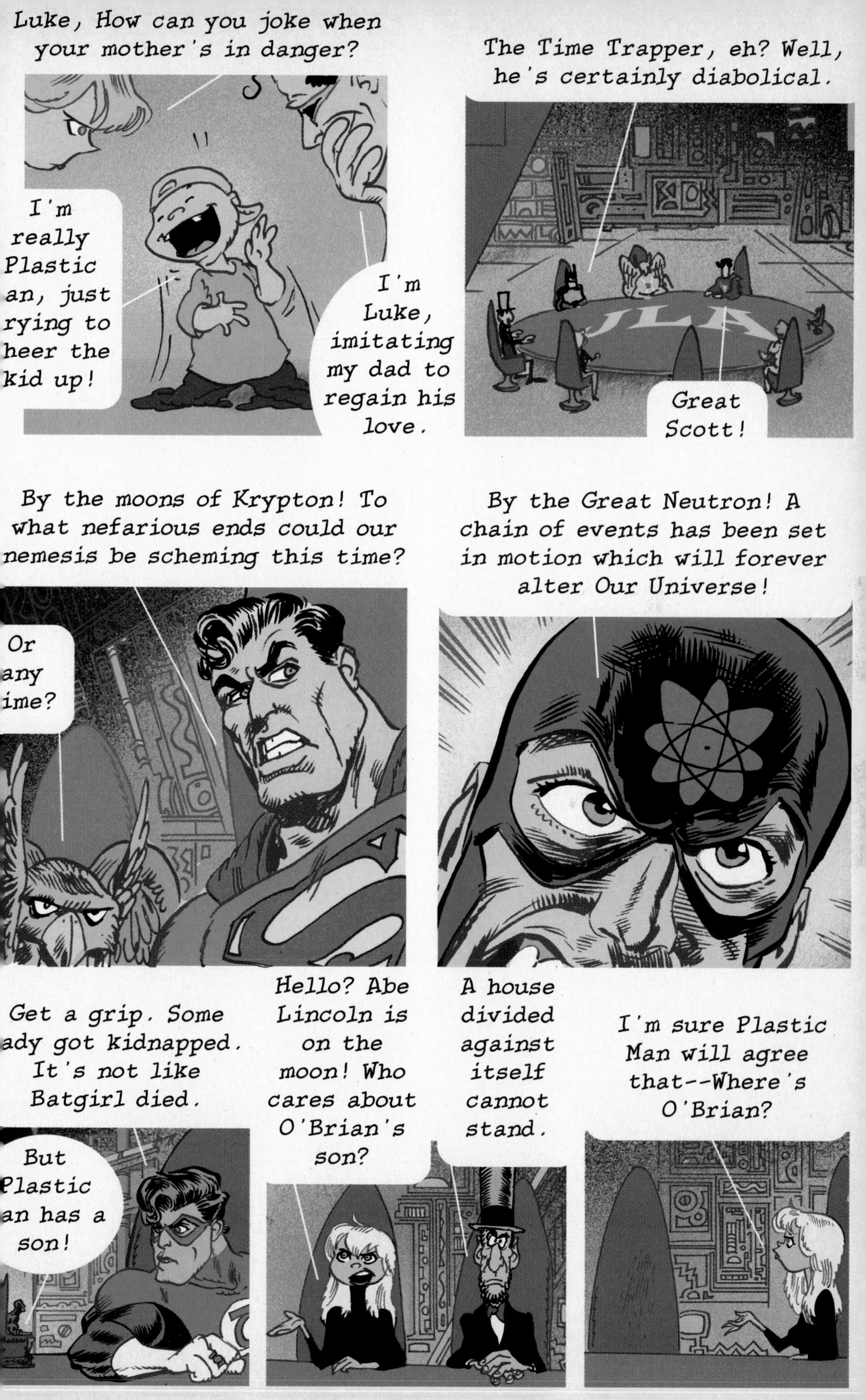

Luke, How can you joke when your mother's in danger?
I'm really Plastic an, just rying to heer the kid up!
I'm Luke, imitating my dad to regain his love.
The Time Trapper, eh? Well, he's certainly diabolical.
Great Scott!
By the moons of Krypton! To what nefarious ends could our nemesis be scheming this time?
Or any ime?
By the Great Neutron! A chain of events has been set in motion which will forever alter Our Universe!
Get a grip. Some ady got kidnapped. It's not like Batgirl died.
But Plastic an has a son!
Hello? Abe Lincoln is on the moon! Who cares about O'Brian's son?
A house divided against itself cannot stand.
I'm sure Plastic Man will agree that--Where's O'Brian?

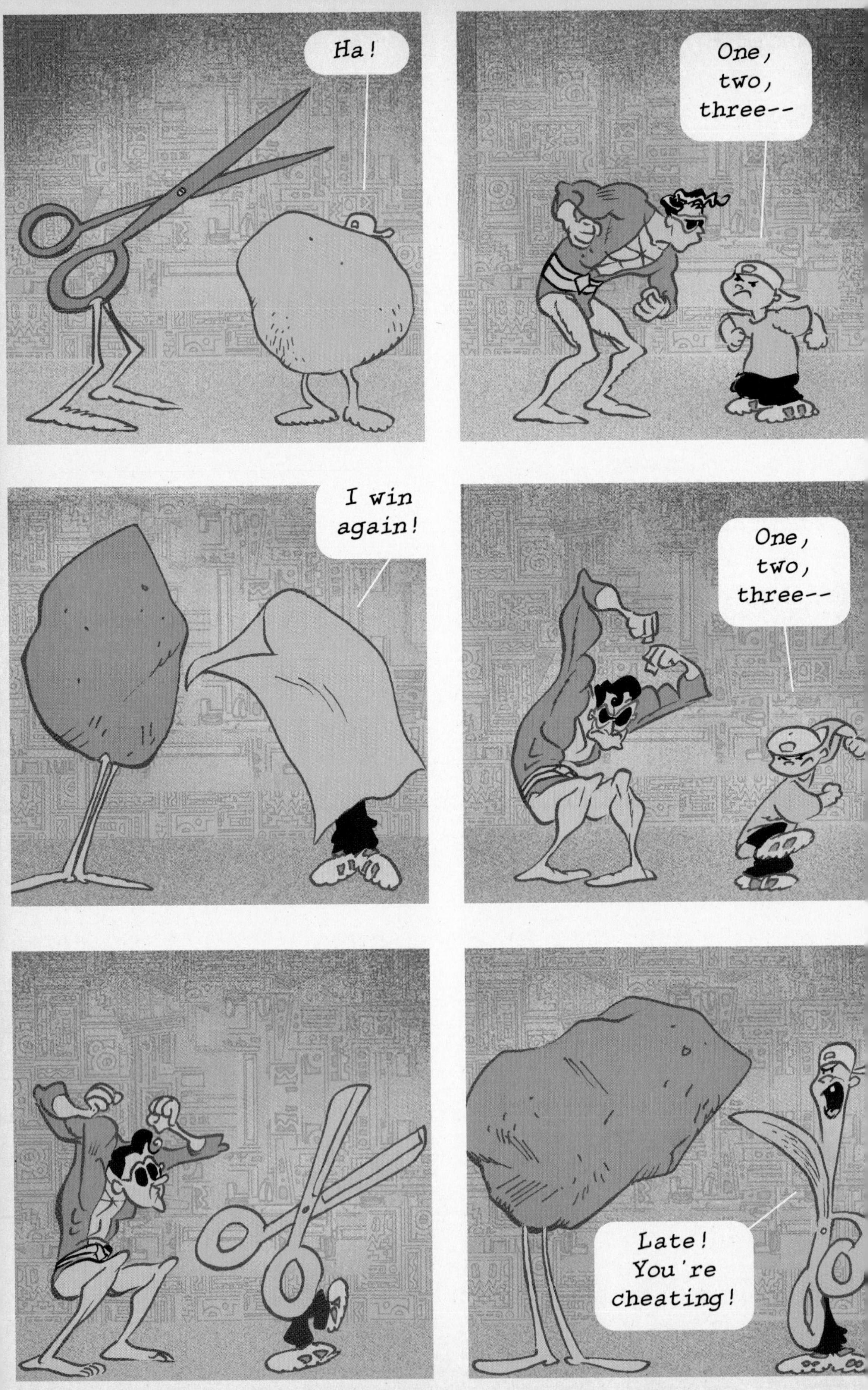
Ha!
One, two, three--
I win again!
One, two, three--
Late! You're cheating!

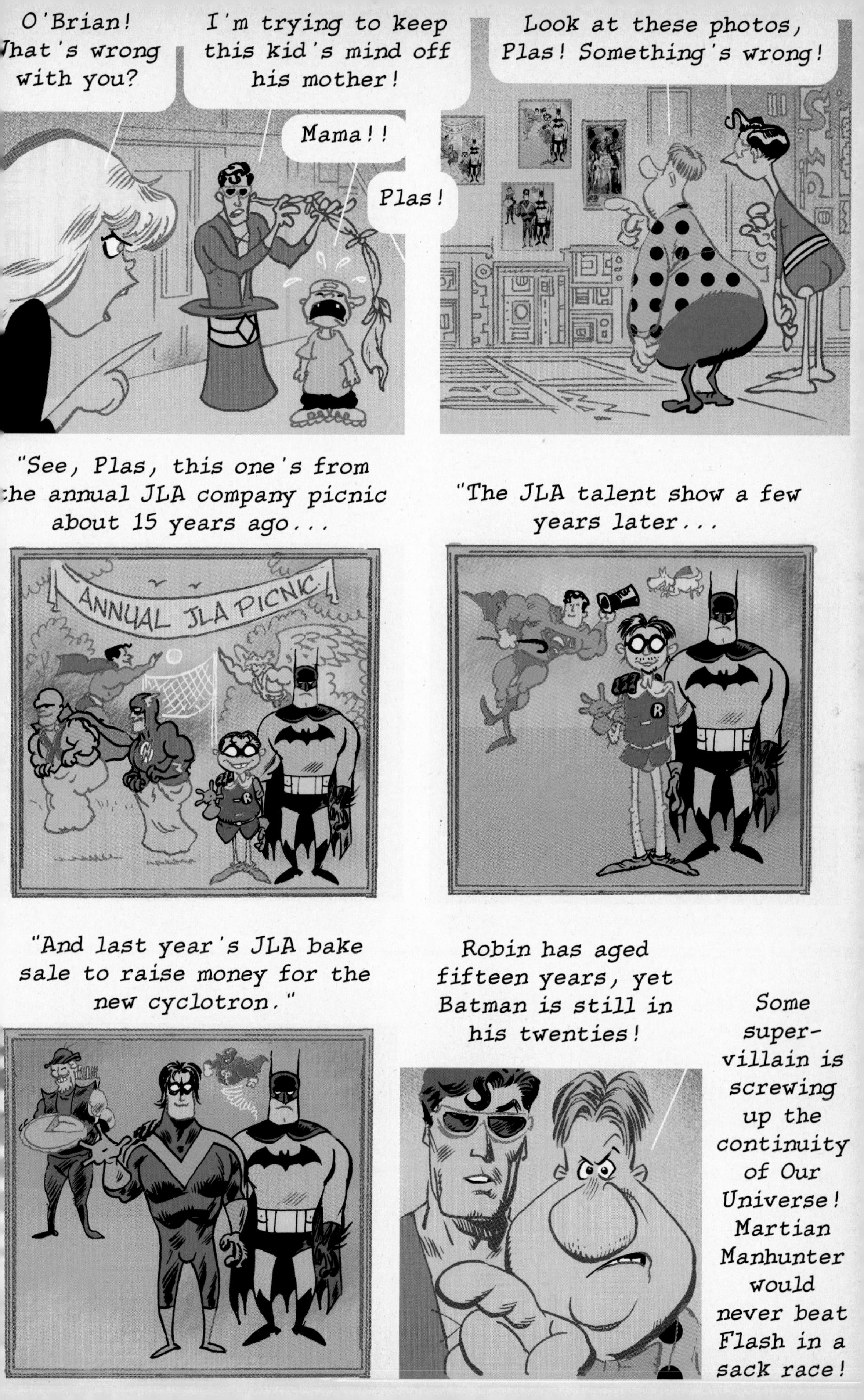
O'Brian!
What's wrong
with you?
I'm trying to keep
this kid's mind off
his mother!
Mama!!
Plas!
Look at these photos,
Plas! Something's wrong!
"See, Plas, this one's from
the annual JLA company picnic
about 15 years ago...
ANNUAL JLA PICNIC
"The JLA talent show a few
years later...
"And last year's JLA bake
sale to raise money for the
new cyclotron."
Robin has aged
fifteen years, yet
Batman is still in
his twenties!
Some
super-
villain is
screwing
up the
continuity
of Our
Universe!
Martian
Manhunter
would
never beat
Flash in a
sack race!

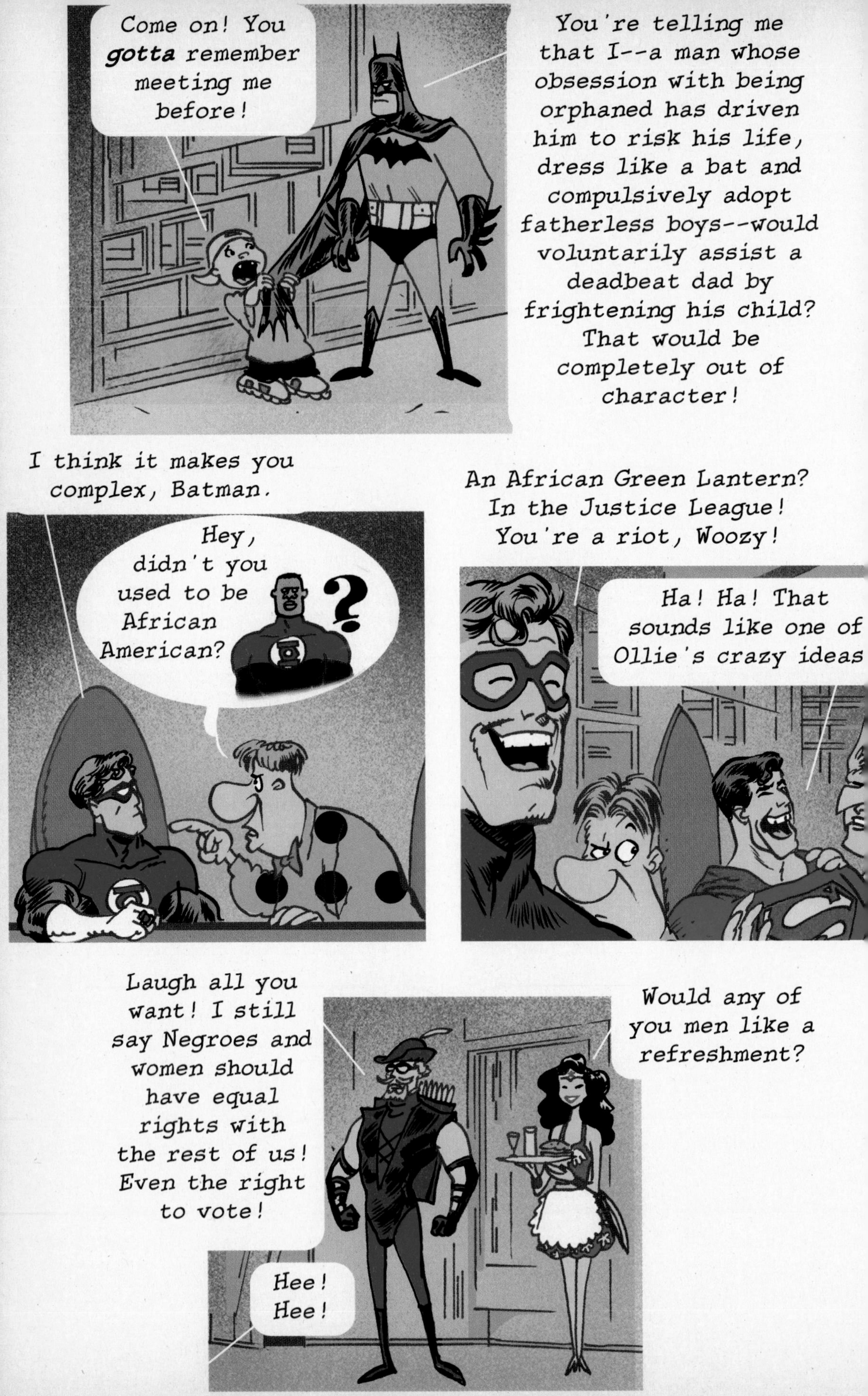
Come on! You **gotta** remember meeting me before!
You're telling me that I--a man whose obsession with being orphaned has driven him to risk his life, dress like a bat and compulsively adopt fatherless boys--would voluntarily assist a deadbeat dad by frightening his child? That would be completely out of character!
I think it makes you complex, Batman.
Hey, didn't you used to be African American?
?
An African Green Lantern? In the Justice League! You're a riot, Woozy!
Ha! Ha! That sounds like one of Ollie's crazy ideas
Laugh all you want! I still say Negroes and women should have equal rights with the rest of us! Even the right to vote!
Would any of you men like a refreshment?
Hee! Hee!

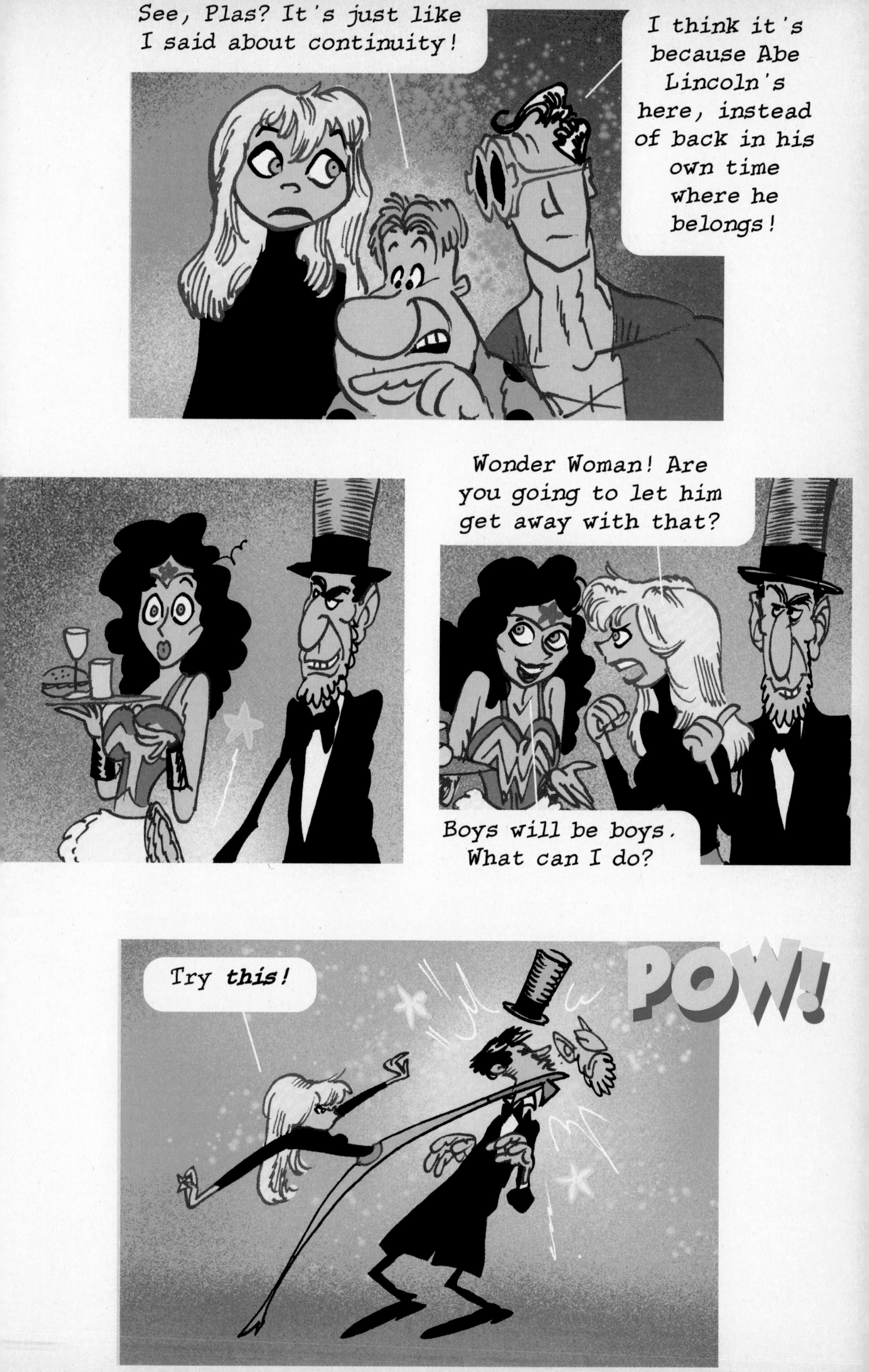
See, Plas? It's just like I said about continuity!
I think it's because Abe Lincoln's here, instead of back in his own time where he belongs!
Wonder Woman! Are you going to let him get away with that?
Boys will be boys. What can I do?
Try ***this!***
POW!

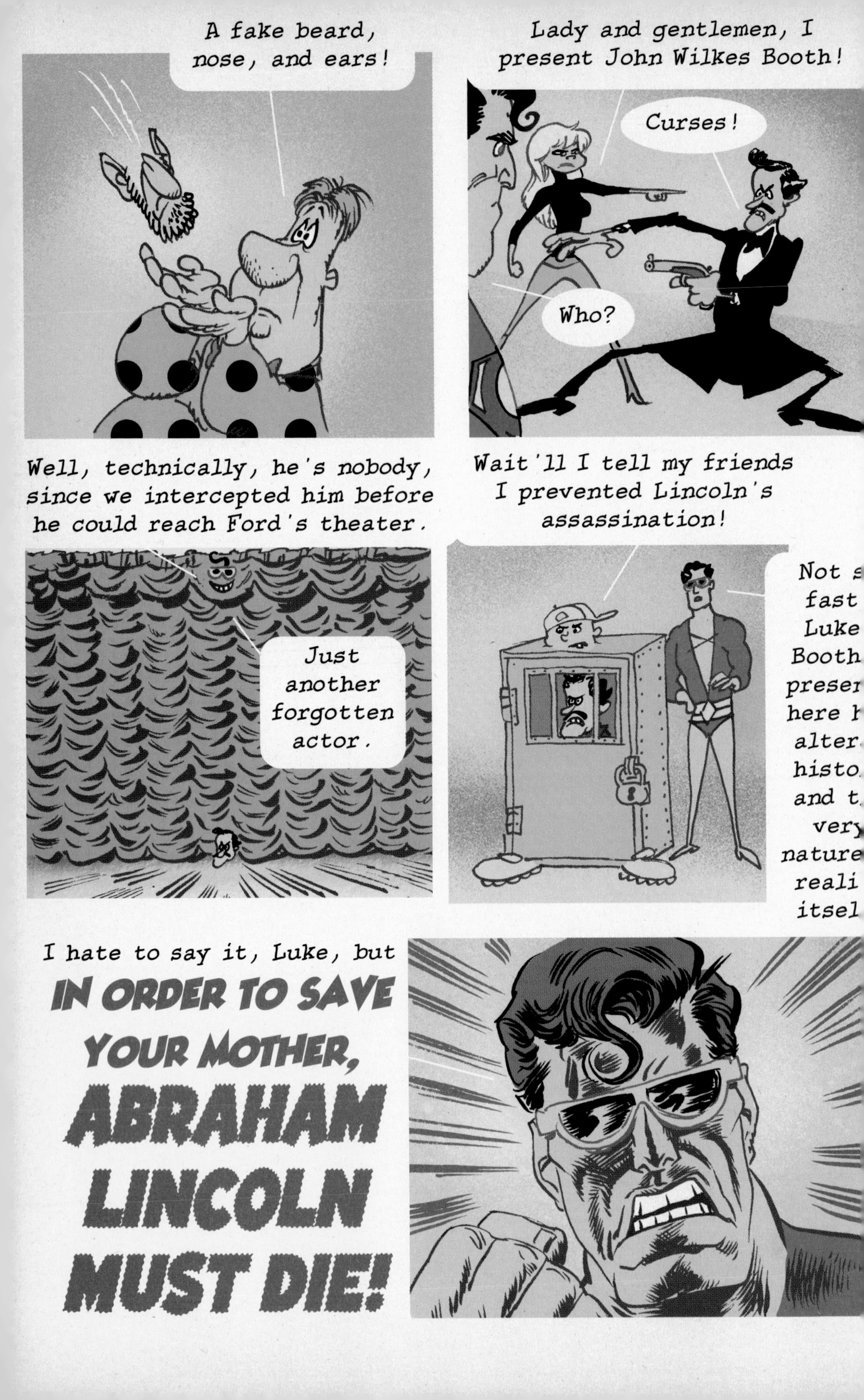
A fake beard, nose, and ears!
Lady and gentlemen, I present John Wilkes Booth!
Curses!
Who?
Well, technically, he's nobody, since we intercepted him before he could reach Ford's theater.
Just another forgotten actor.
Wait'll I tell my friends I prevented Lincoln's assassination!
Not s fast Luke Booth prese here h alter histo and t ver nature reali itsel
I hate to say it, Luke, but
IN ORDER TO SAVE YOUR MOTHER, ABRAHAM LINCOLN MUST DIE!

CONTINUITY BANDIT PART 2

ABRAHAM LINCOLN MUST DIE!

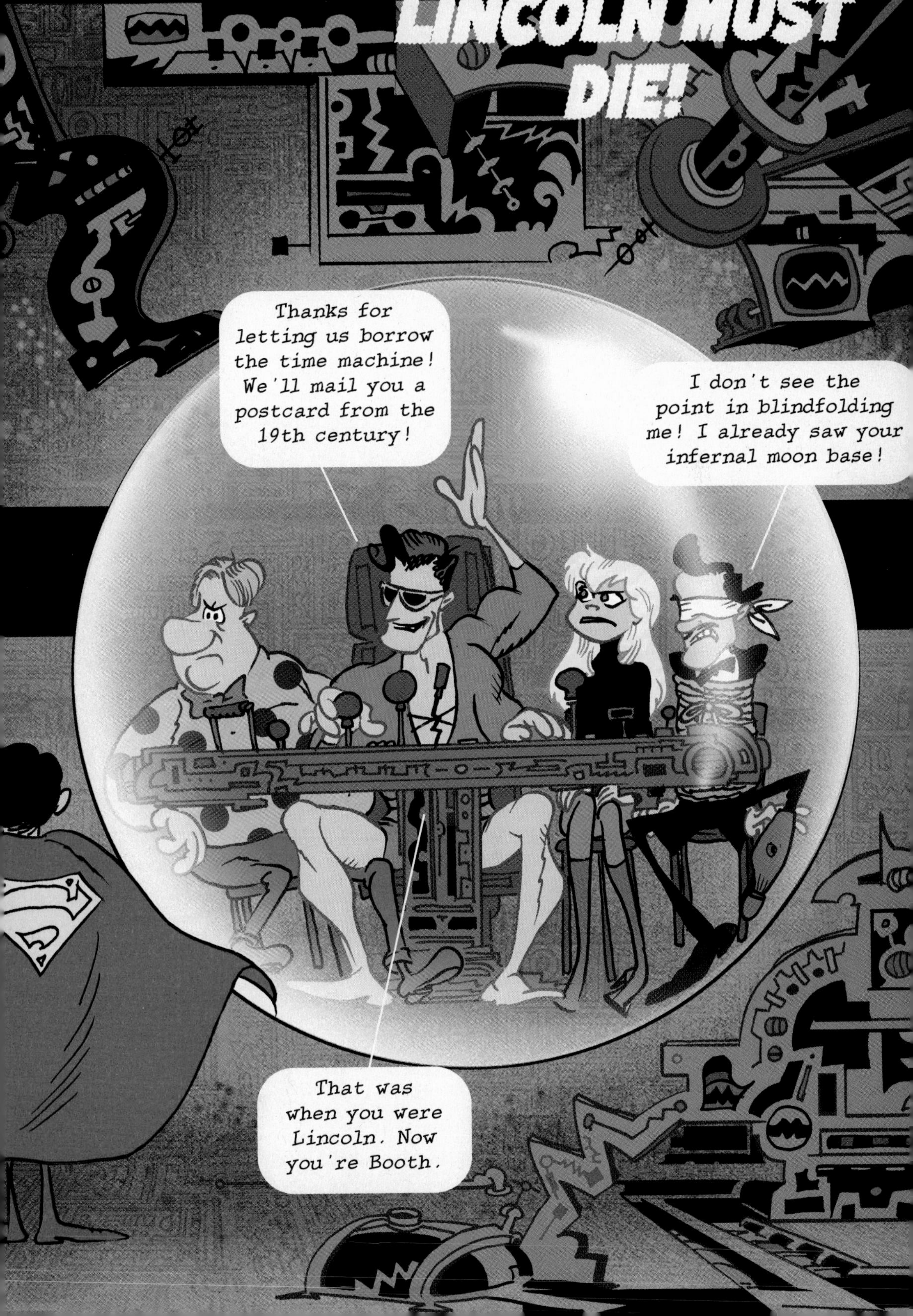
Thanks for letting us borrow the time machine! We'll mail you a postcard from the 19th century!
I don't see the point in blindfolding me! I already saw your infernal moon base!
That was when you were Lincoln. Now you're Booth.

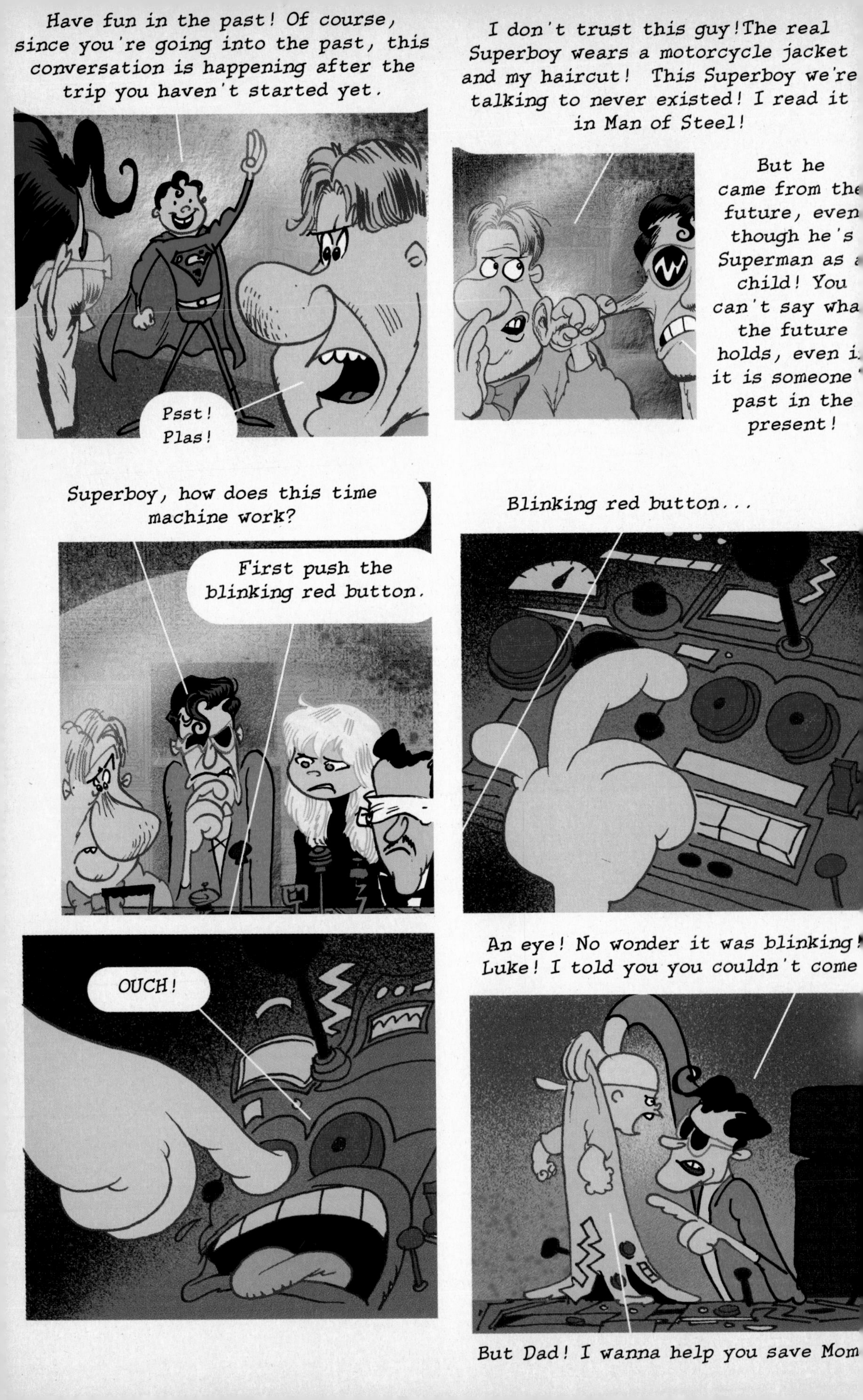
Have fun in the past! Of course, since you're going into the past, this conversation is happening after the trip you haven't started yet.
Psst! Plas!
I don't trust this guy! The real Superboy wears a motorcycle jacket and my haircut! This Superboy we're talking to never existed! I read it in Man of Steel!
But he came from th future, even though he's Superman as child! You can't say wha the future holds, even i it is someone past in the present!
Superboy, how does this time machine work?
First push the blinking red button.
Blinking red button...
OUCH!
An eye! No wonder it was blinking Luke! I told you you couldn't come
But Dad! I wanna help you save Mom

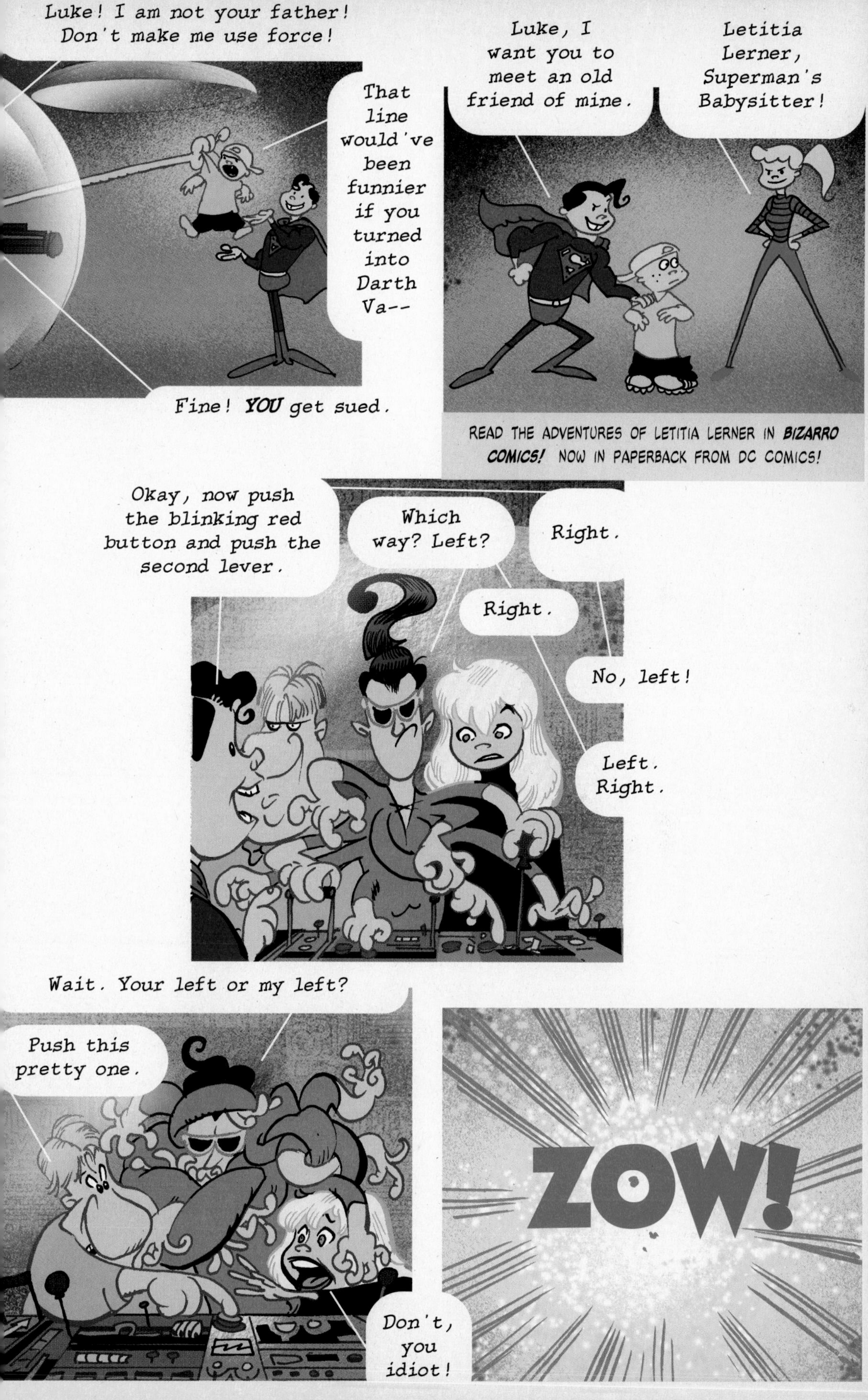
Luke! I am not your father! Don't make me use force!
That line would've been funnier if you turned into Darth Va--
Fine! YOU get sued.
Luke, I want you to meet an old friend of mine.
Letitia Lerner, Superman's Babysitter!
READ THE ADVENTURES OF LETITIA LERNER IN BIZARRO COMICS! NOW IN PAPERBACK FROM DC COMICS!
Okay, now push the blinking red button and push the second lever.
Which way? Left?
Right.
Right.
No, left!
Left. Right.
Wait. Your left or my left?
Push this pretty one.
Don't, you idiot!
ZOW!

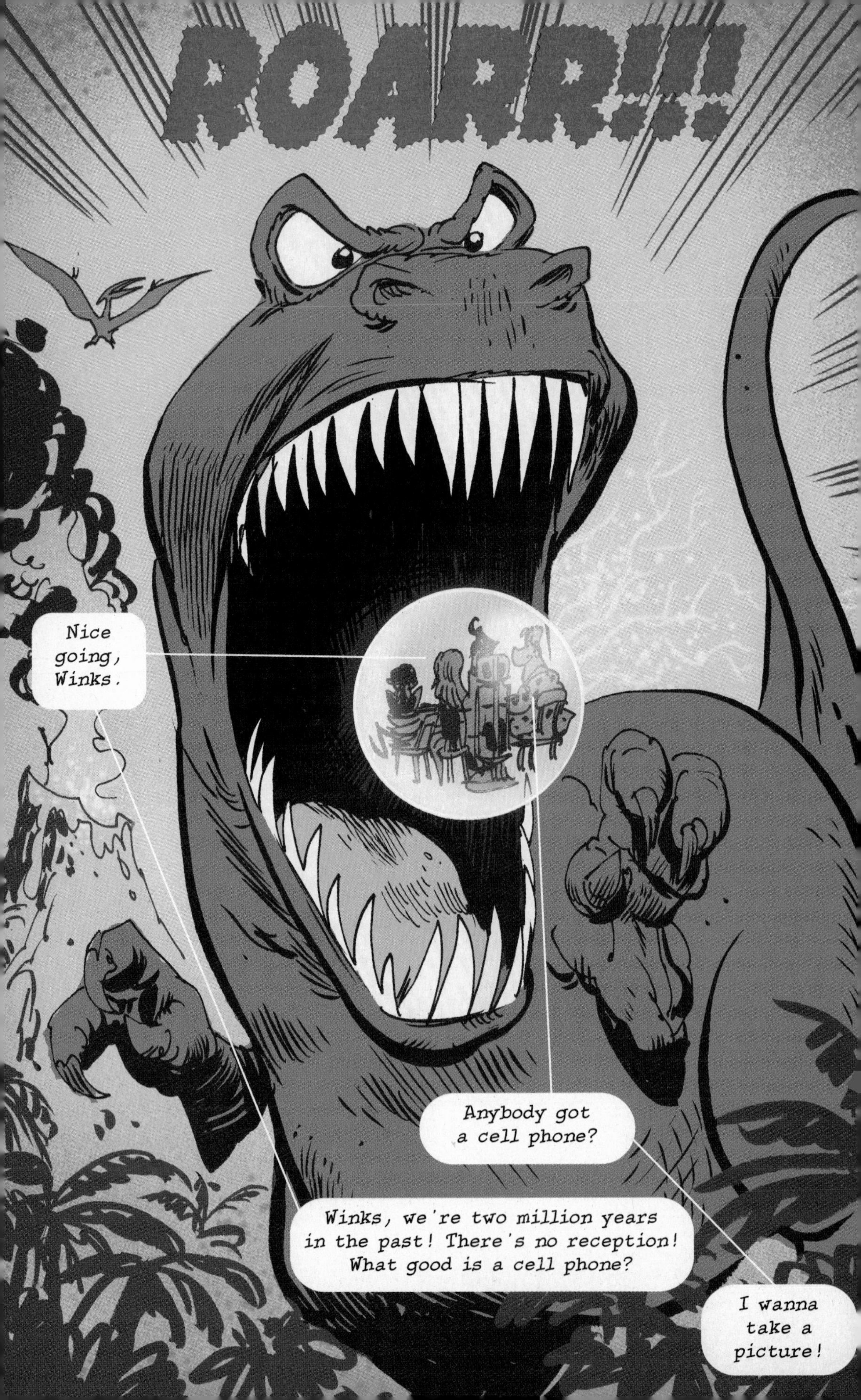
ROARR!!!
Nice going, Winks.
Anybody got a cell phone?
Winks, we're two million years in the past! There's no reception! What good is a cell phone?
I wanna take a picture!

I can't hold his teeth back! Either get us out of here or figure out what jewelry you want for all your new body piercings!

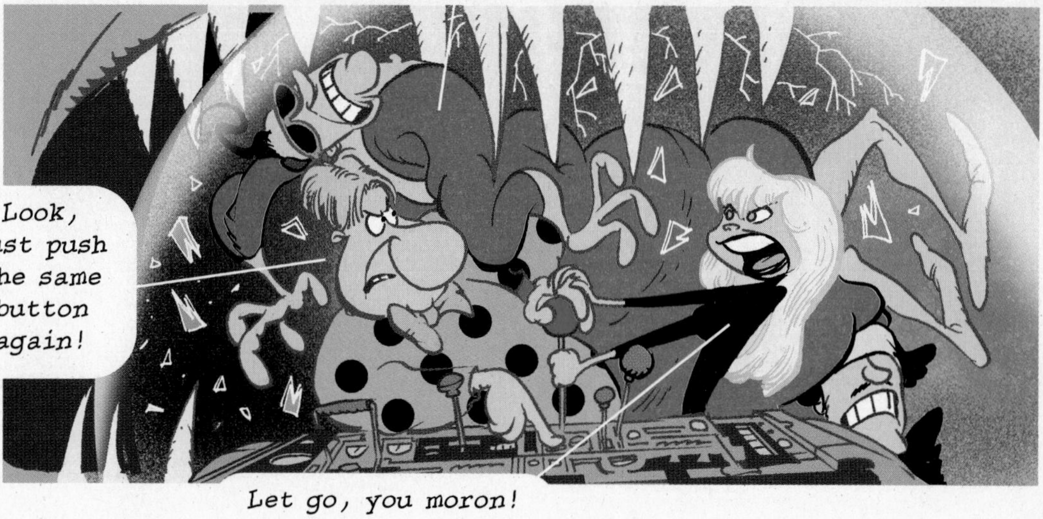
Look, just push the same button again!
Let go, you moron!

'm not a moron. I'm just big boned.

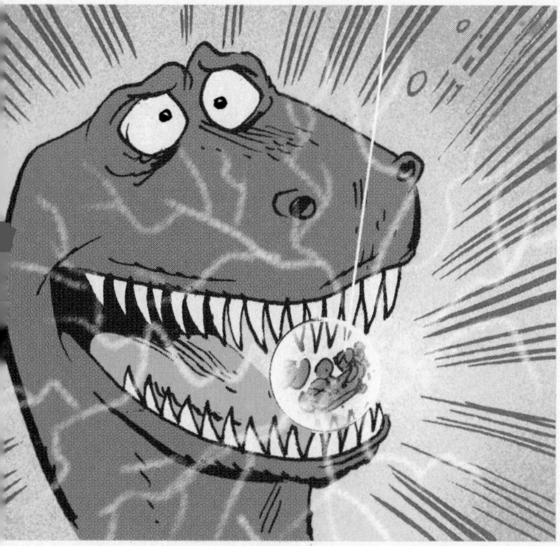

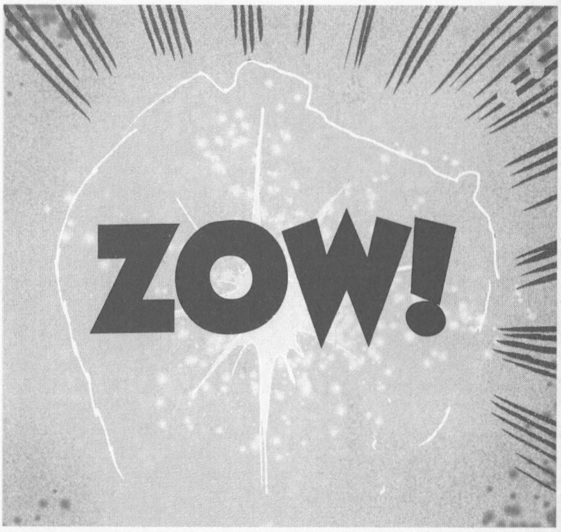
ZOW!

Draw, yuh yella belly lily-livered owlhoot! This town ain't big enough for the -- JUMPIN' JEHOSEPHAT!

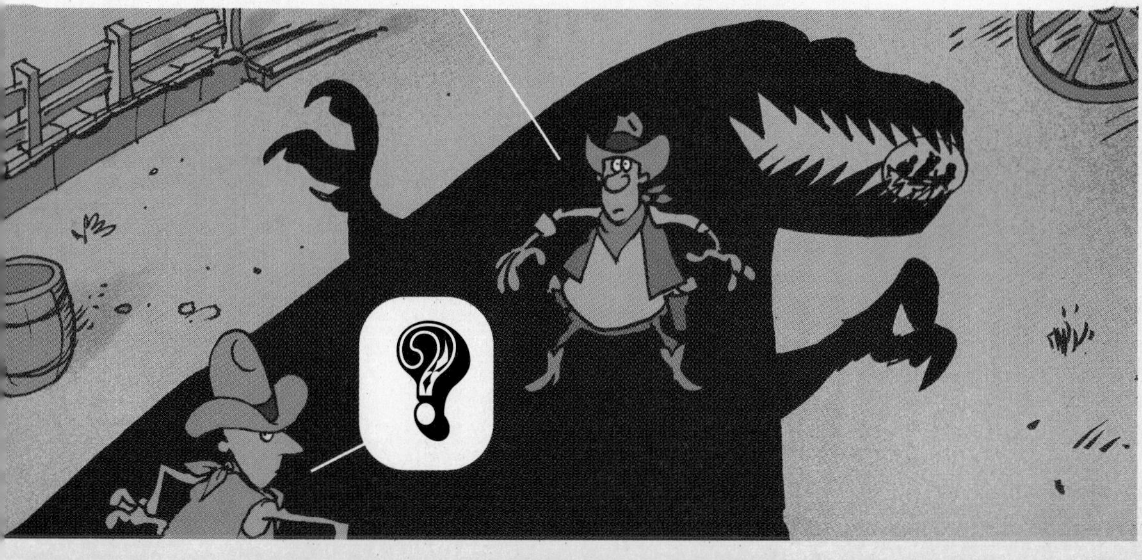
?

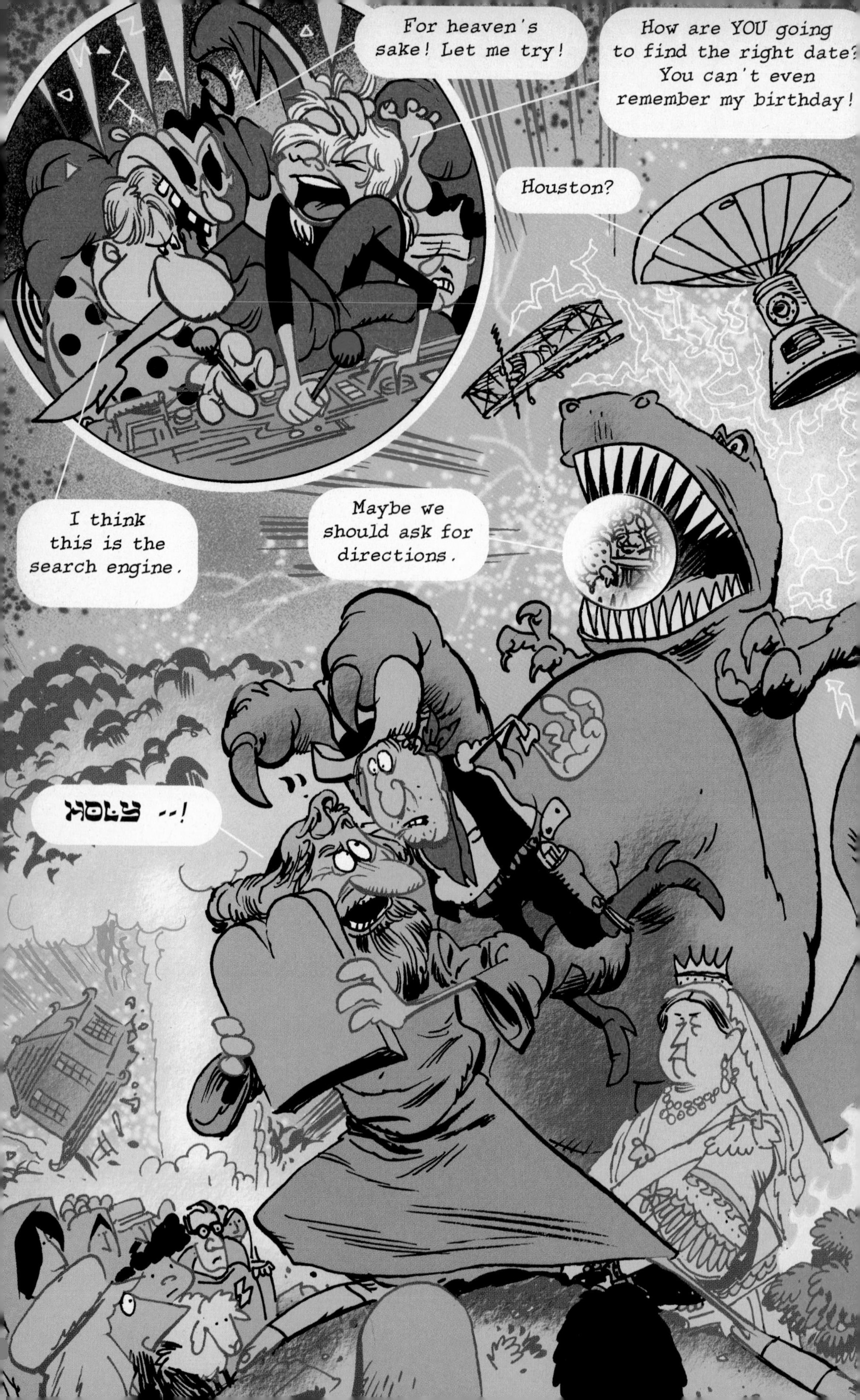
For heaven's sake! Let me try!
How are YOU going to find the right date? You can't even remember my birthday!
Houston?
I think this is the search engine.
Maybe we should ask for directions.
HOLY --!

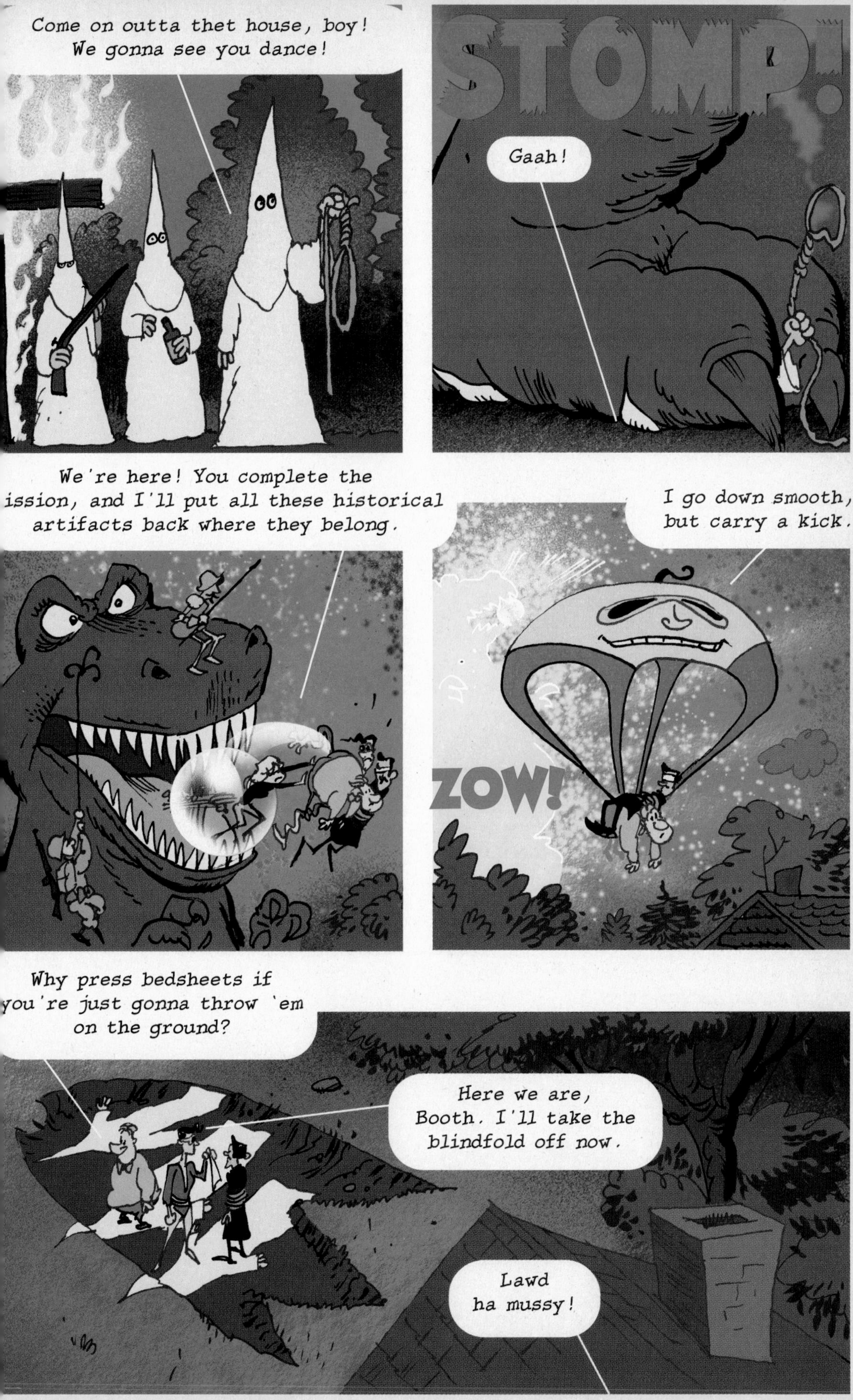
Come on outta thet house, boy! We gonna see you dance!
STOMP!
Gaah!
We're here! You complete the ission, and I'll put all these historical artifacts back where they belong.
I go down smooth, but carry a kick.
ZOW!
Why press bedsheets if you're just gonna throw 'em on the ground?
Here we are, Booth. I'll take the blindfold off now.
Lawd ha mussy!

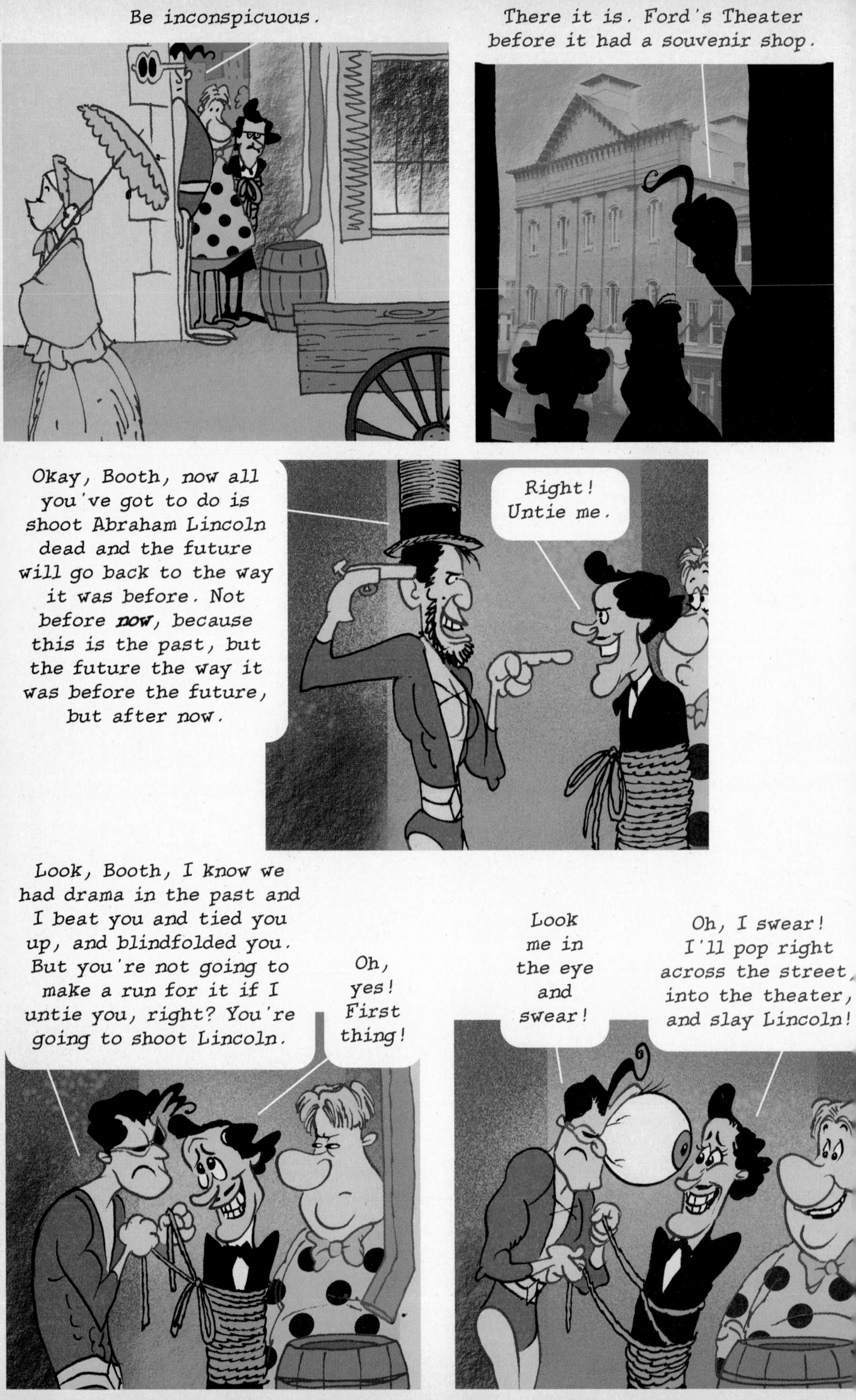
Be inconspicuous.
There it is. Ford's Theater before it had a souvenir shop.
Okay, Booth, now all you've got to do is shoot Abraham Lincoln dead and the future will go back to the way it was before. Not before **now**, because this is the past, but the future the way it was before the future, but after now.
Right! Untie me.
Look, Booth, I know we had drama in the past and I beat you and tied you up, and blindfolded you. But you're not going to make a run for it if I untie you, right? You're going to shoot Lincoln.
Oh, yes! First thing!
Look me in the eye and swear!
Oh, I swear! I'll pop right across the street, into the theater, and slay Lincoln!

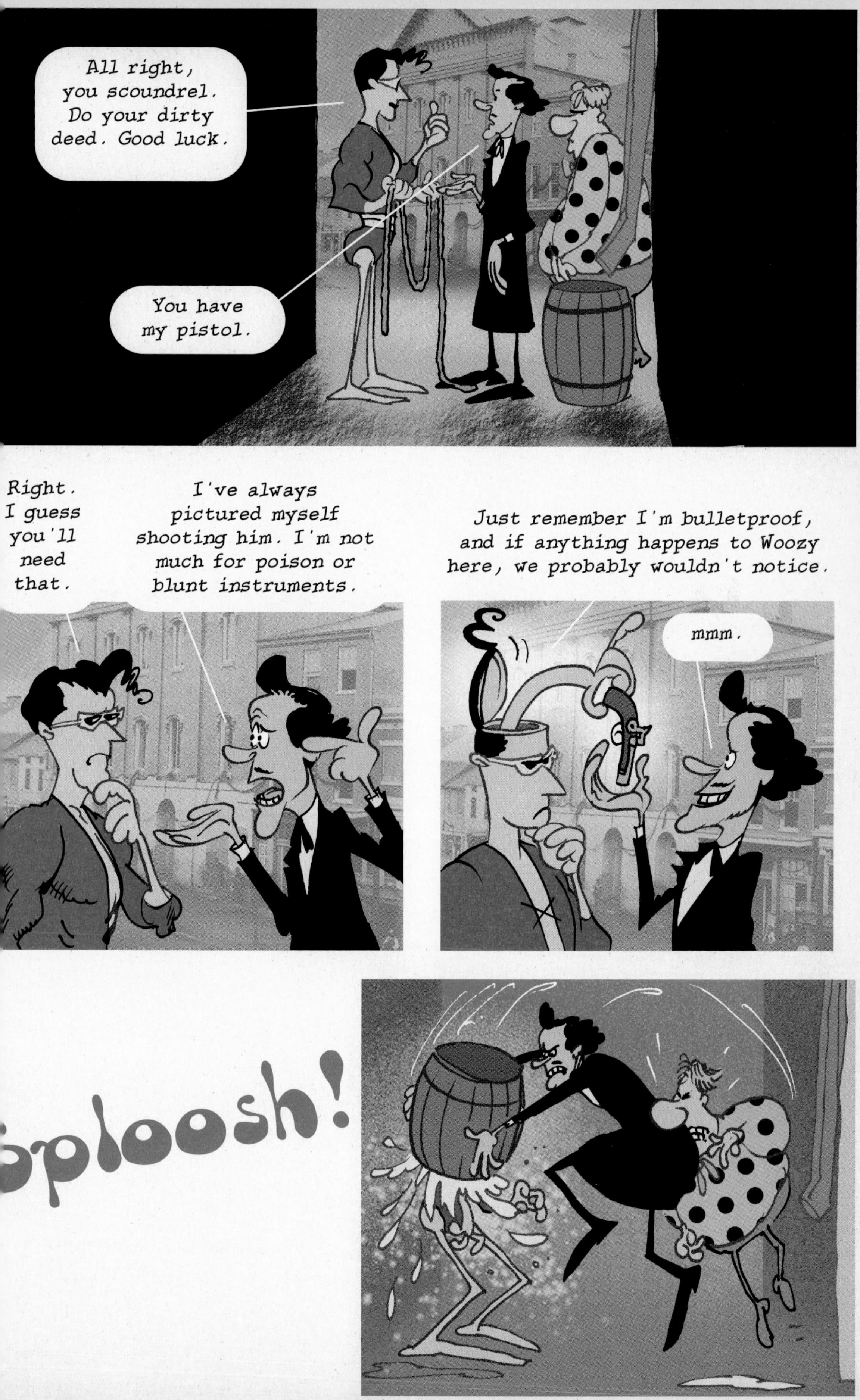
All right, you scoundrel. Do your dirty deed. Good luck.
You have my pistol.
Right. I guess you'll need that.
I've always pictured myself shooting him. I'm not much for poison or blunt instruments.
Just remember I'm bulletproof, and if anything happens to Woozy here, we probably wouldn't notice.
mmm.
Sploosh!

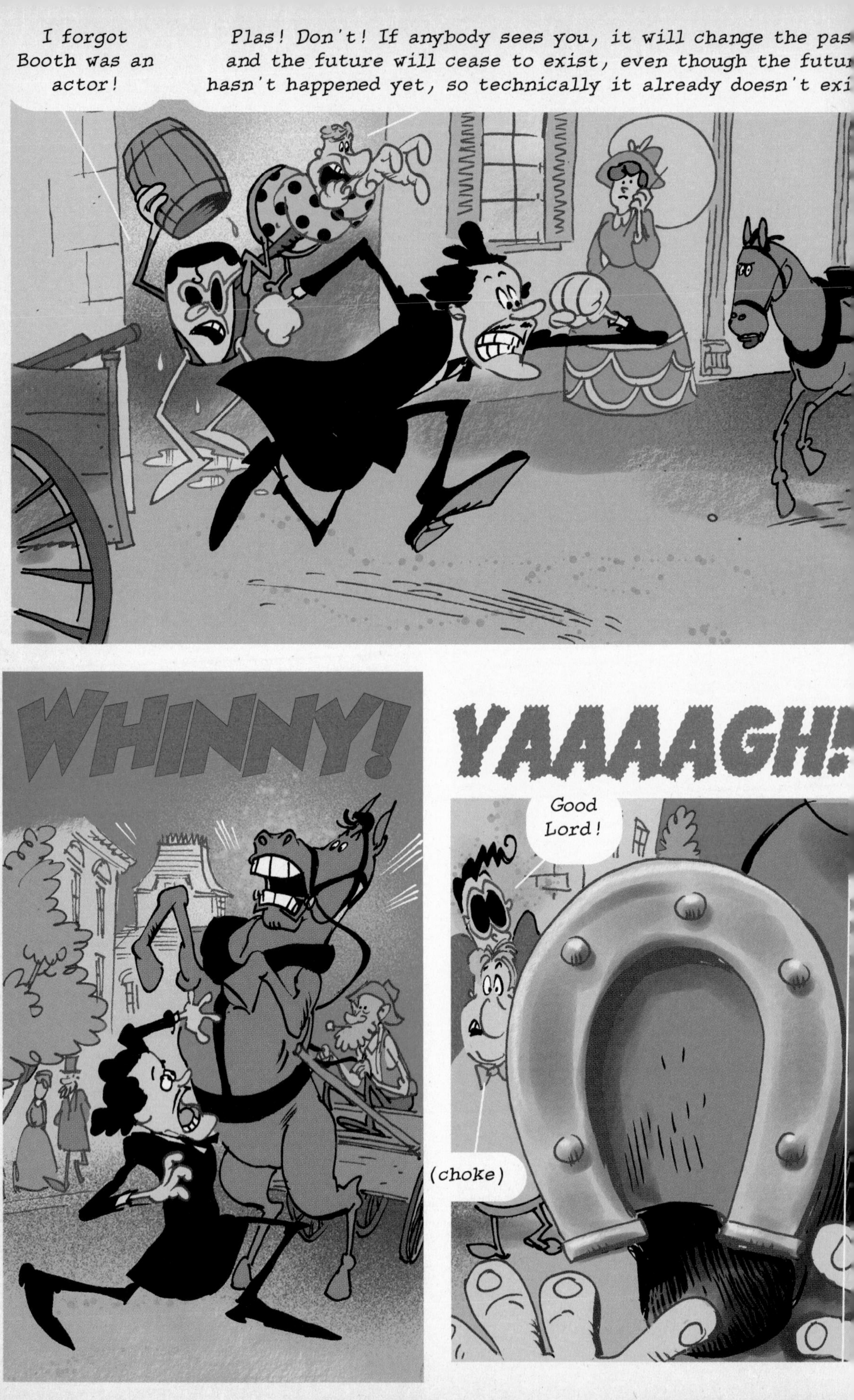
I forgot Booth was an actor!
Plas! Don't! If anybody sees you, it will change the pas
and the future will cease to exist, even though the futu
hasn't happened yet, so technically it already doesn't exi
WHINNY!
YAAAAGH!
Good Lord!
(choke)

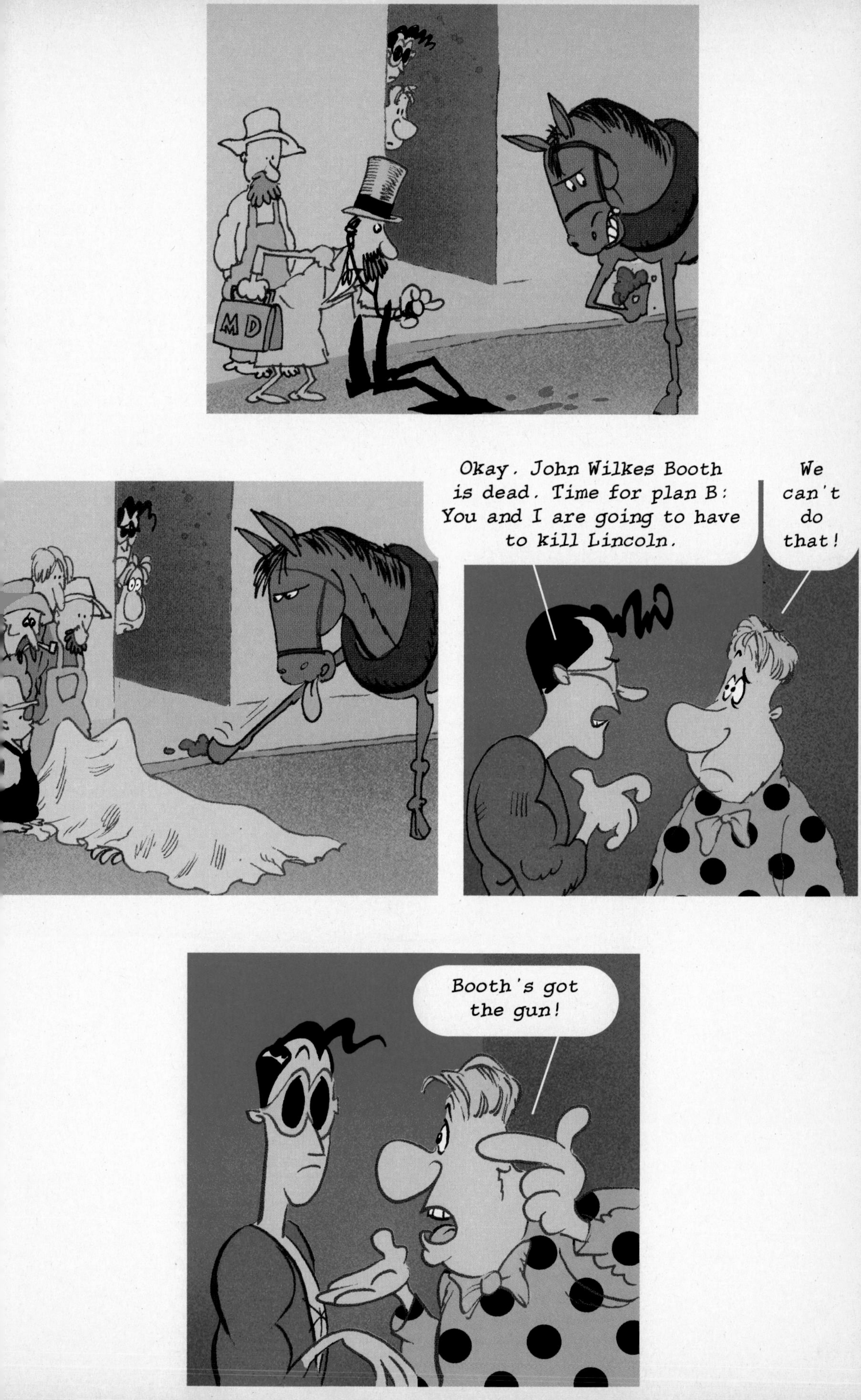

MD
Okay. John Wilkes Booth is dead. Time for plan B: You and I are going to have to kill Lincoln.
We can't do that!
Booth's got the gun!

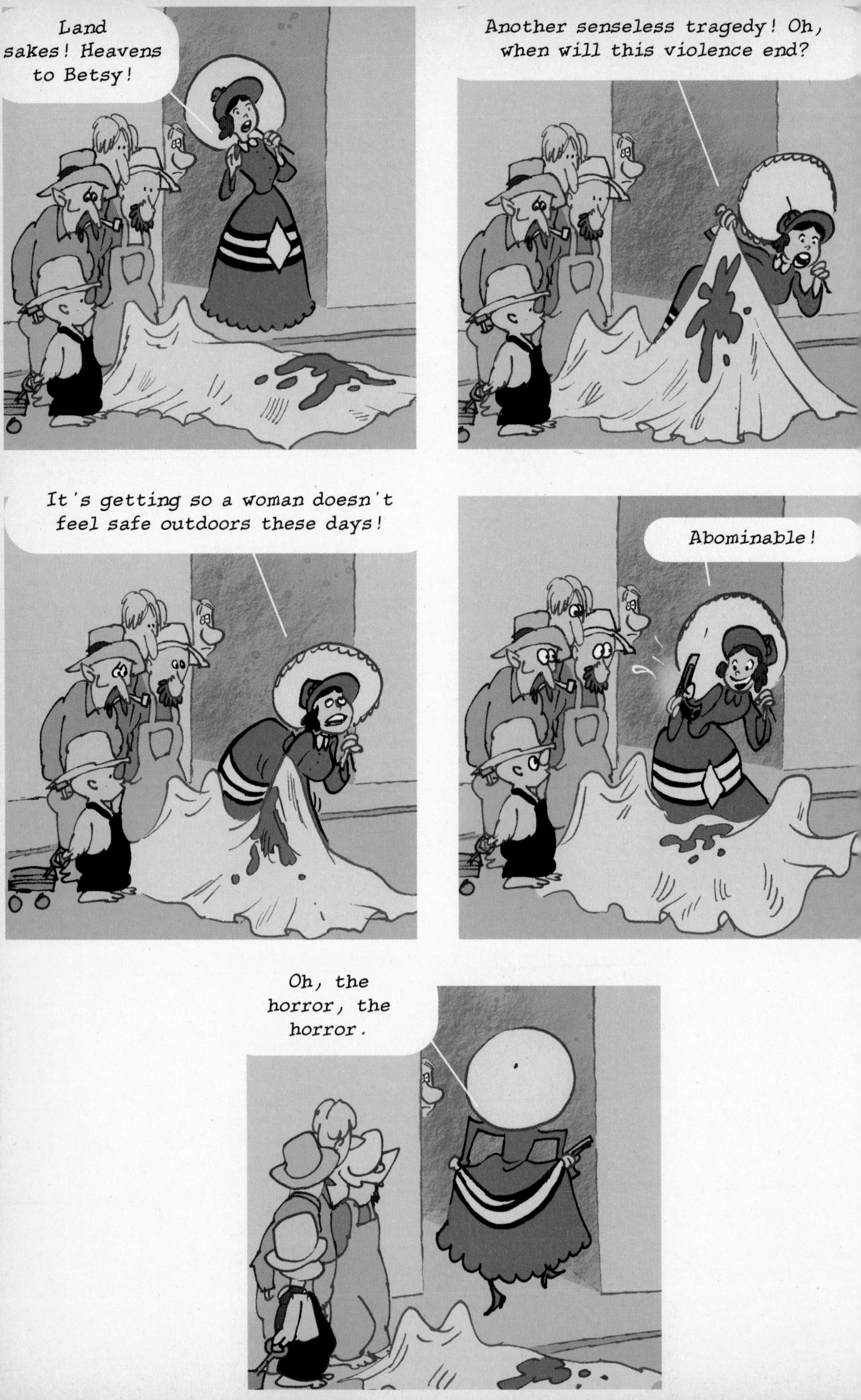
Land sakes! Heavens to Betsy!
Another senseless tragedy! Oh, when will this violence end?
It's getting so a woman doesn't feel safe outdoors these days!
Abominable!
Oh, the horror, the horror.

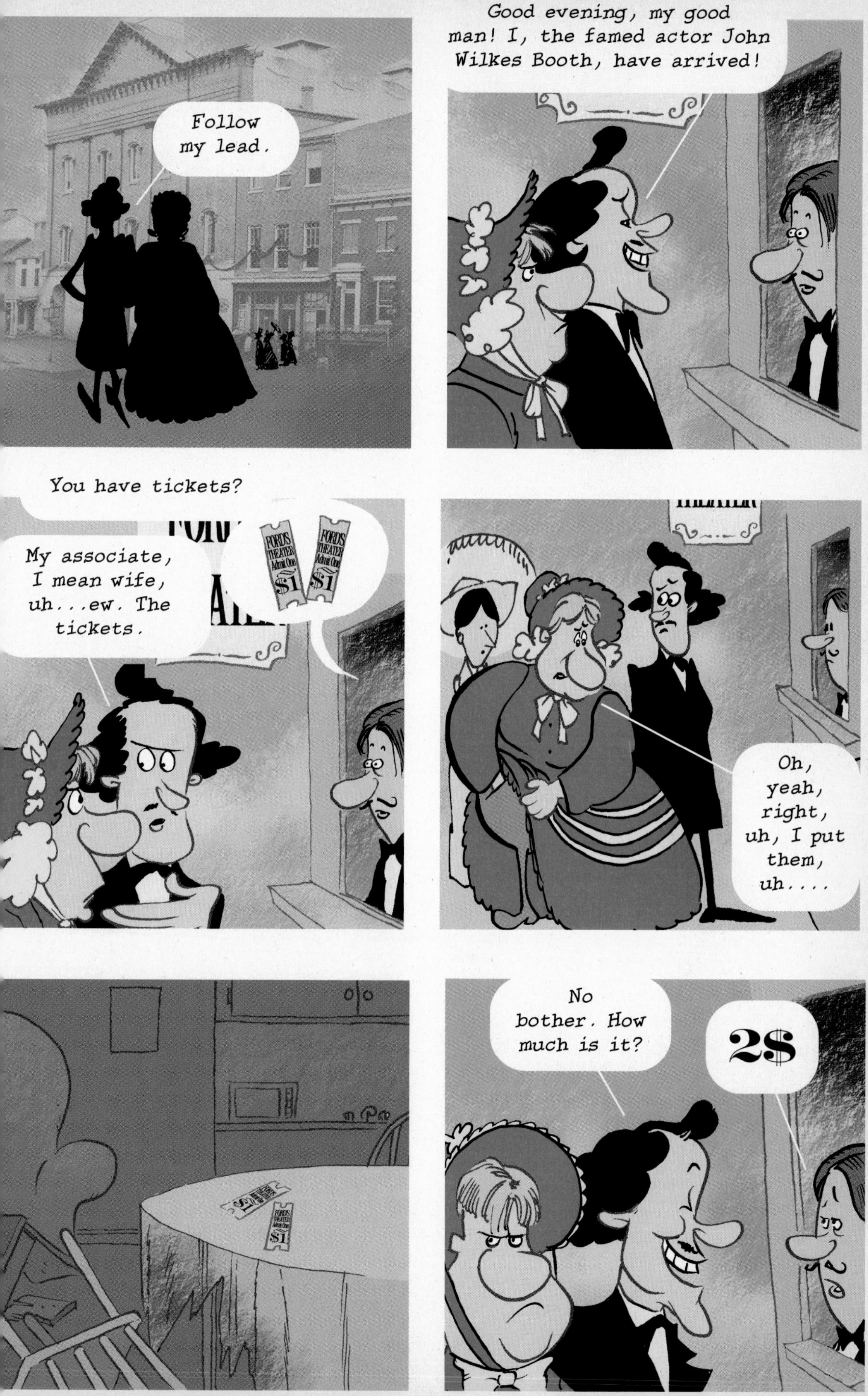
Follow my lead.
Good evening, my good man! I, the famed actor John Wilkes Booth, have arrived!
You have tickets?
My associate, I mean wife, uh...ew. The tickets.
FORDS THEATER Admit One $1
Oh, yeah, right, uh, I put them, uh....
No bother. How much is it?
2$

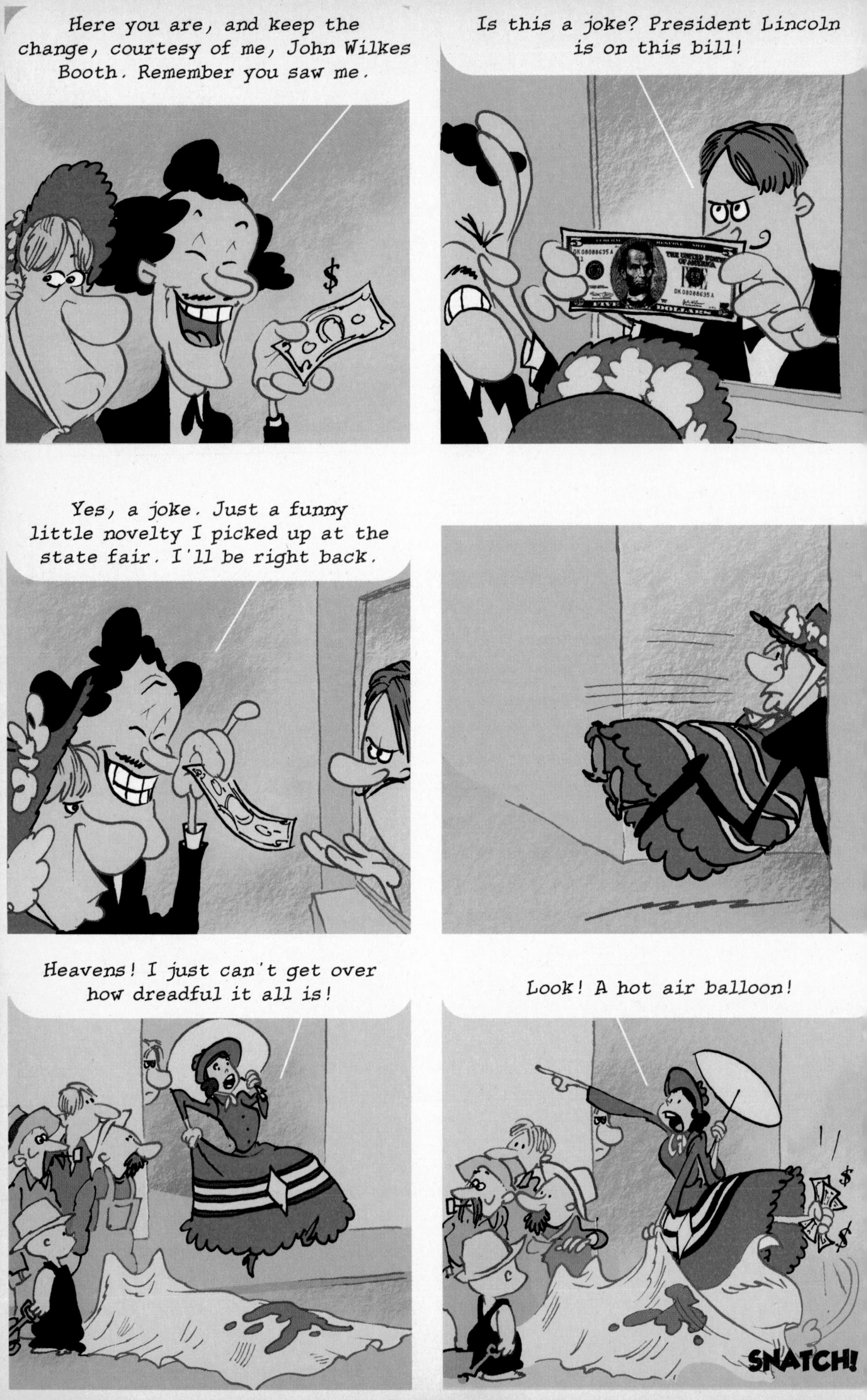
Here you are, and keep the change, courtesy of me, John Wilkes Booth. Remember you saw me.
$
Is this a joke? President Lincoln is on this bill!
Yes, a joke. Just a funny little novelty I picked up at the state fair. I'll be right back.
Heavens! I just can't get over how dreadful it all is!
Look! A hot air balloon!
SNATCH!

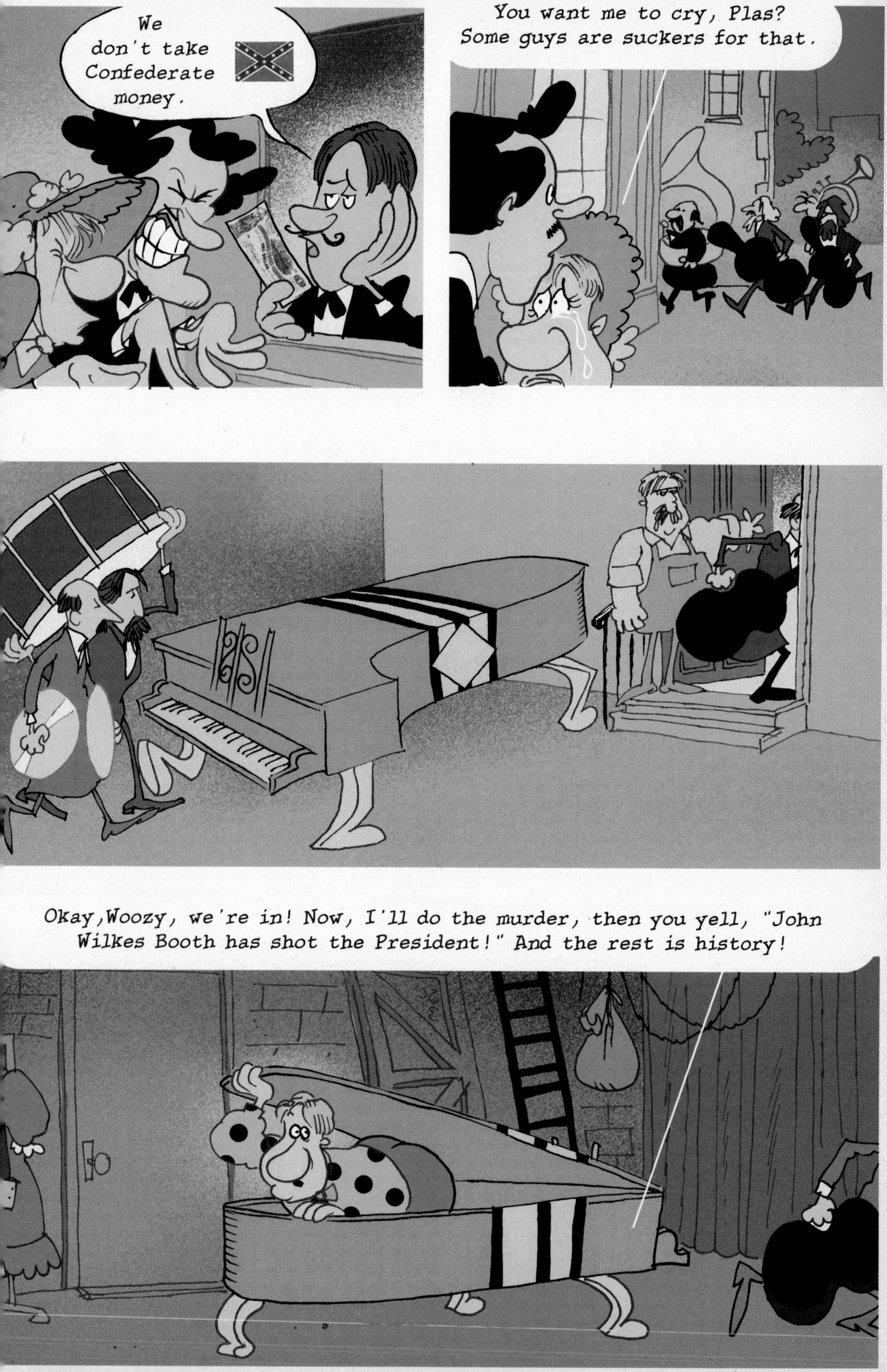
We don't take Confederate money.
You want me to cry, Plas? Some guys are suckers for that.
Okay, Woozy, we're in! Now, I'll do the murder, then you yell, "John Wilkes Booth has shot the President!" And the rest is history!

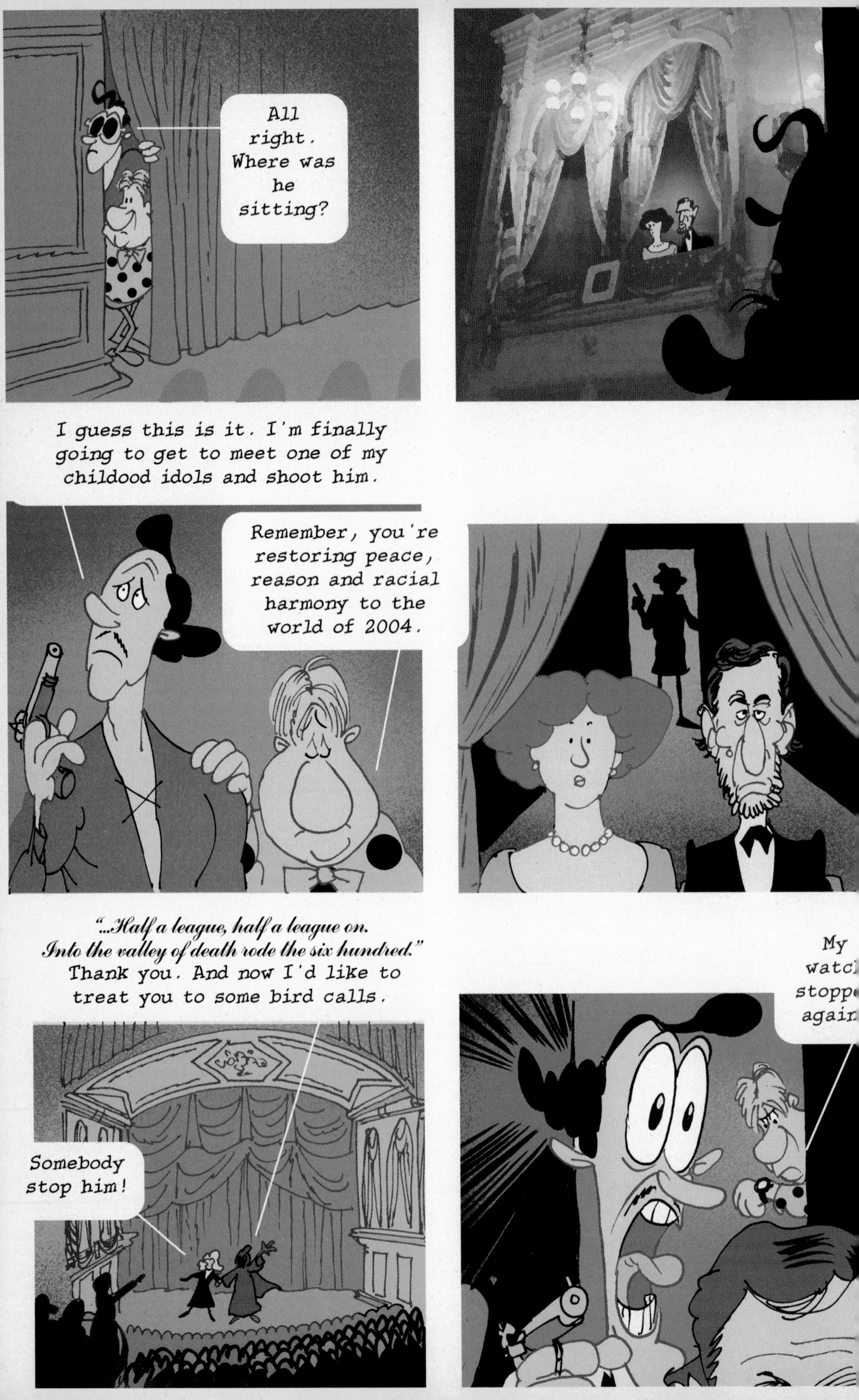
All right. Where was he sitting?
I guess this is it. I'm finally going to get to meet one of my childood idols and shoot him.
Remember, you're restoring peace, reason and racial harmony to the world of 2004.
"...Half a league, half a league on. Into the valley of death rode the six hundred." Thank you. And now I'd like to treat you to some bird calls.
Somebody stop him!
My watc stopp agai

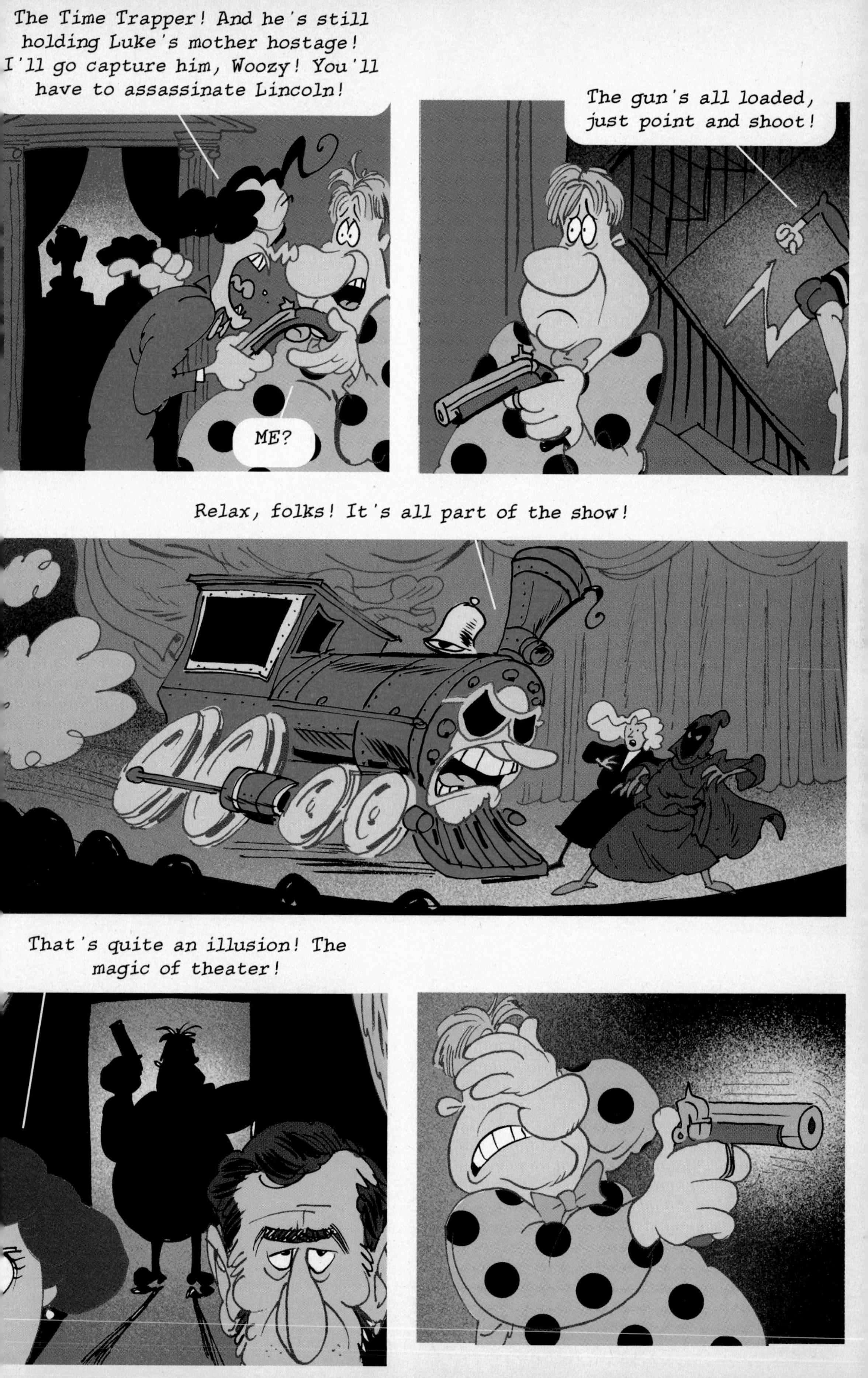

The Time Trapper! And he's still holding Luke's mother hostage! I'll go capture him, Woozy! You'll have to assassinate Lincoln!
ME?
The gun's all loaded, just point and shoot!
Relax, folks! It's all part of the show!
That's quite an illusion! The magic of theater!

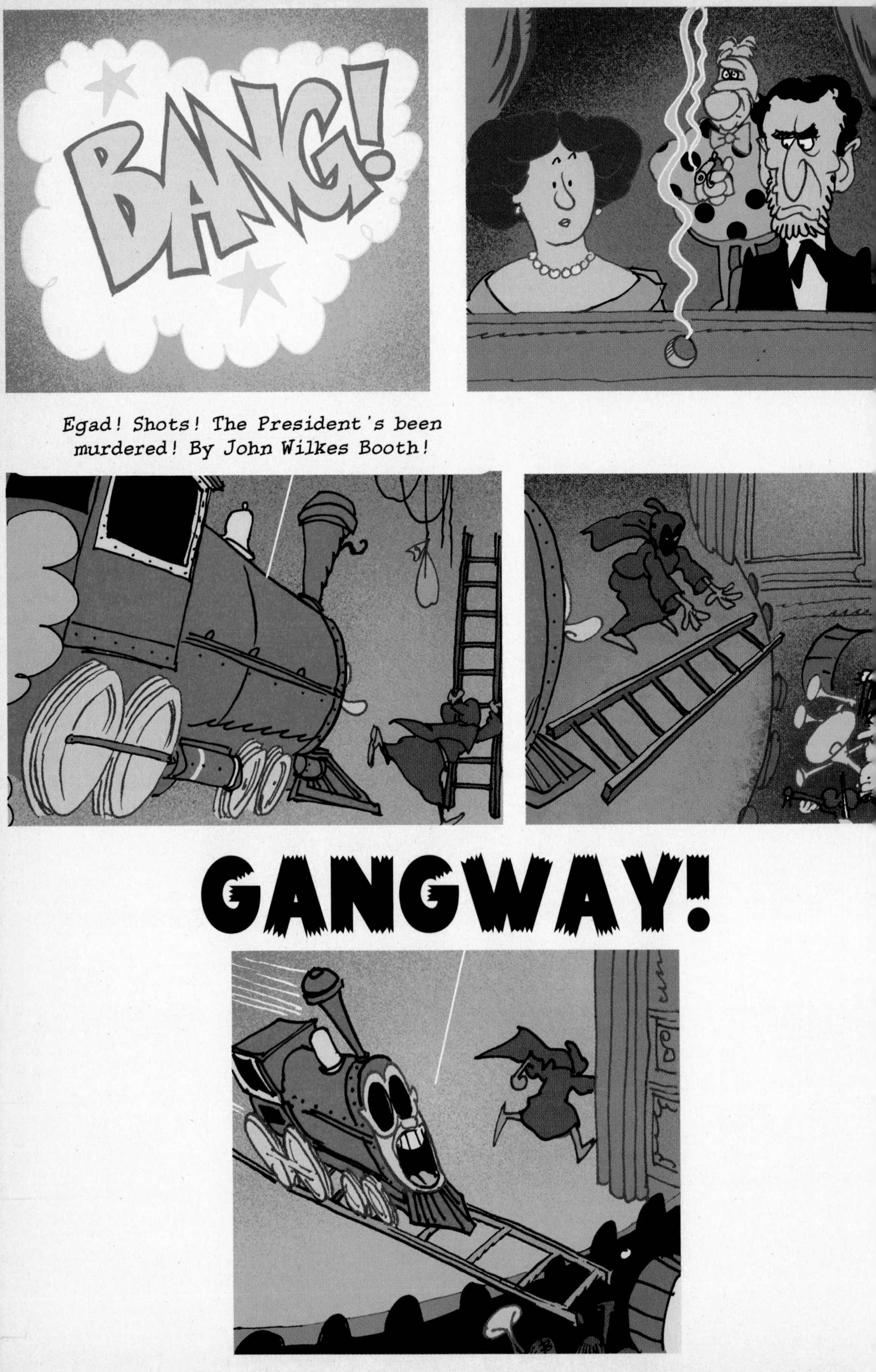
BANG!
Egad! Shots! The President's been murdered! By John Wilkes Booth!
GANGWAY!

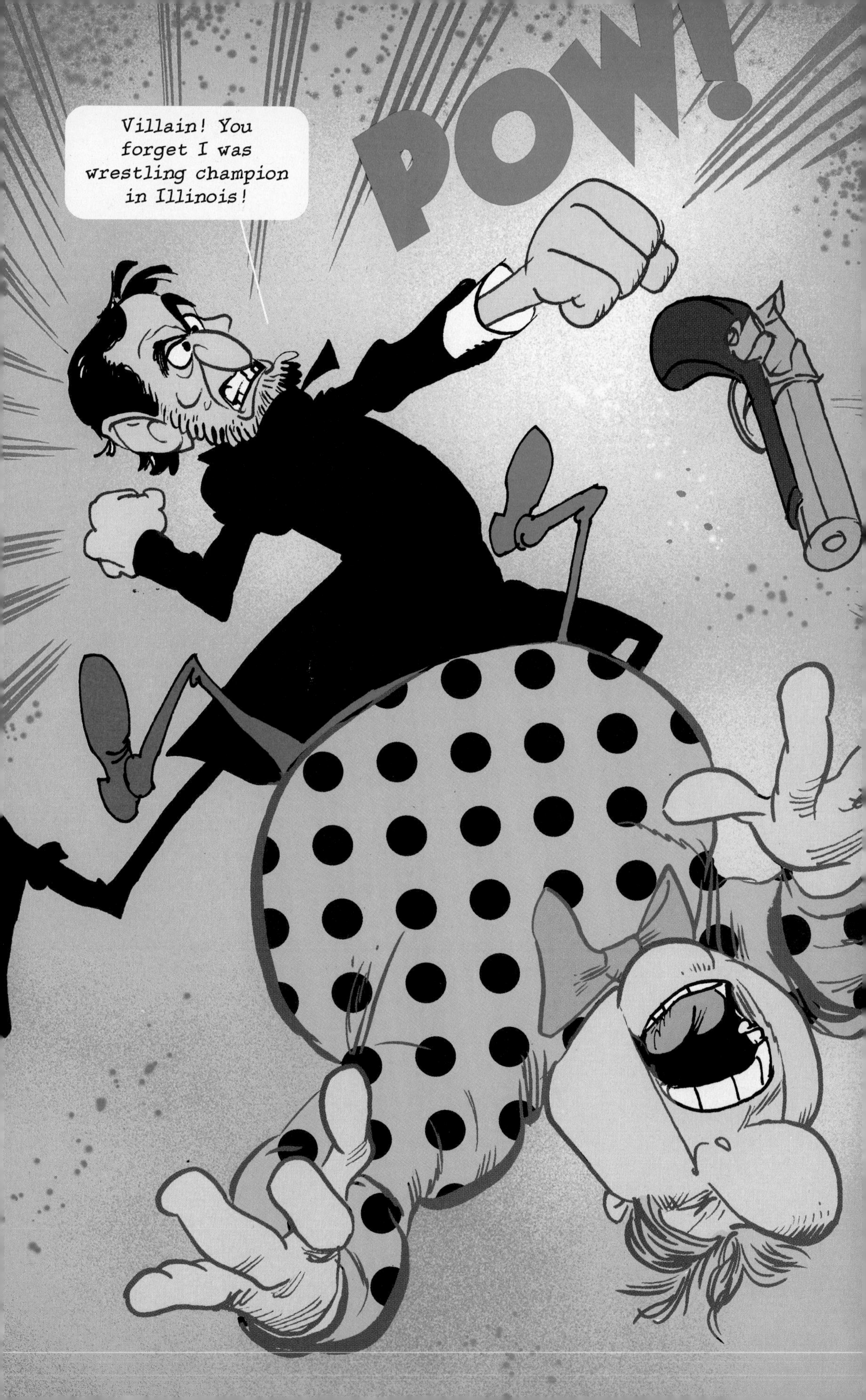
Villain! You forget I was wrestling champion in Illinois!
POW!

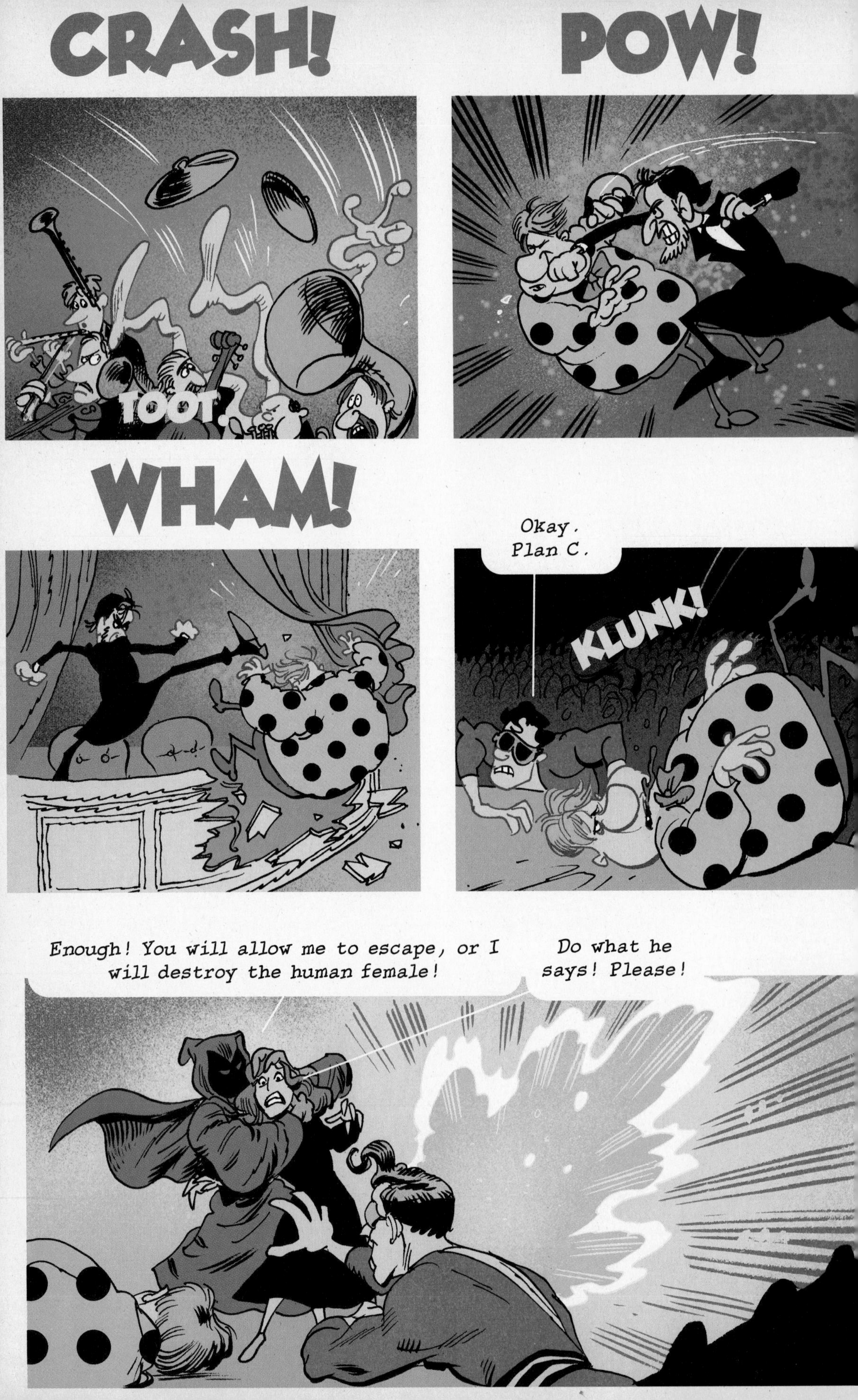
CRASH!
TOOT.
POW!
WHAM!
Okay. Plan C.
KLUNK!
Enough! You will allow me to escape, or I will destroy the human female!
Do what he says! Please!

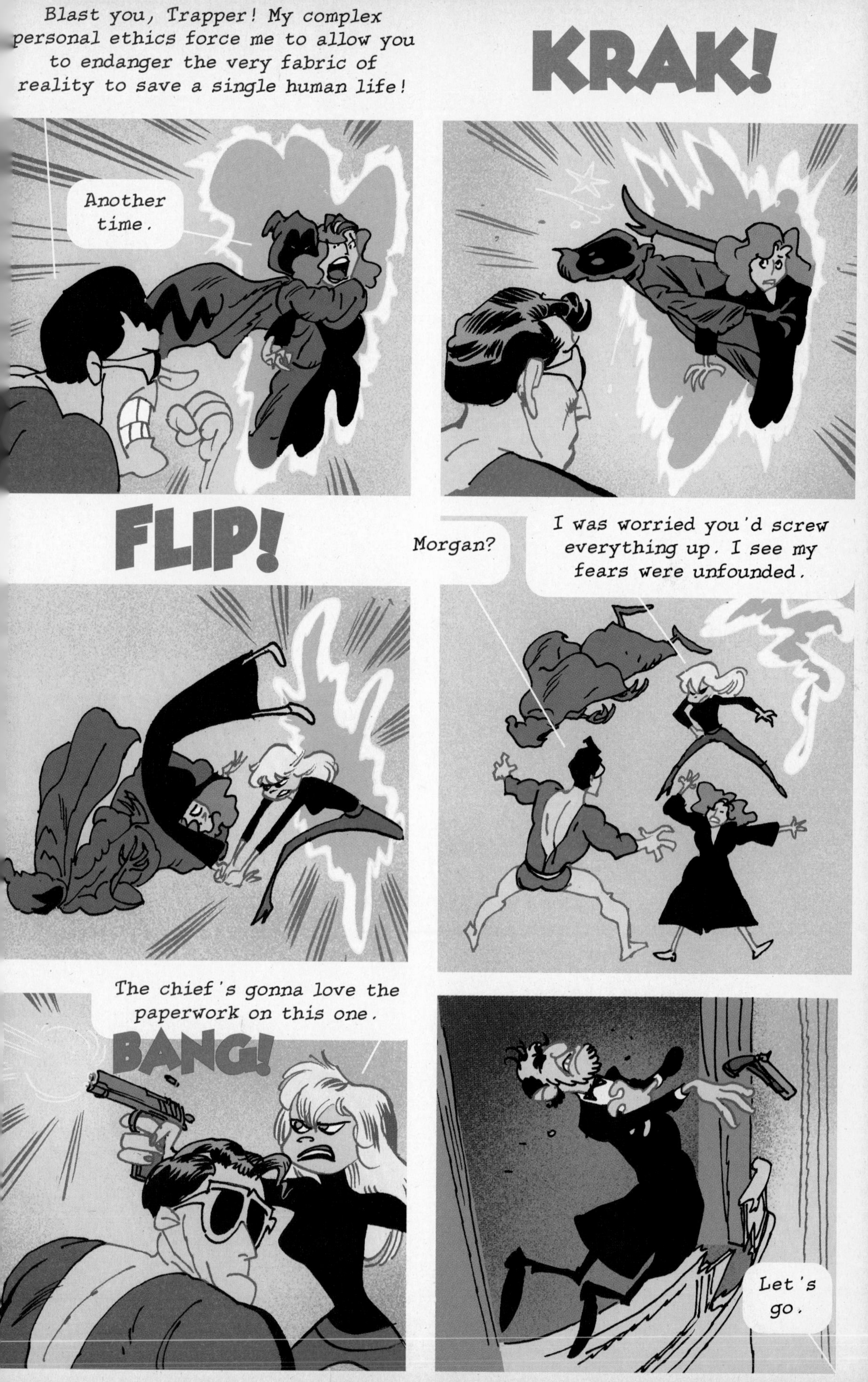
Blast you, Trapper! My complex personal ethics force me to allow you to endanger the very fabric of reality to save a single human life!
KRAK!
Another time.
FLIP!
Morgan?
I was worried you'd screw everything up. I see my fears were unfounded.
The chief's gonna love the paperwork on this one.
BANG!
Let's go.

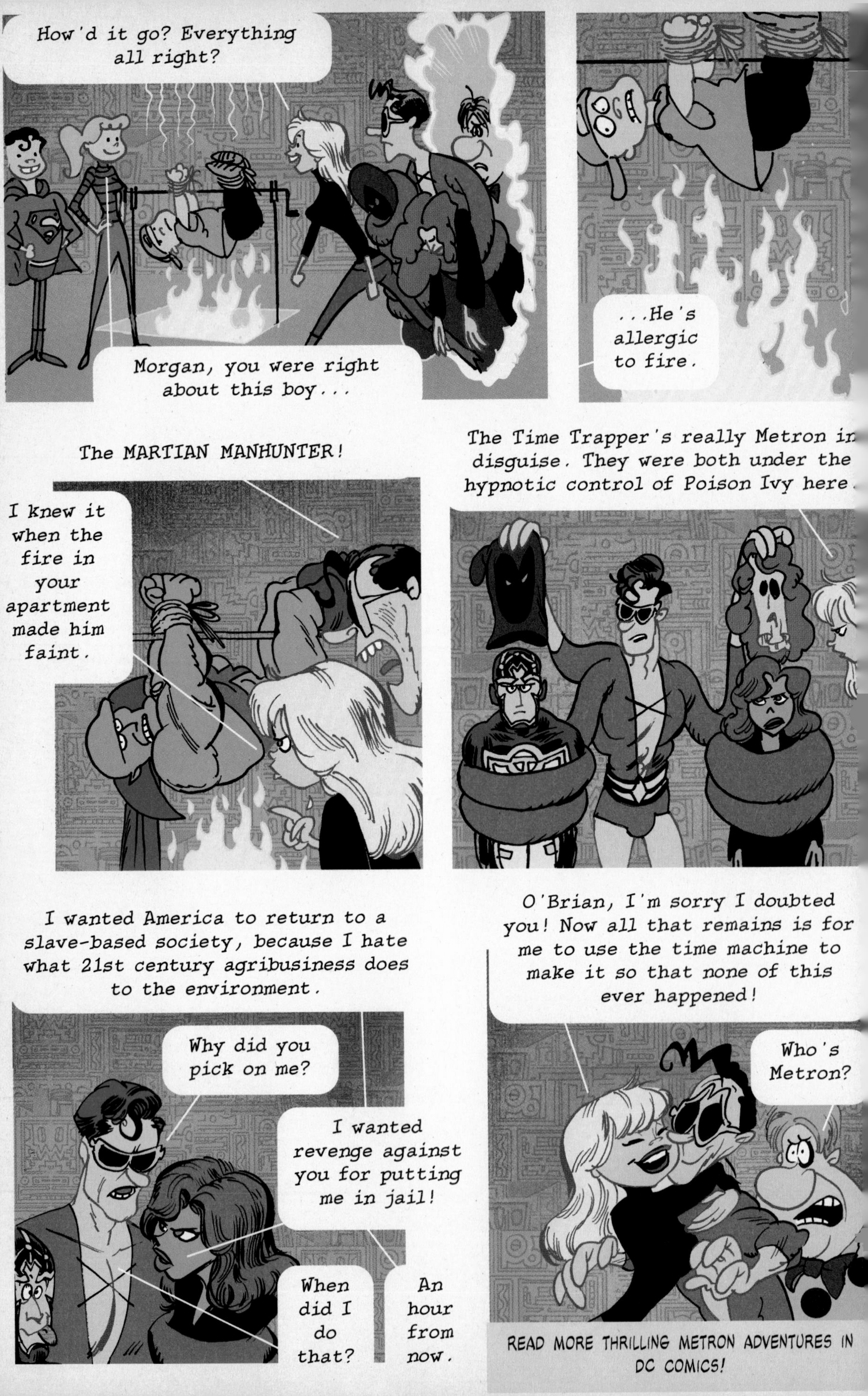
How'd it go? Everything all right?
Morgan, you were right about this boy...
...He's allergic to fire.
The MARTIAN MANHUNTER!
I knew it when the fire in your apartment made him faint.
The Time Trapper's really Metron in disguise. They were both under the hypnotic control of Poison Ivy here.
I wanted America to return to a slave-based society, because I hate what 21st century agribusiness does to the environment.
Why did you pick on me?
I wanted revenge against you for putting me in jail!
When did I do that?
An hour from now.
O'Brian, I'm sorry I doubted you! Now all that remains is for me to use the time machine to make it so that none of this ever happened!
Who's Metron?
READ MORE THRILLING METRON ADVENTURES IN DC COMICS!

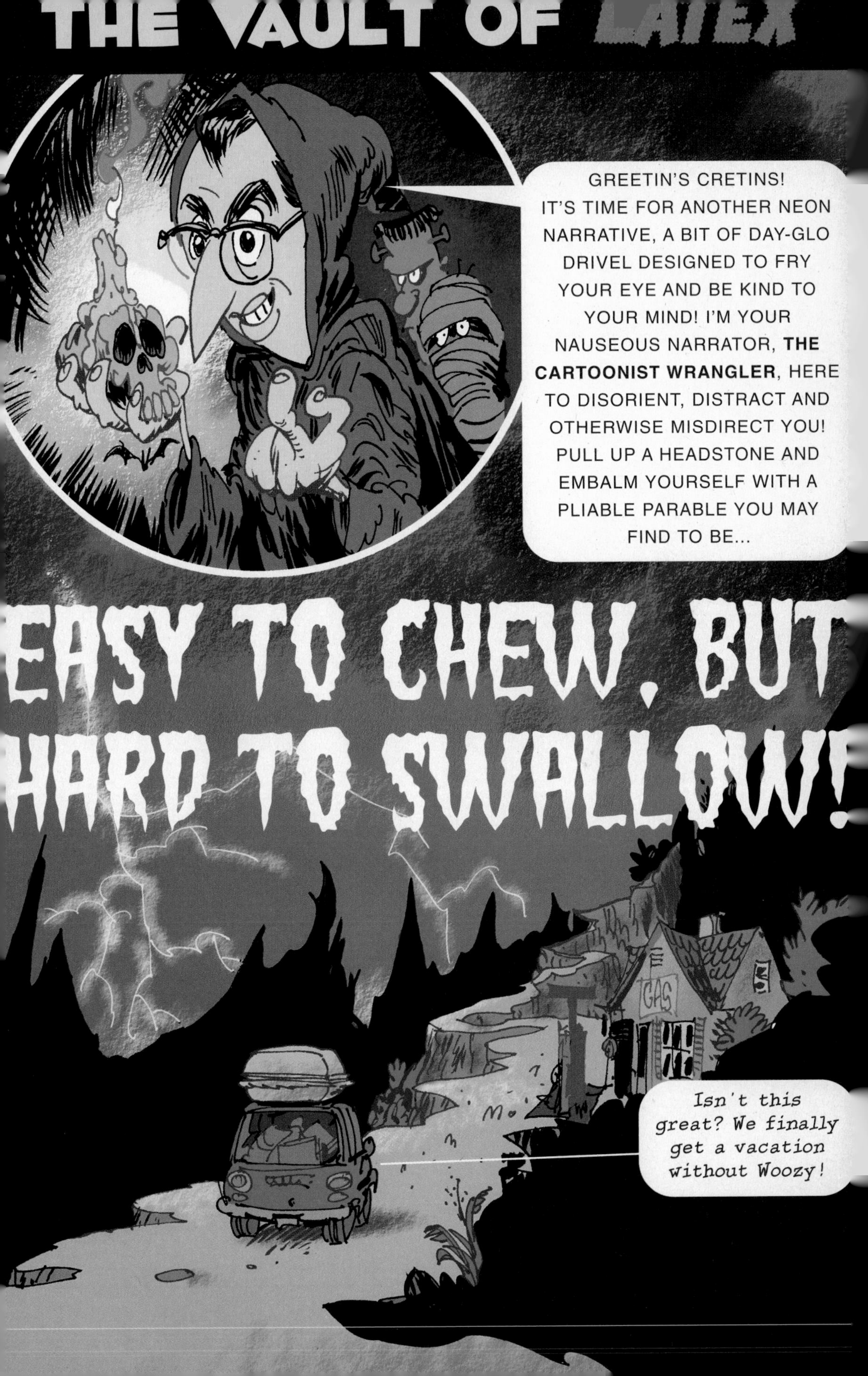
THE VAULT OF LATEX
GREETIN'S CRETINS! IT'S TIME FOR ANOTHER NEON NARRATIVE, A BIT OF DAY-GLO DRIVEL DESIGNED TO FRY YOUR EYE AND BE KIND TO YOUR MIND! I'M YOUR NAUSEOUS NARRATOR, THE CARTOONIST WRANGLER, HERE TO DISORIENT, DISTRACT AND OTHERWISE MISDIRECT YOU! PULL UP A HEADSTONE AND EMBALM YOURSELF WITH A PLIABLE PARABLE YOU MAY FIND TO BE...
EASY TO CHEW, BUT HARD TO SWALLOW!
GAS
Isn't this great? We finally get a vacation without Woozy!

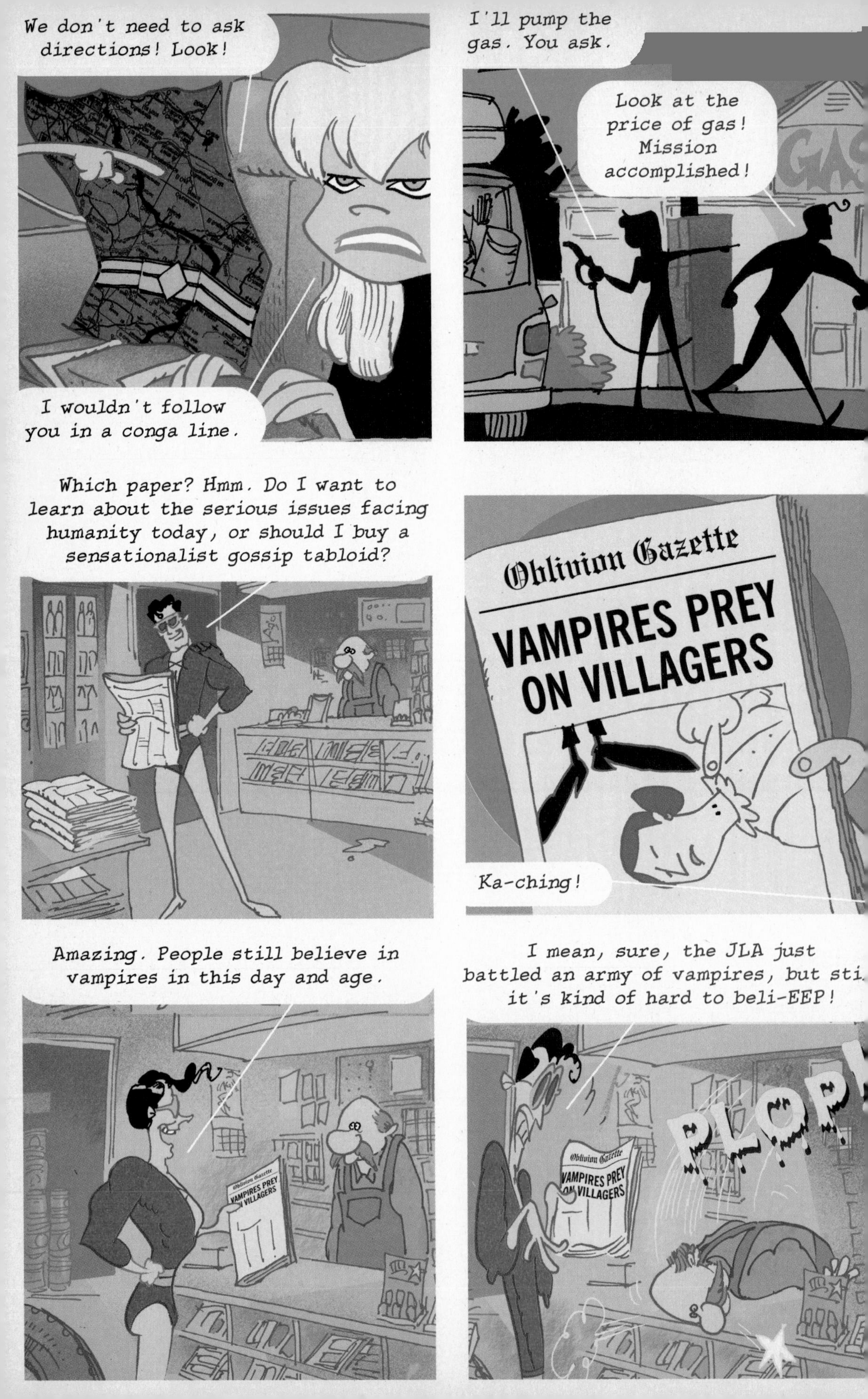
We don't need to ask directions! Look!
I wouldn't follow you in a conga line.
I'll pump the gas. You ask.
Look at the price of gas! Mission accomplished!
GAS
Which paper? Hmm. Do I want to learn about the serious issues facing humanity today, or should I buy a sensationalist gossip tabloid?
Oblivion Gazette
VAMPIRES PREY ON VILLAGERS
Ka-ching!
Amazing. People still believe in vampires in this day and age.
I mean, sure, the JLA just battled an army of vampires, but sti
it's kind of hard to beli-EEP!
PLOP

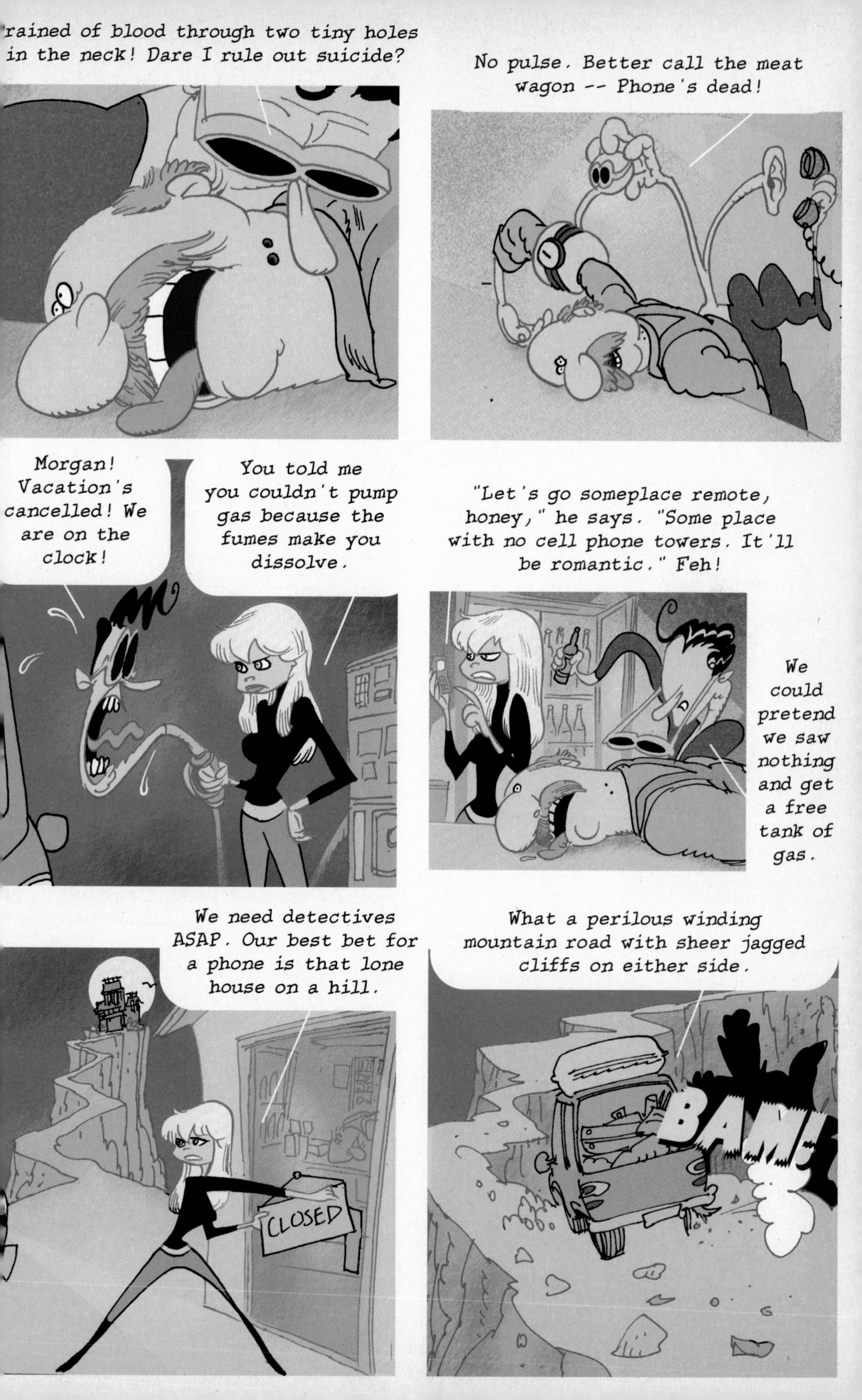

rained of blood through two tiny holes in the neck! Dare I rule out suicide?
No pulse. Better call the meat wagon -- Phone's dead!
Morgan! Vacation's cancelled! We are on the clock!
You told me you couldn't pump gas because the fumes make you dissolve.
"Let's go someplace remote, honey," he says. "Some place with no cell phone towers. It'll be romantic." Feh!
We could pretend we saw nothing and get a free tank of gas.
We need detectives ASAP. Our best bet for a phone is that lone house on a hill.
CLOSED
What a perilous winding mountain road with sheer jagged cliffs on either side.
BAM!

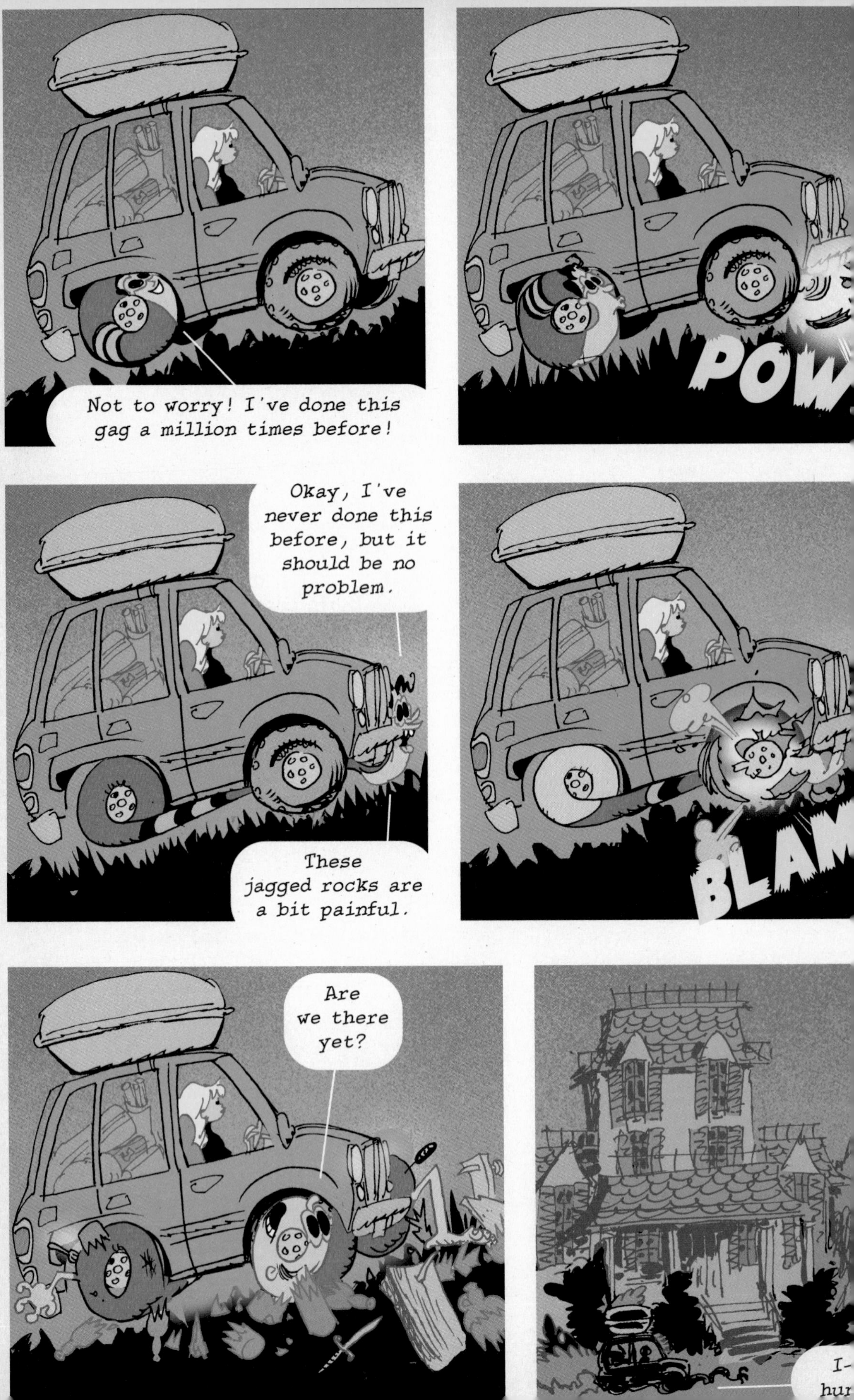
Not to worry! I've done this gag a million times before!
POW
Okay, I've never done this before, but it should be no problem.
These jagged rocks are a bit painful.
BLAM
Are we there yet?

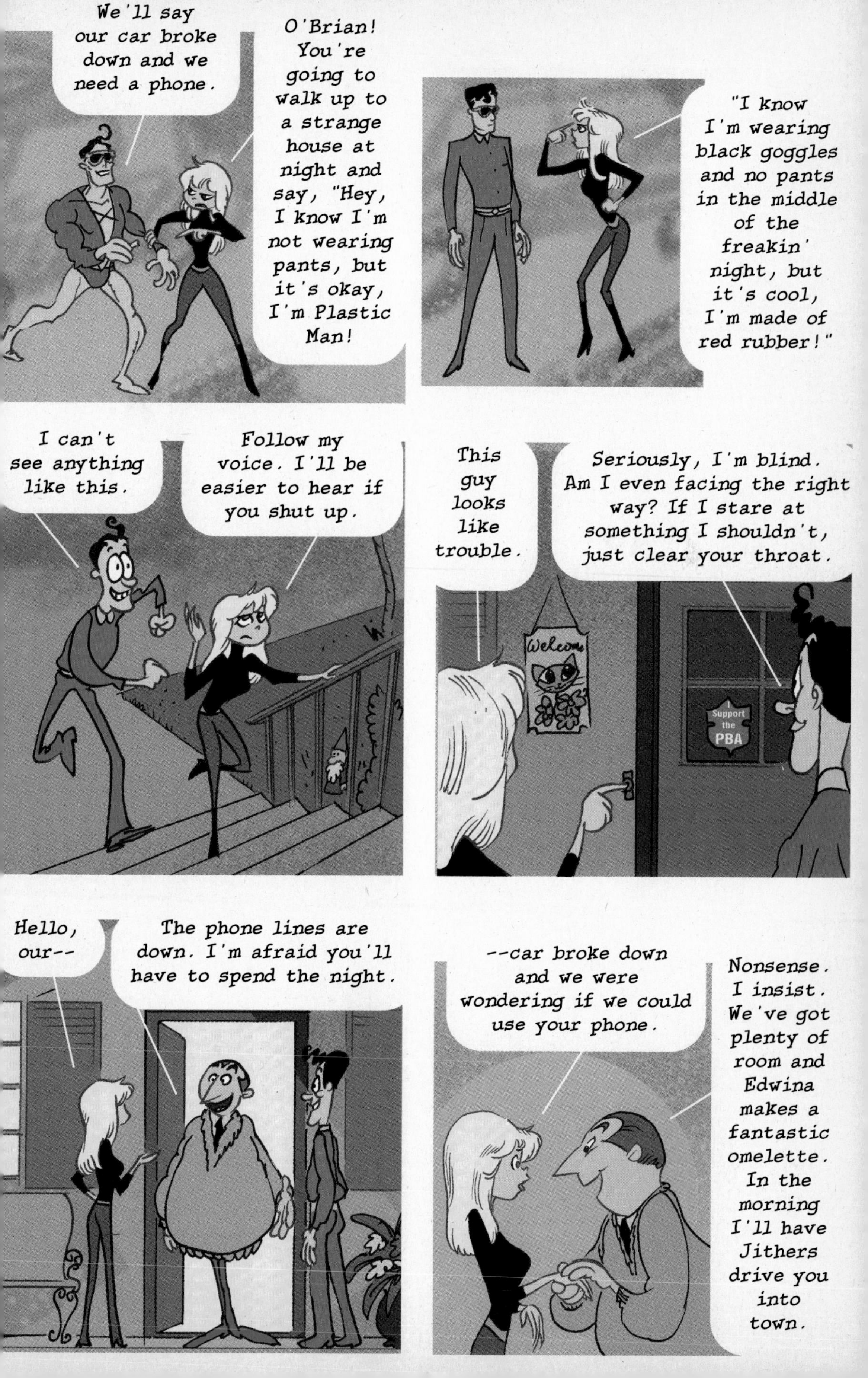
We'll say our car broke down and we need a phone.
O'Brian! You're going to walk up to a strange house at night and say, "Hey, I know I'm not wearing pants, but it's okay, I'm Plastic Man!
"I know I'm wearing black goggles and no pants in the middle of the freakin' night, but it's cool, I'm made of red rubber!"
I can't see anything like this.
Follow my voice. I'll be easier to hear if you shut up.
This guy looks like trouble.
Seriously, I'm blind. Am I even facing the right way? If I stare at something I shouldn't, just clear your throat.
Welcome
I Support the PBA
Hello, our--
The phone lines are down. I'm afraid you'll have to spend the night.
--car broke down and we were wondering if we could use your phone.
Nonsense. I insist. We've got plenty of room and Edwina makes a fantastic omelette. In the morning I'll have Jithers drive you into town.

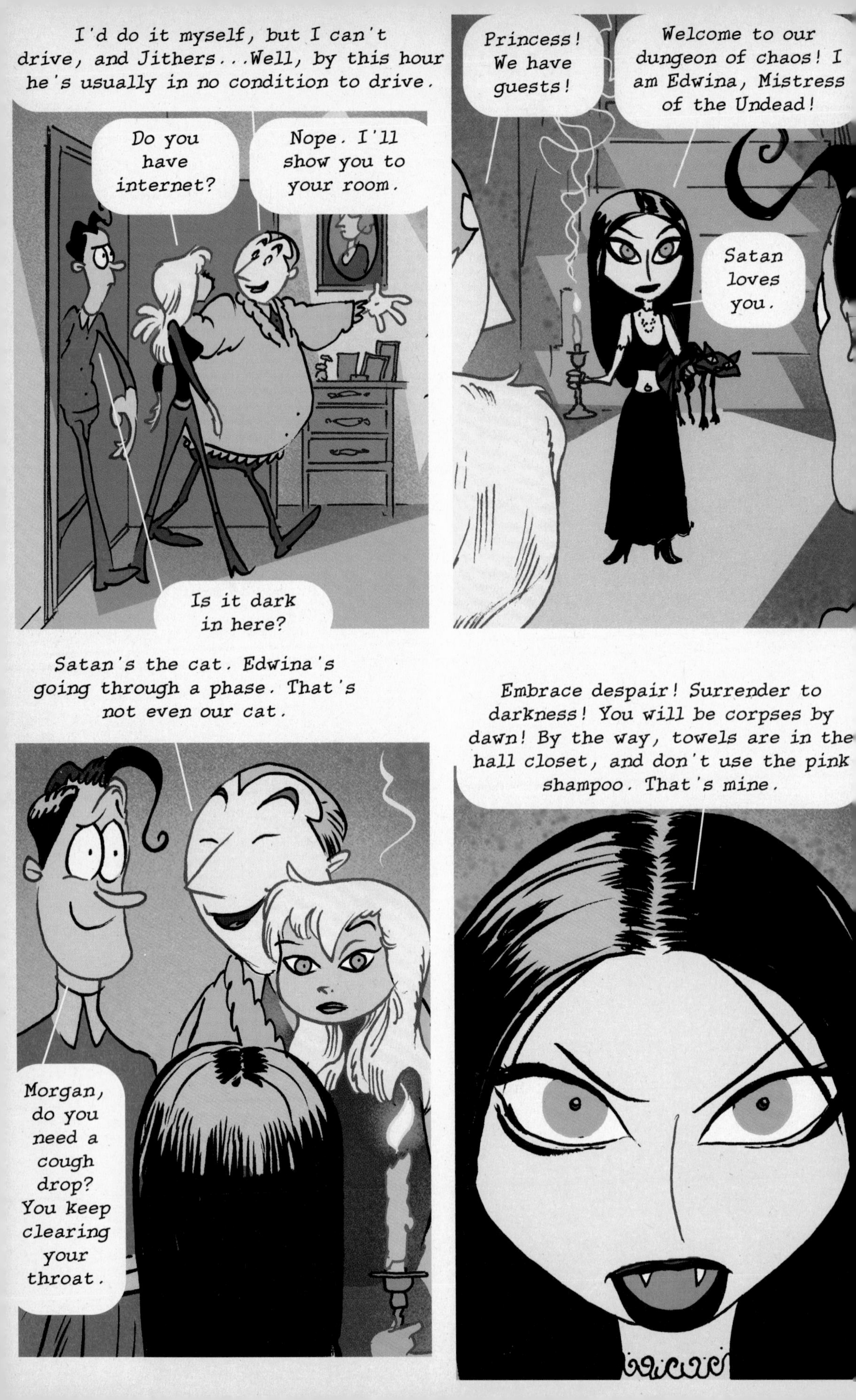
I'd do it myself, but I can't drive, and Jithers...Well, by this hour he's usually in no condition to drive.
Do you have internet?
Nope. I'll show you to your room.
Is it dark in here?
Princess! We have guests!
Welcome to our dungeon of chaos! I am Edwina, Mistress of the Undead!
Satan loves you.
Satan's the cat. Edwina's going through a phase. That's not even our cat.
Morgan, do you need a cough drop? You keep clearing your throat.
Embrace despair! Surrender to darkness! You will be corpses by dawn! By the way, towels are in the hall closet, and don't use the pink shampoo. That's mine.

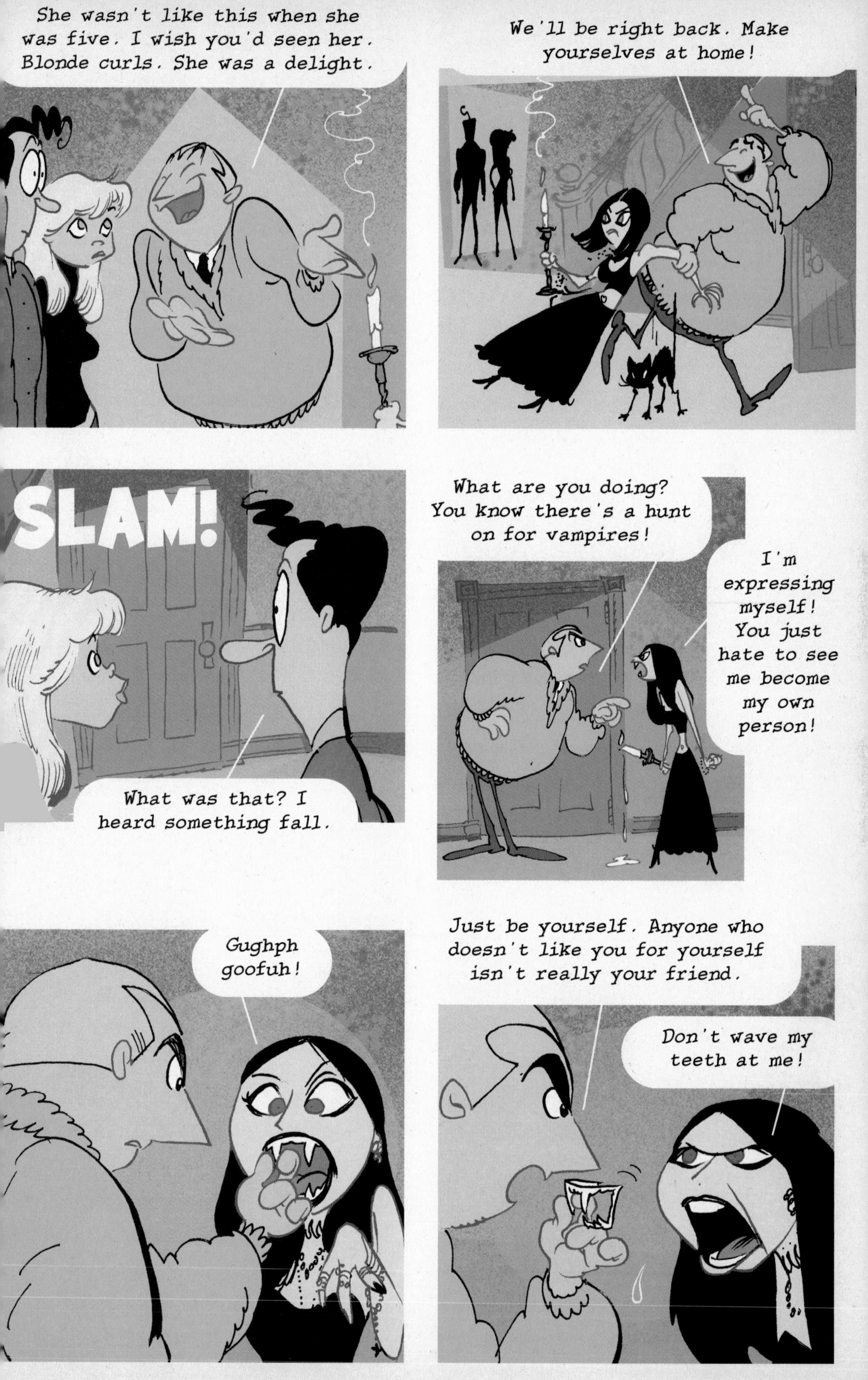
She wasn't like this when she was five. I wish you'd seen her. Blonde curls. She was a delight.
We'll be right back. Make yourselves at home!
SLAM!
What was that? I heard something fall.
What are you doing? You know there's a hunt on for vampires!
I'm expressing myself! You just hate to see me become my own person!
Gughph goofuh!
Just be yourself. Anyone who doesn't like you for yourself isn't really your friend.
Don't wave my teeth at me!

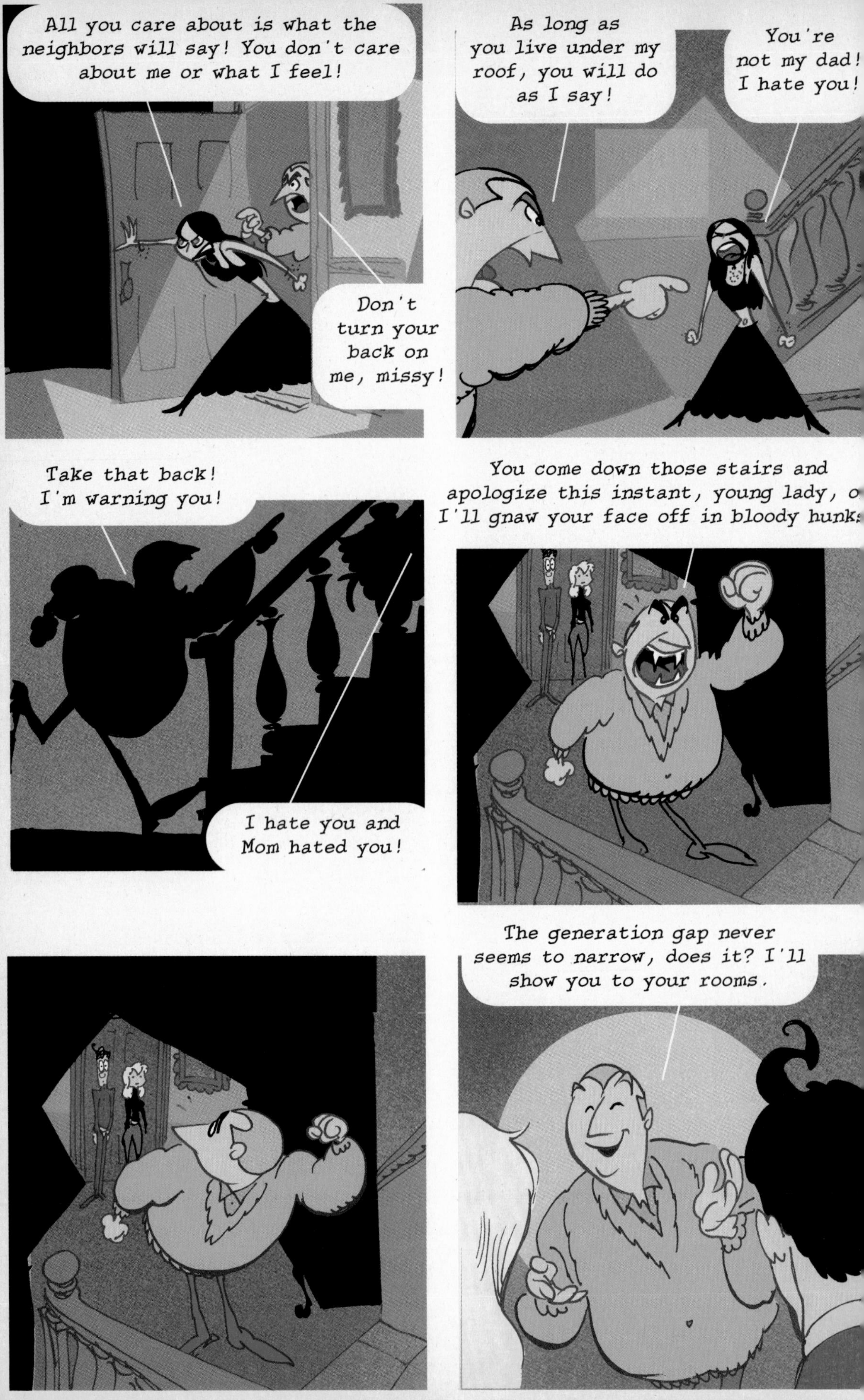
All you care about is what the neighbors will say! You don't care about me or what I feel!
Don't turn your back on me, missy!
As long as you live under my roof, you will do as I say!
You're not my dad! I hate you!
Take that back! I'm warning you!
I hate you and Mom hated you!
You come down those stairs and apologize this instant, young lady,
I'll gnaw your face off in bloody hunk
The generation gap never seems to narrow, does it? I'll show you to your rooms.

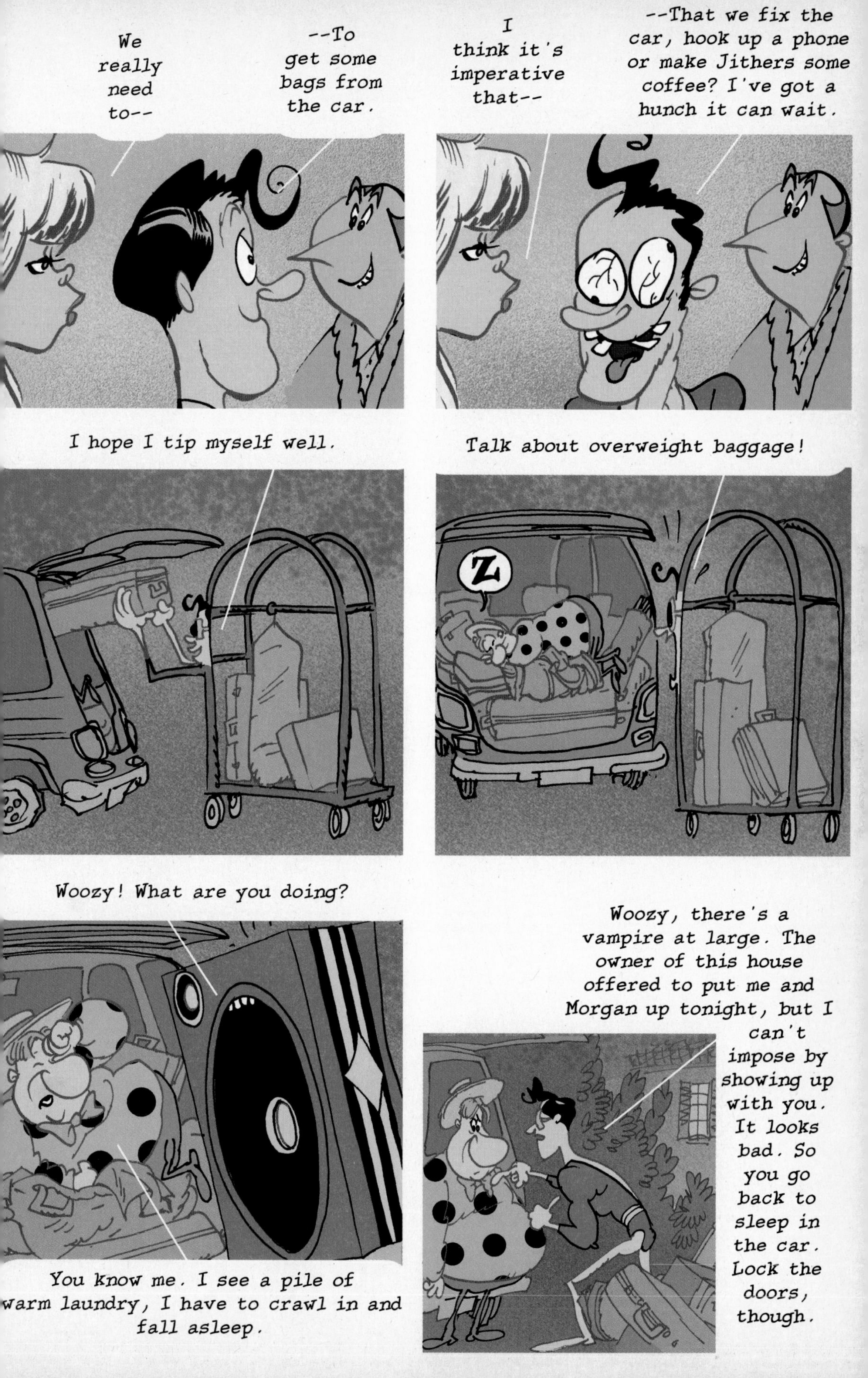
We really need to--
--To get some bags from the car.
I think it's imperative that--
--That we fix the car, hook up a phone or make Jithers some coffee? I've got a hunch it can wait.
I hope I tip myself well.
Talk about overweight baggage!
Z
Woozy! What are you doing?
You know me. I see a pile of warm laundry, I have to crawl in and fall asleep.
Woozy, there's a vampire at large. The owner of this house offered to put me and Morgan up tonight, but I can't impose by showing up with you. It looks bad. So you go back to sleep in the car. Lock the doors, though.

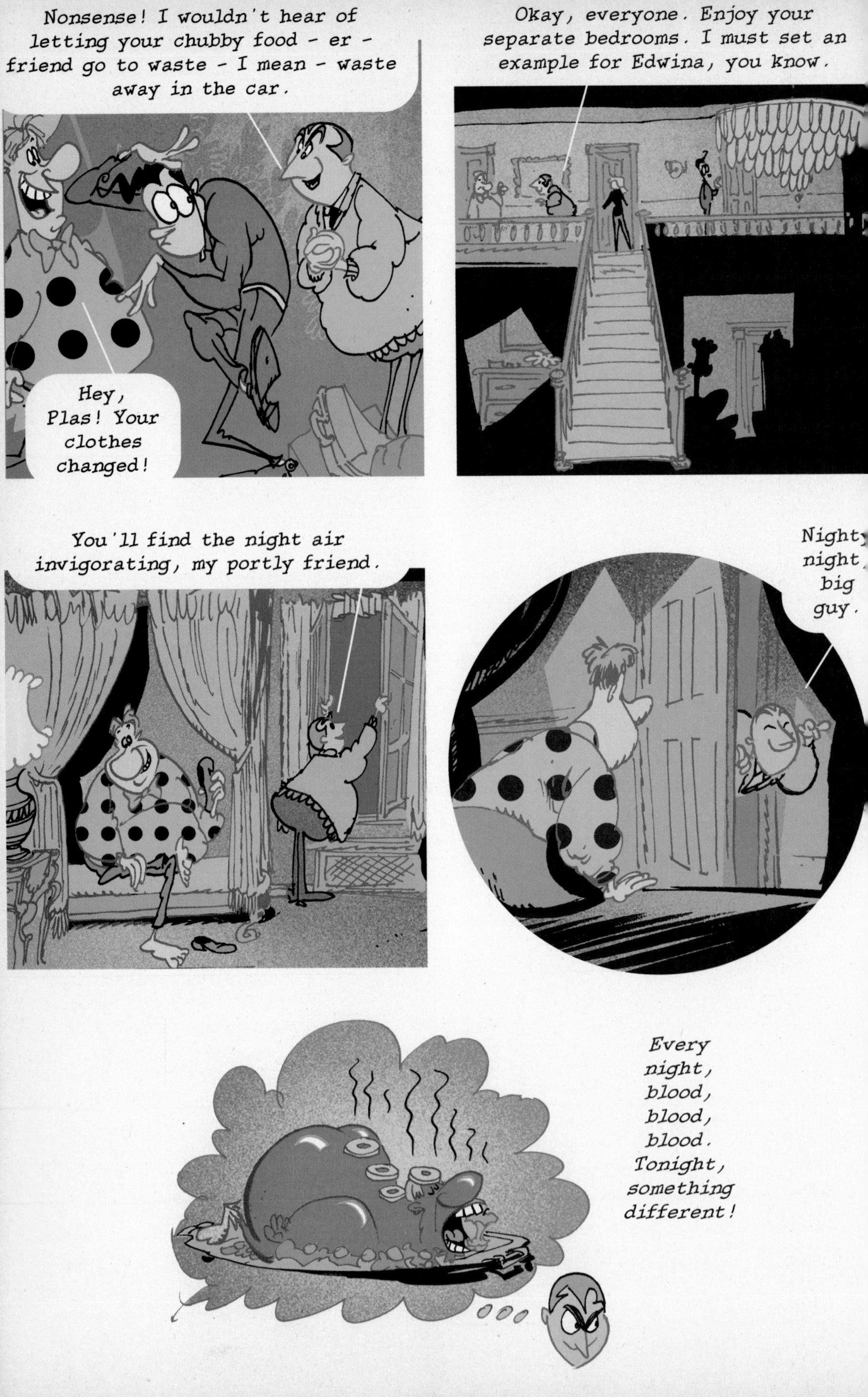
Nonsense! I wouldn't hear of letting your chubby food - er - friend go to waste - I mean - waste away in the car.
Hey, Plas! Your clothes changed!
Okay, everyone. Enjoy your separate bedrooms. I must set an example for Edwina, you know.
You'll find the night air invigorating, my portly friend.
Night night, big guy.
Every night, blood, blood, blood. Tonight, something different!

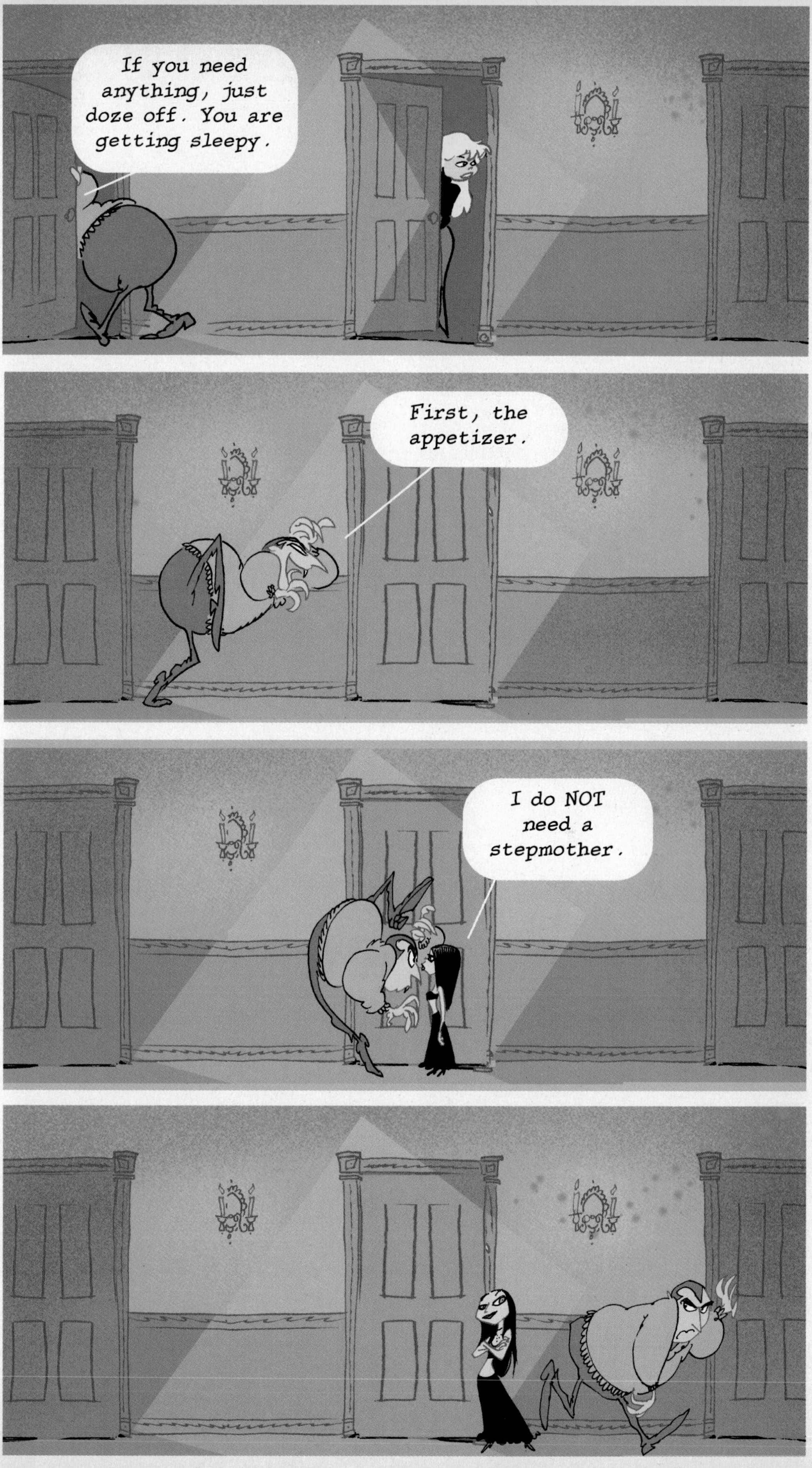
If you need anything, just doze off. You are getting sleepy.
First, the appetizer.
I do NOT need a stepmother.

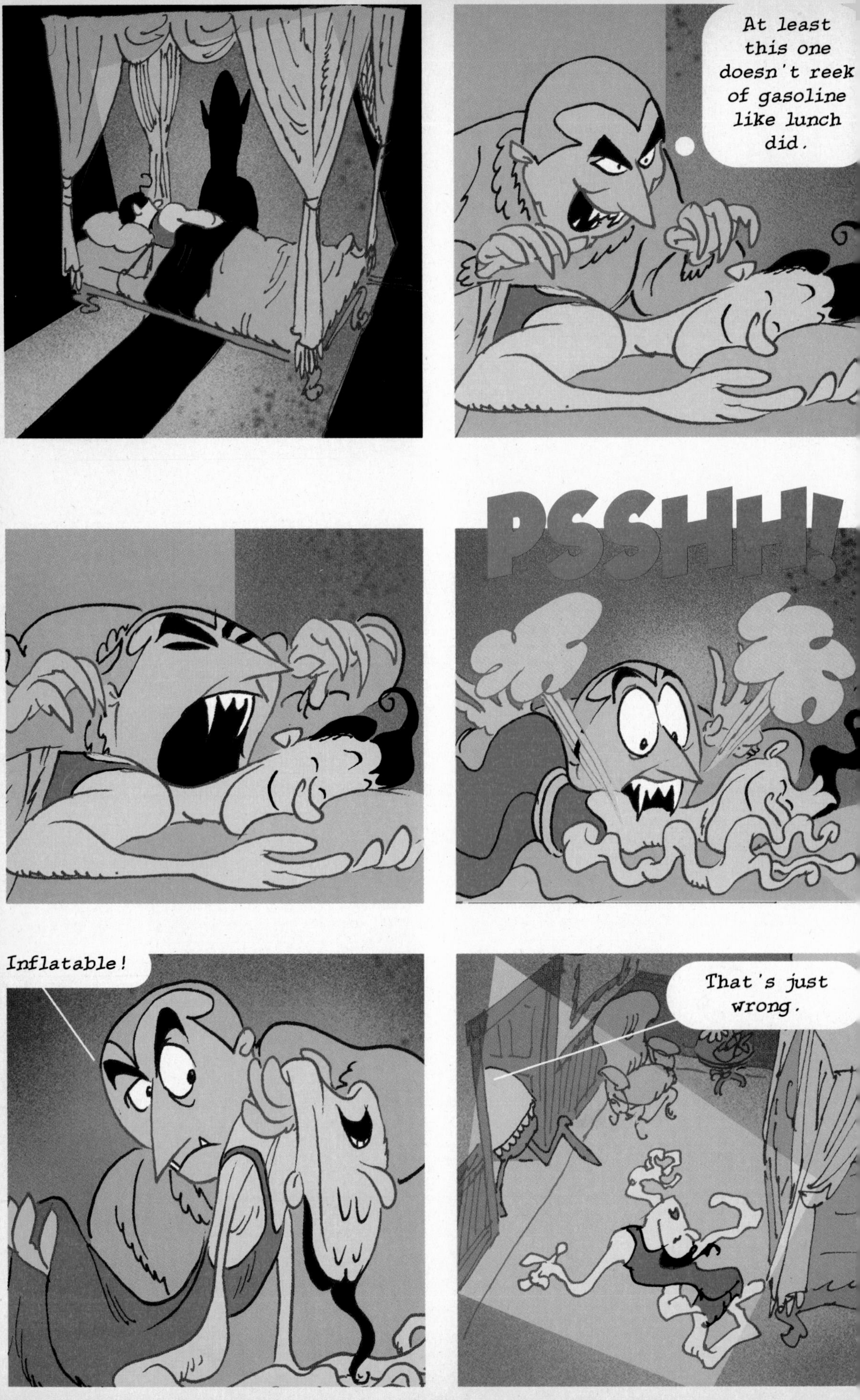
At least this one doesn't reek of gasoline like lunch did.
PSSHH!
Inflatable!
That's just wrong.

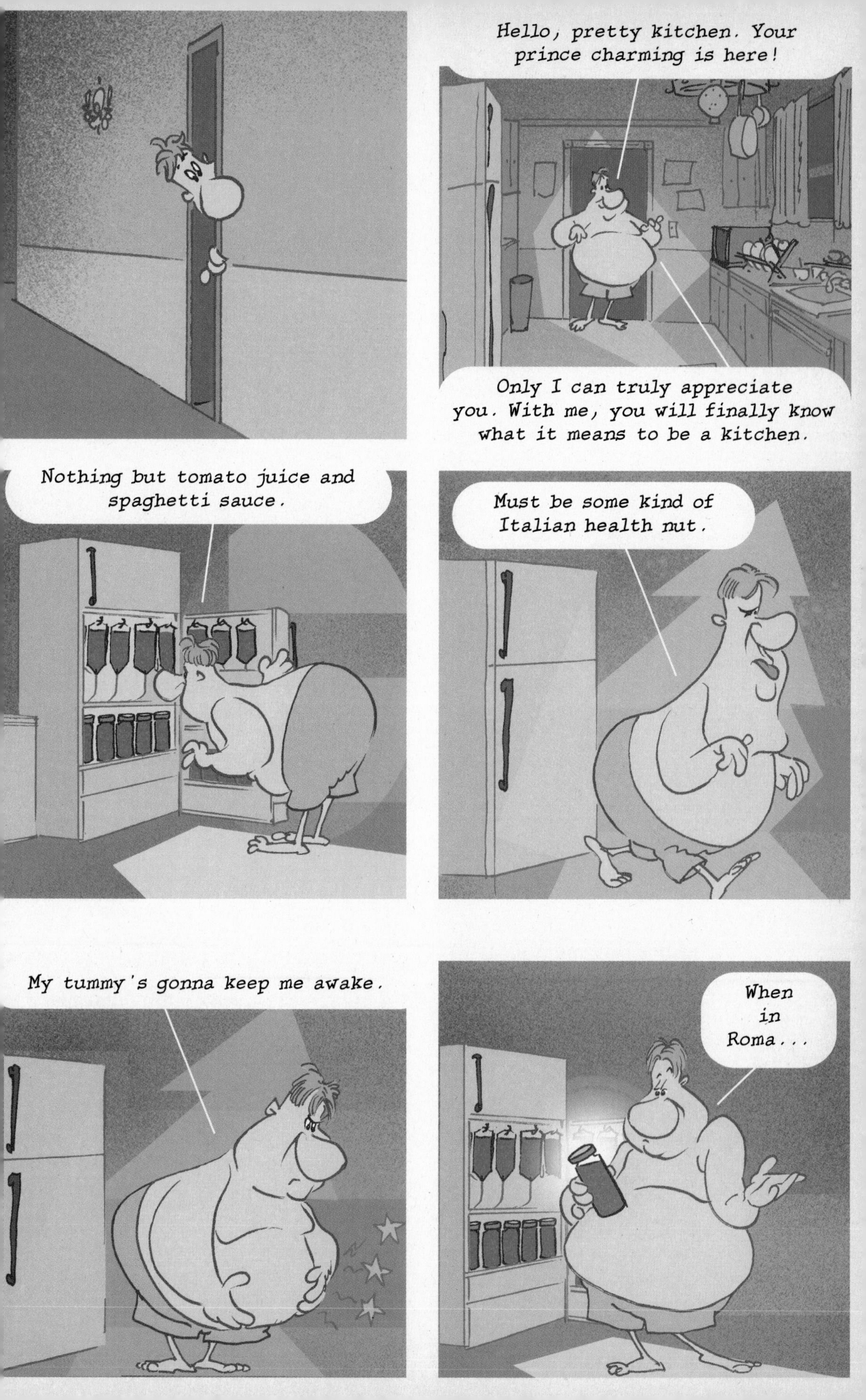
Hello, pretty kitchen. Your prince charming is here!
Only I can truly appreciate you. With me, you will finally know what it means to be a kitchen.
Nothing but tomato juice and spaghetti sauce.
Must be some kind of Italian health nut.
My tummy's gonna keep me awake.
When in Roma...

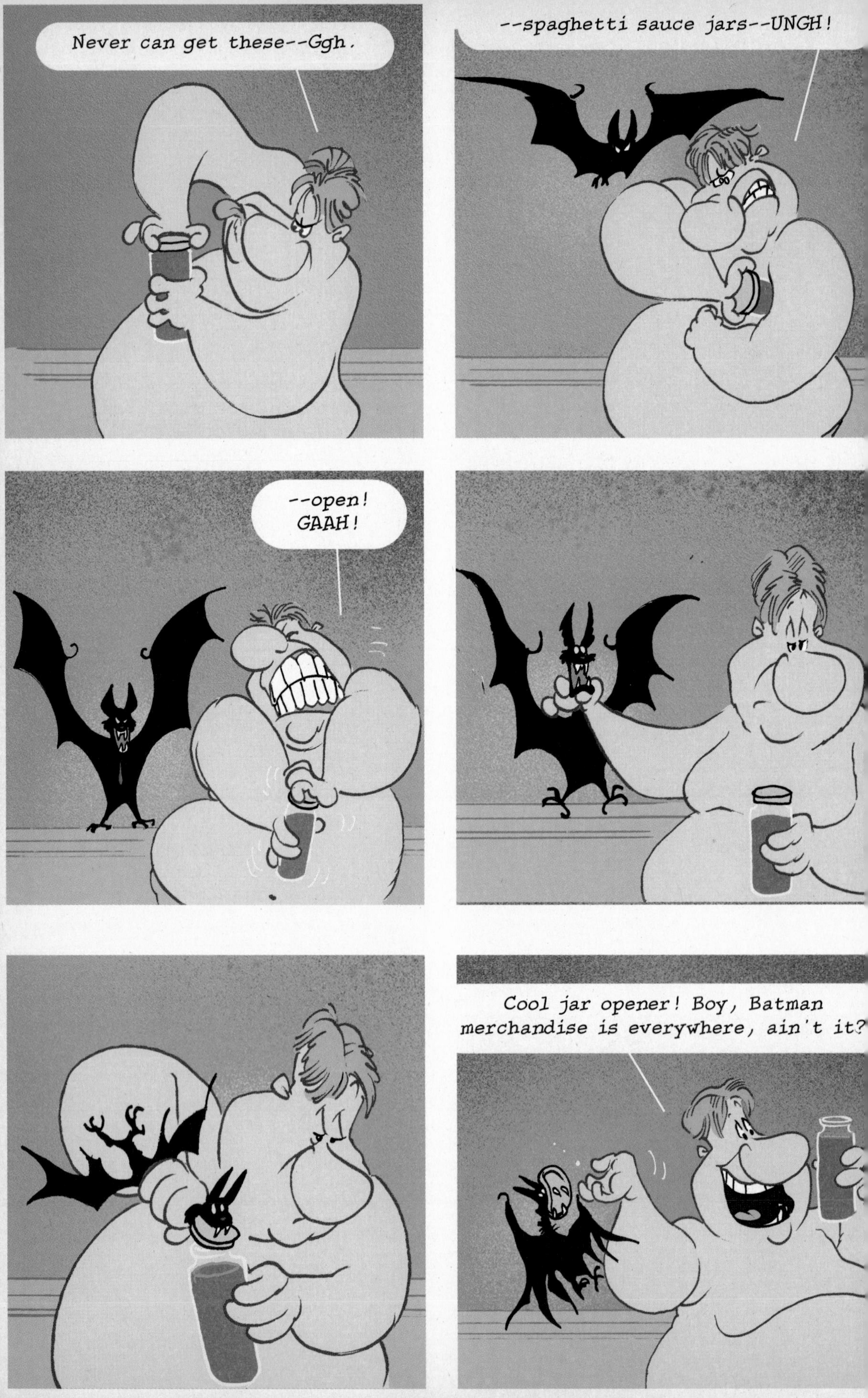
Never can get these--Ggh.
--spaghetti sauce jars--UNGH!
--open!
GAAH!
Cool jar opener! Boy, Batman merchandise is everywhere, ain't it?

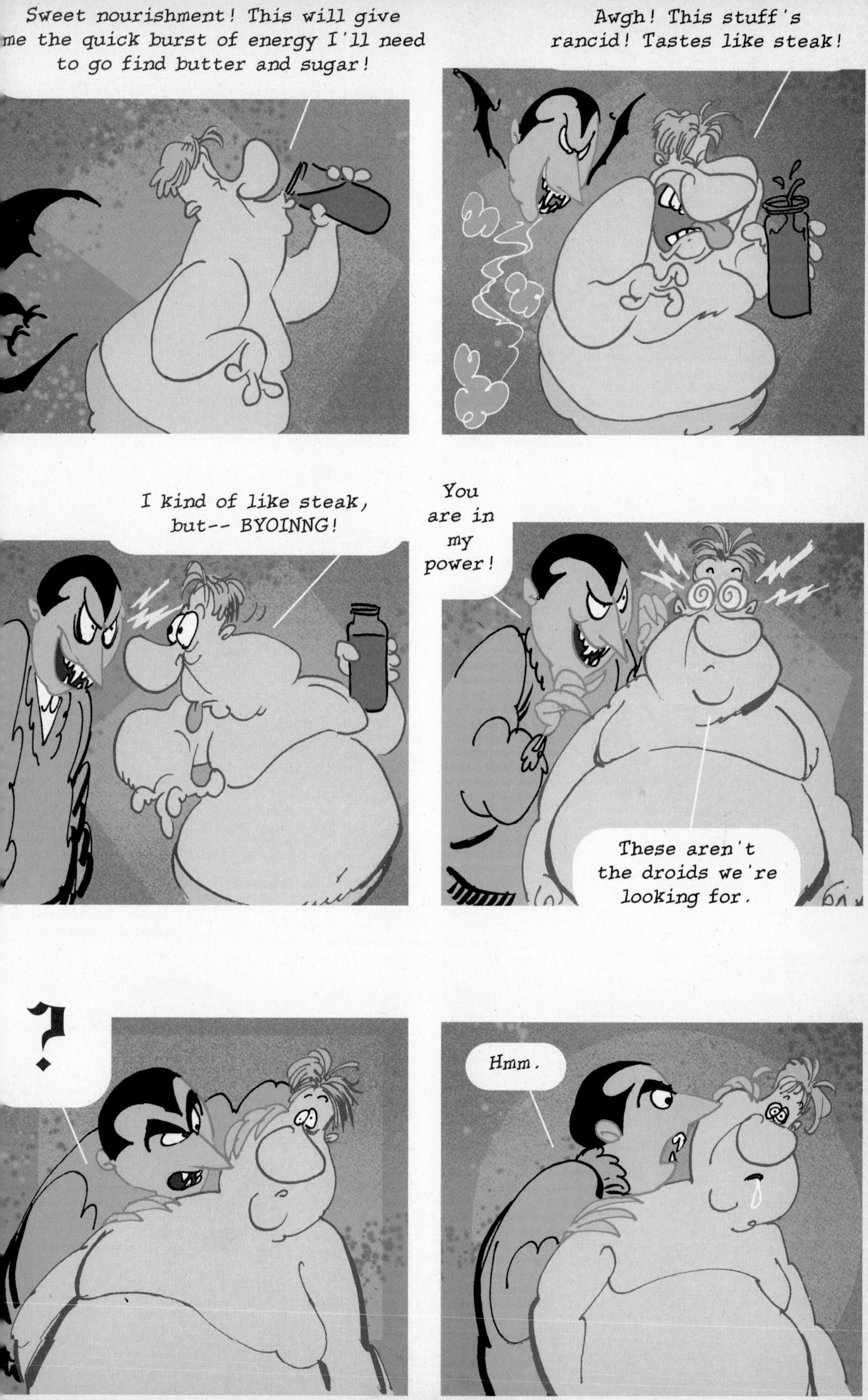
Sweet nourishment! This will give me the quick burst of energy I'll need to go find butter and sugar!
Awgh! This stuff's rancid! Tastes like steak!
I kind of like steak, but-- BYOINNG!
You are in my power!
These aren't the droids we're looking for.
?
Hmm.

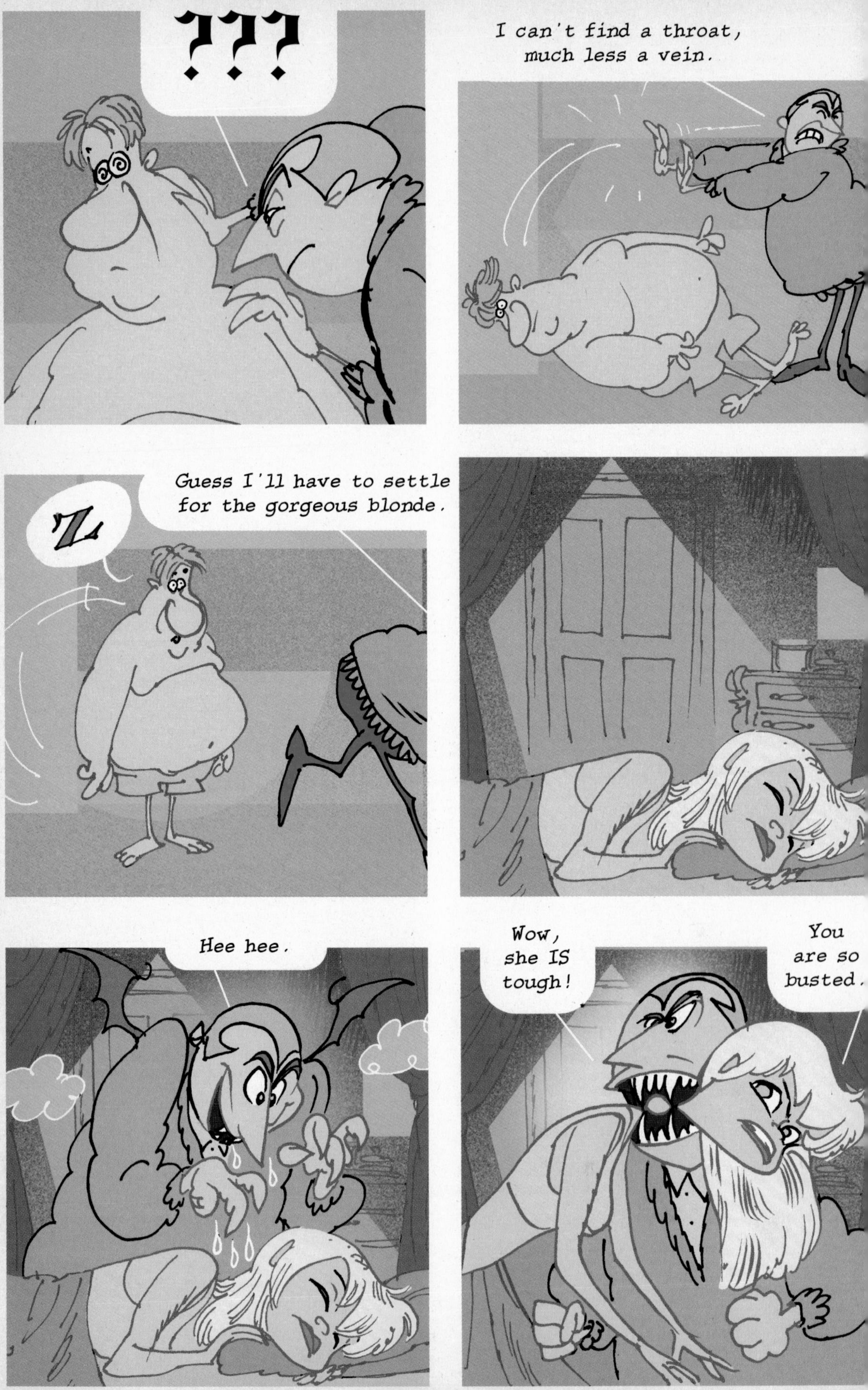
???
I can't find a throat, much less a vein.
Z
Guess I'll have to settle for the gorgeous blonde.
Hee hee.
Wow, she IS tough!
You are so busted.

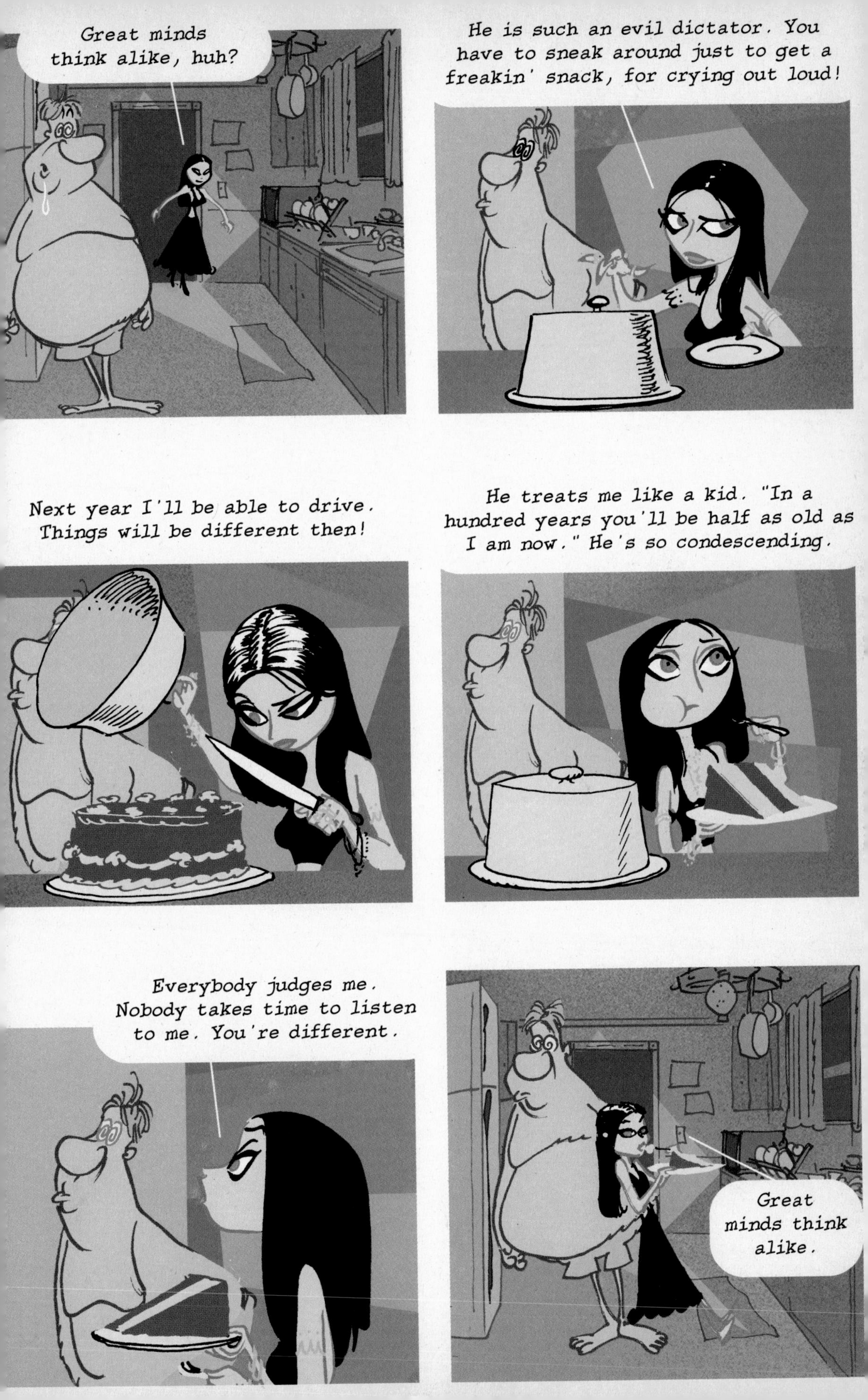
Great minds think alike, huh?
He is such an evil dictator. You have to sneak around just to get a freakin' snack, for crying out loud!
Next year I'll be able to drive. Things will be different then!
He treats me like a kid. "In a hundred years you'll be half as old as I am now." He's so condescending.
Everybody judges me. Nobody takes time to listen to me. You're different.
Great minds think alike.

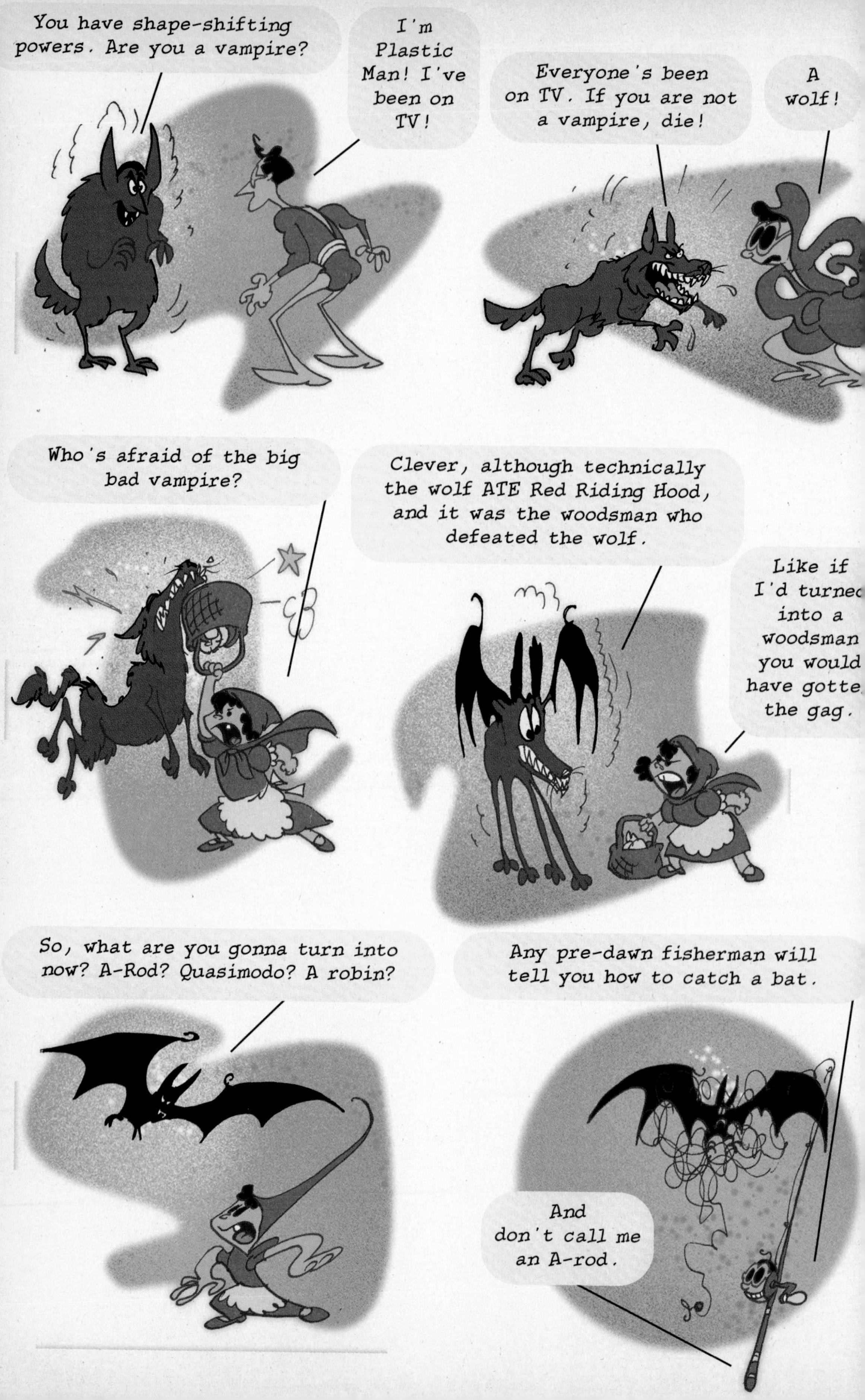
You have shape-shifting powers. Are you a vampire?
I'm Plastic Man! I've been on TV!
Everyone's been on TV. If you are not a vampire, die!
A wolf!
Who's afraid of the big bad vampire?
Clever, although technically the wolf ATE Red Riding Hood, and it was the woodsman who defeated the wolf.
Like if I'd turne into a woodsman you would have gotte the gag.
So, what are you gonna turn into now? A-Rod? Quasimodo? A robin?
Any pre-dawn fisherman will tell you how to catch a bat.
And don't call me an A-rod.

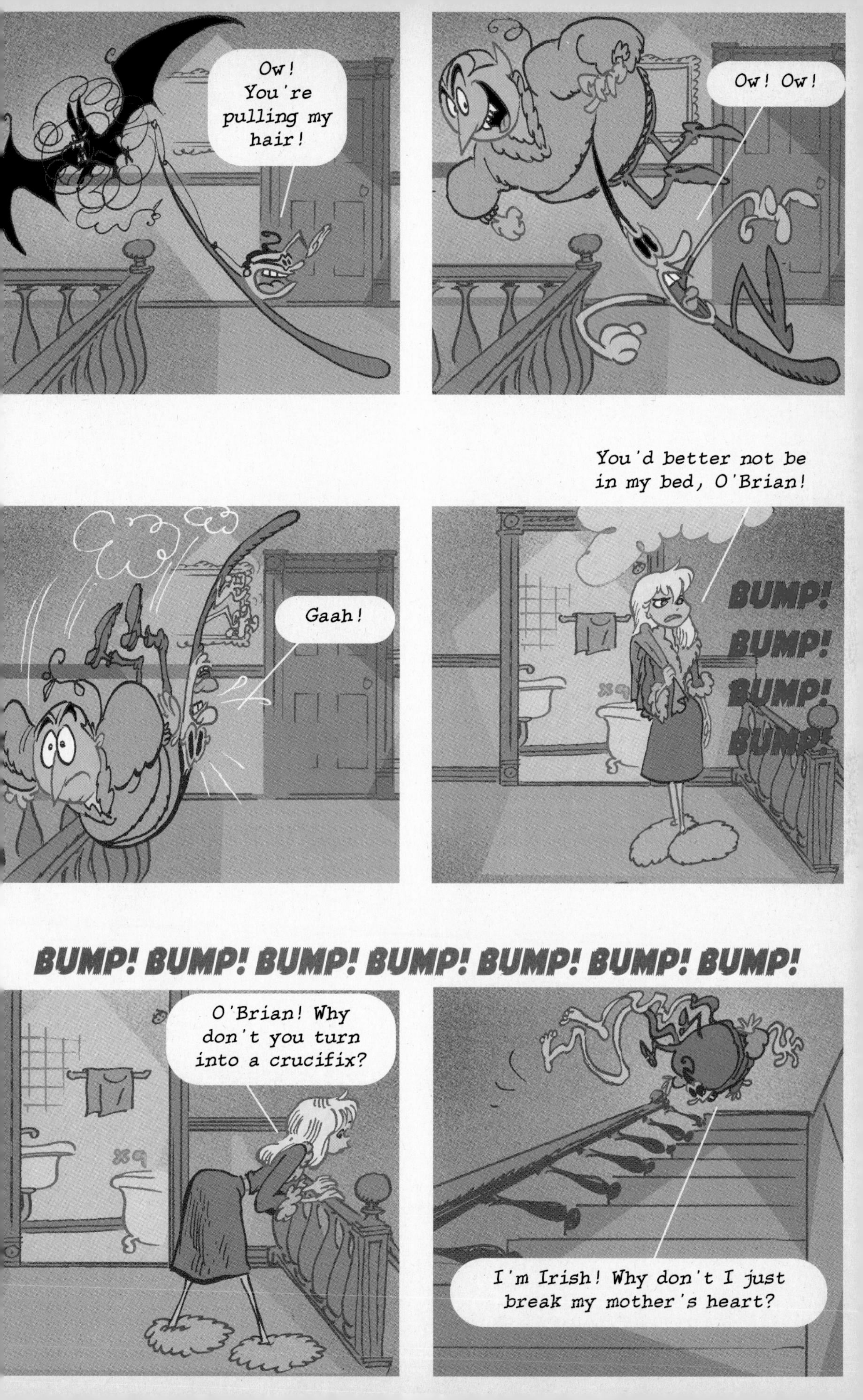
Ow! You're pulling my hair!
Ow! Ow!
Gaah!
You'd better not be in my bed, O'Brian!
BUMP! BUMP! BUMP! BUMP!
BUMP! BUMP! BUMP! BUMP! BUMP! BUMP! BUMP!
O'Brian! Why don't you turn into a crucifix?
I'm Irish! Why don't I just break my mother's heart?

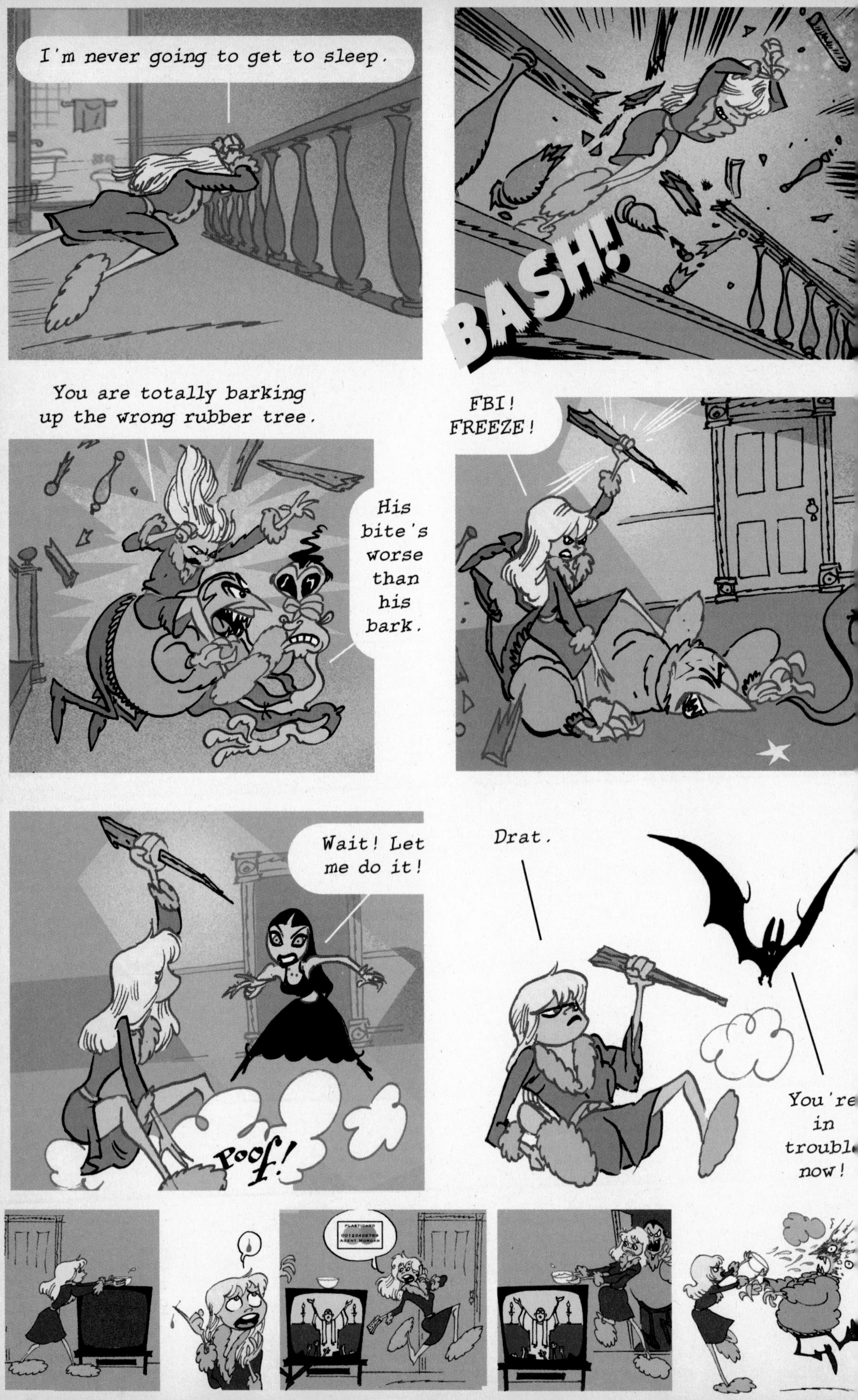
I'm never going to get to sleep.
BASH!
You are totally barking up the wrong rubber tree.
His bite's worse than his bark.
FBI! FREEZE!
Wait! Let me do it!
Poof!
Drat.
You're in troubl
now!
PLASTICARD
00123456789
AGENT MORGAN

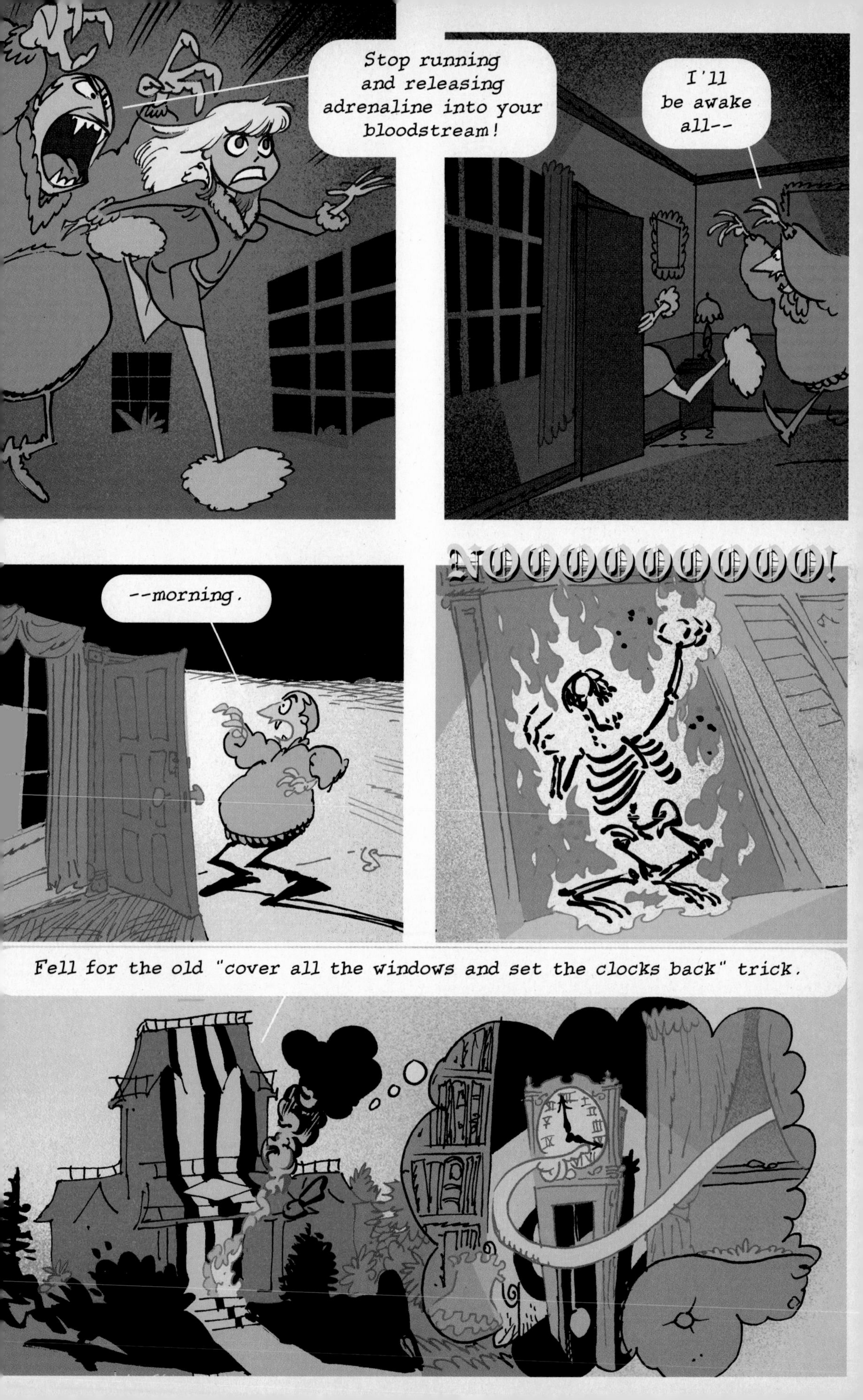
Stop running and releasing adrenaline into your bloodstream!
I'll be awake all--
--morning.
NOOOOOOOOOO!
Fell for the old "cover all the windows and set the clocks back" trick.

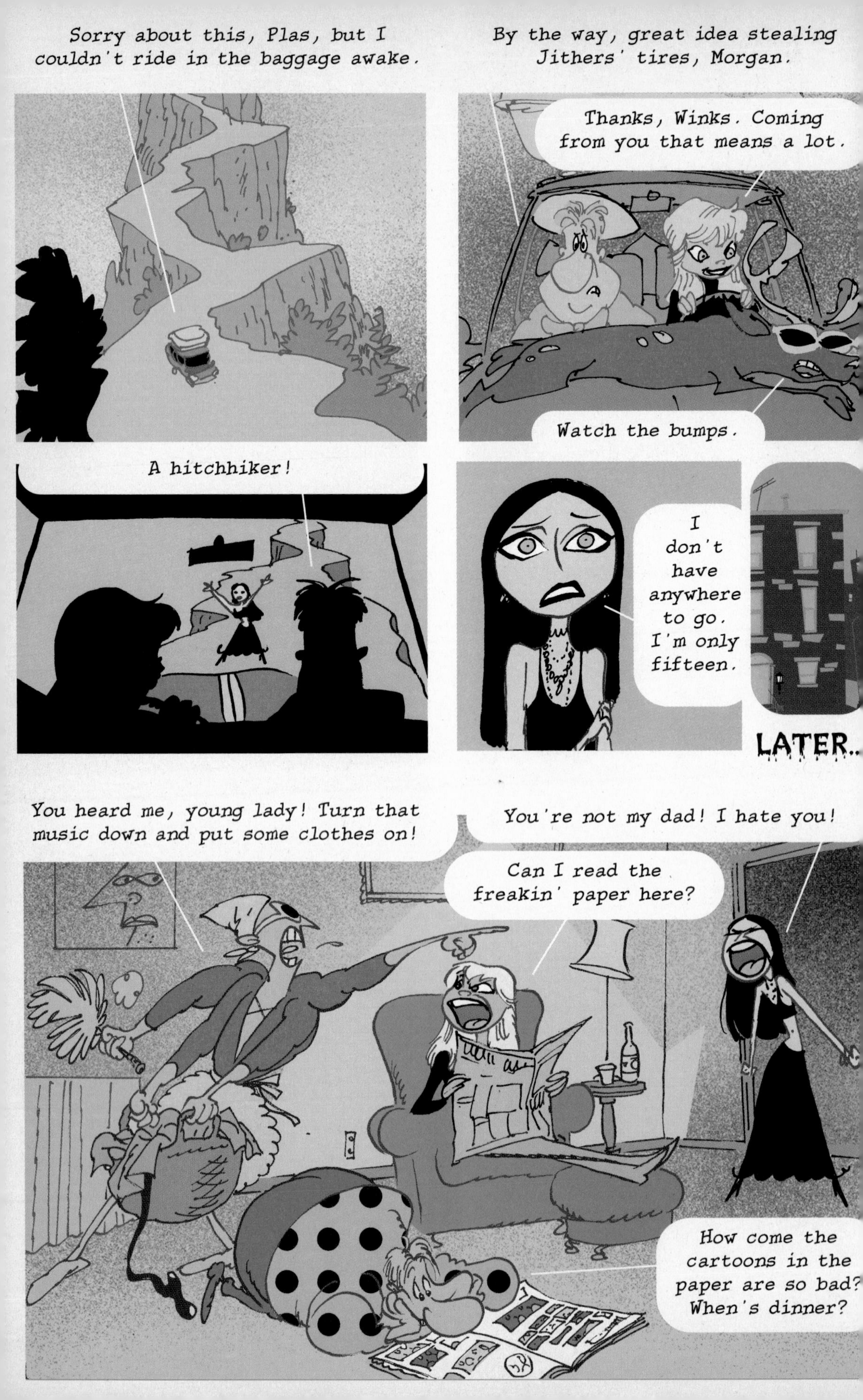
Sorry about this, Plas, but I couldn't ride in the baggage awake.
By the way, great idea stealing Jithers' tires, Morgan.
Thanks, Winks. Coming from you that means a lot.
Watch the bumps.
A hitchhiker!
I don't have anywhere to go. I'm only fifteen.
LATER...
You heard me, young lady! Turn that music down and put some clothes on!
You're not my dad! I hate you!
Can I read the freakin' paper here?
How come the cartoons in the paper are so bad? When's dinner?

INTELLIGENCE FAILURE

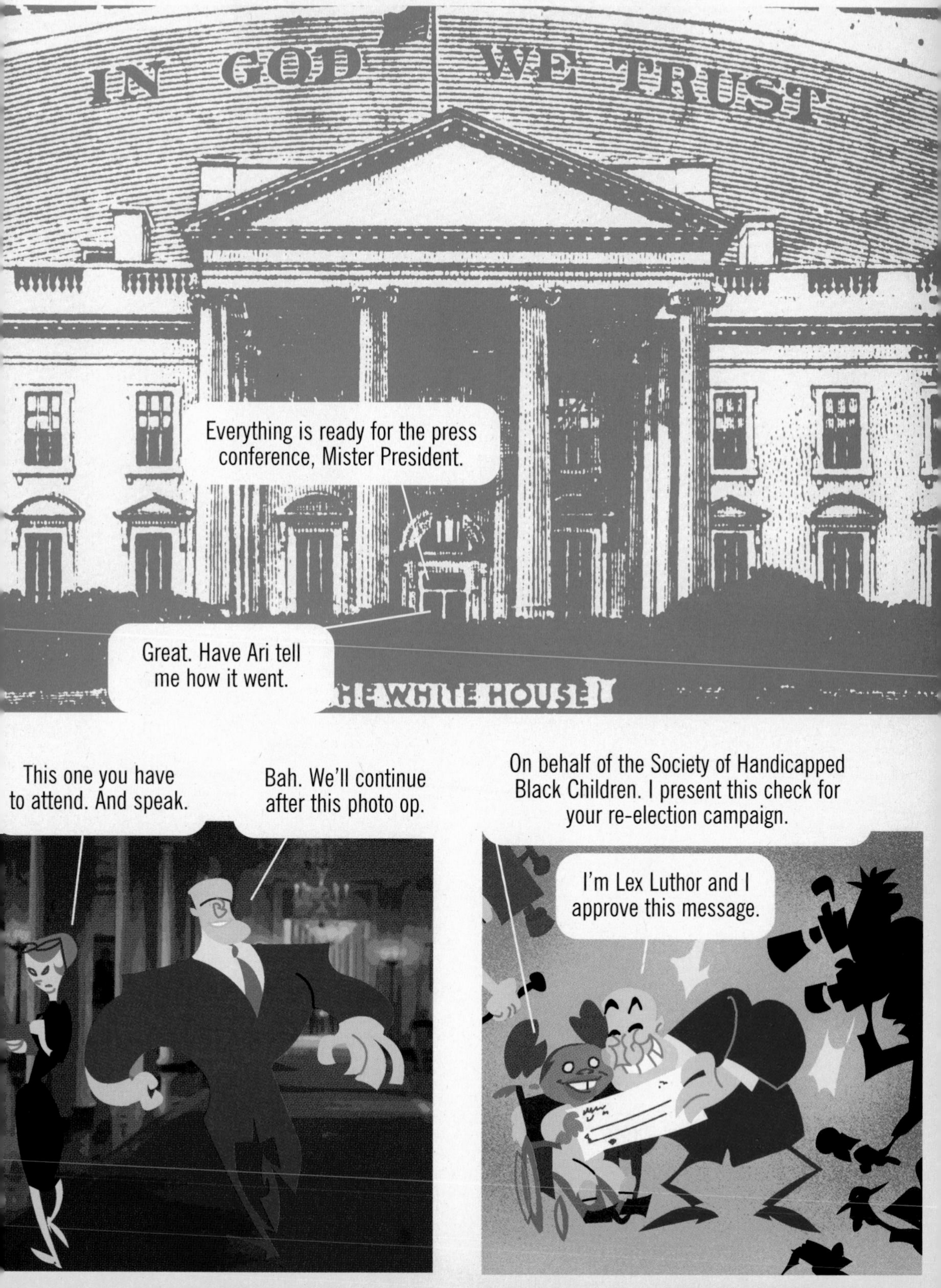
IN GOD WE TRUST
Everything is ready for the press conference, Mister President.
Great. Have Ari tell me how it went.
THE WHITE HOUSE
This one you have to attend. And speak.
Bah. We'll continue after this photo op.
On behalf of the Society of Handicapped Black Children. I present this check for your re-election campaign.
I'm Lex Luthor and I approve this message.

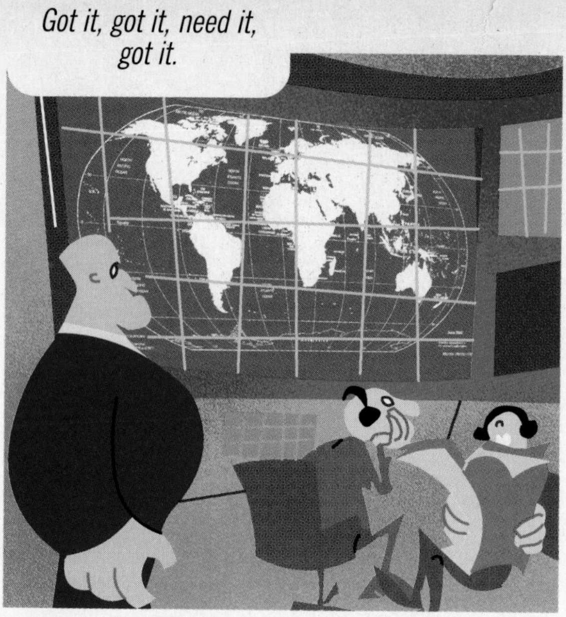
Got it, got it, need it, got it.

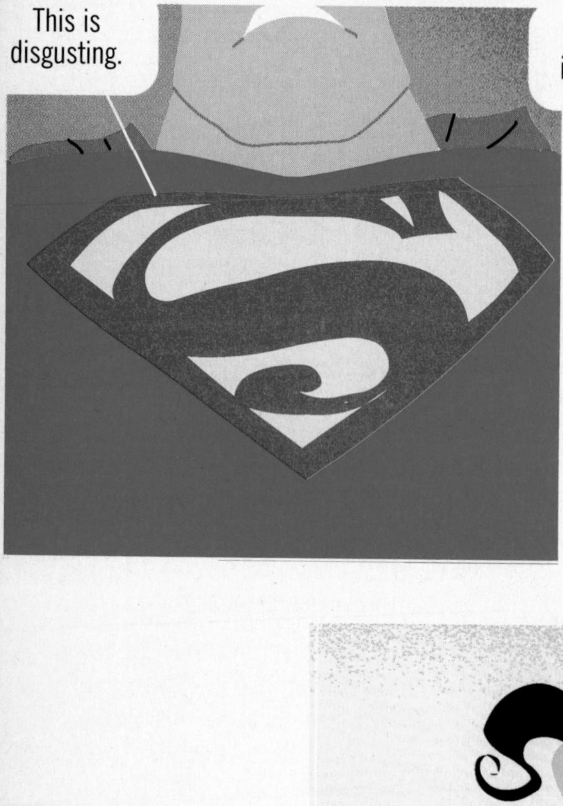
This is disgusting.

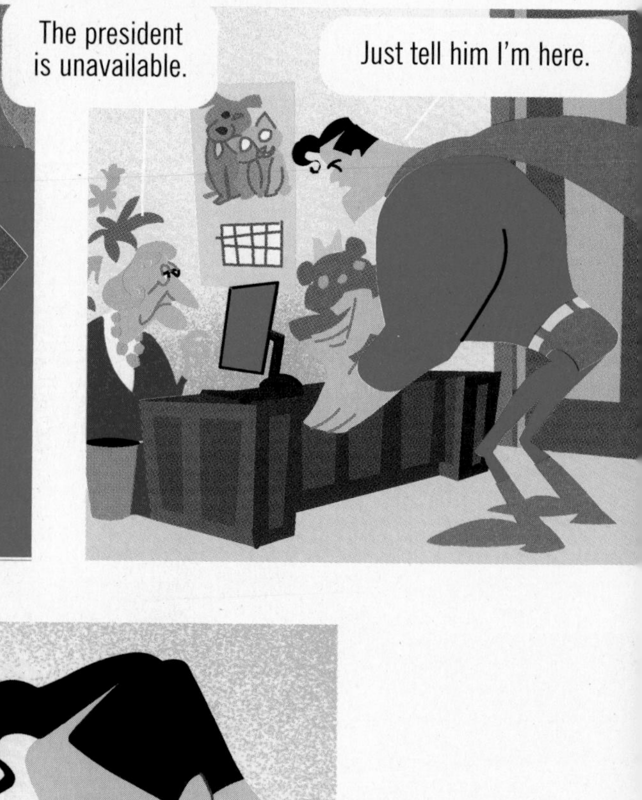
The president is unavailable.
Just tell him I'm here.

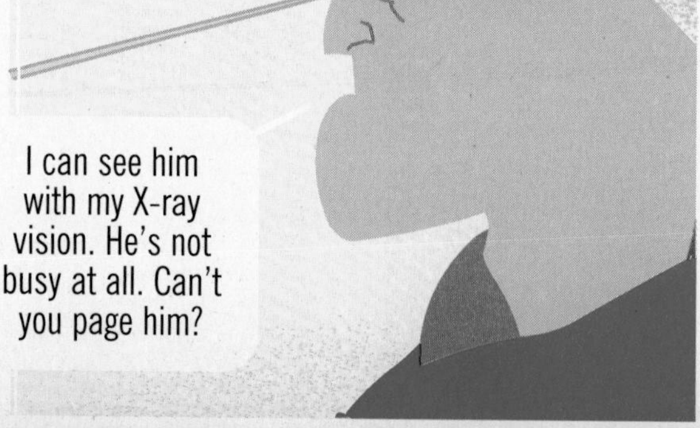
I can see him with my X-ray vision. He's not busy at all. Can't you page him?

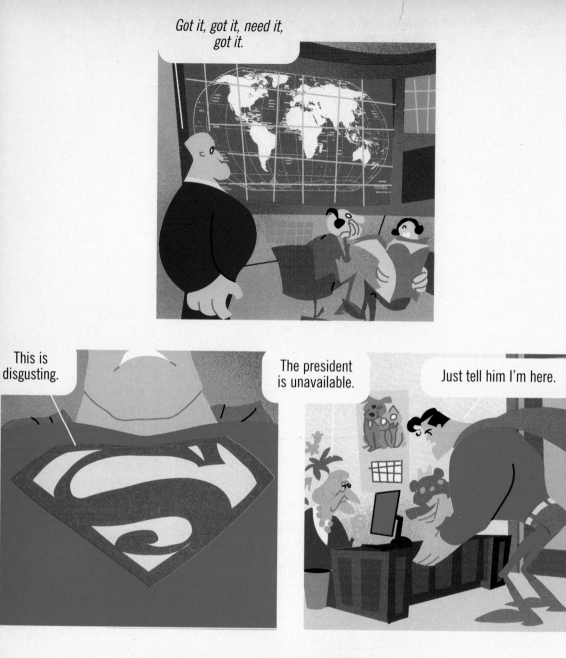

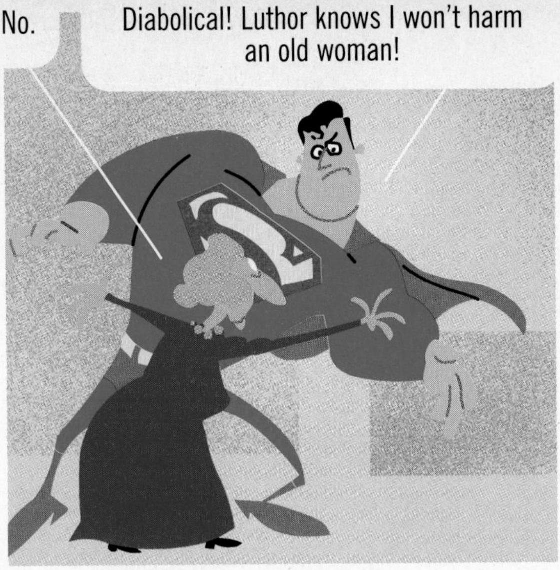
No.
Diabolical! Luthor knows I won't harm an old woman!

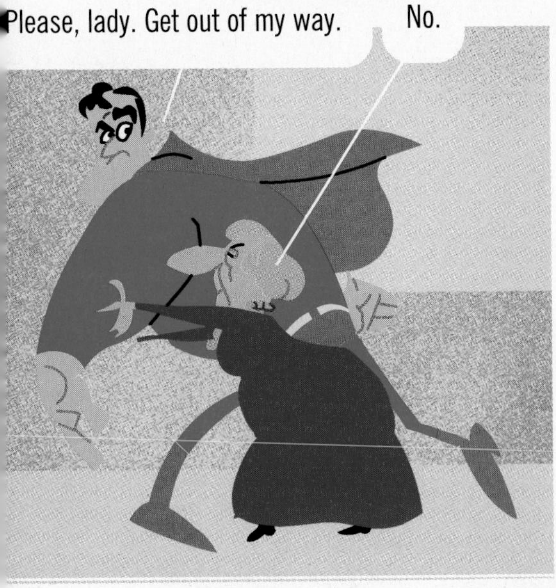
Please, lady. Get out of my way.
No.

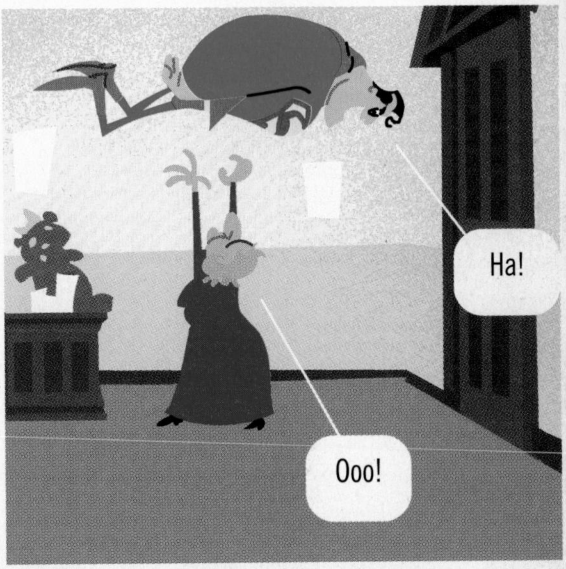
Ha!
Ooo!

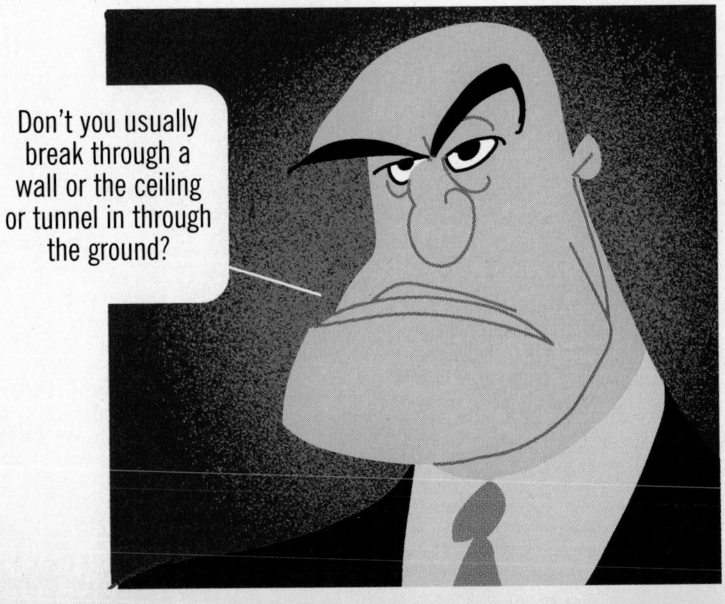
Don't you usually break through a wall or the ceiling or tunnel in through the ground?

I'm trying not to destroy so much taxpayer property these days. The whole Identity Crisis Saga has made me reexamine my values and habits.

I know nothing about it. I'm waiting for the paperback collection.

That's not why I'm here. Is it, Luthor?

You have call me Mister President think it's law.

That's funny coming from an insidious super-criminal like you!

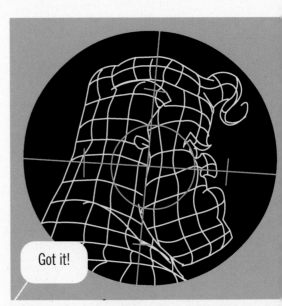

Got it!

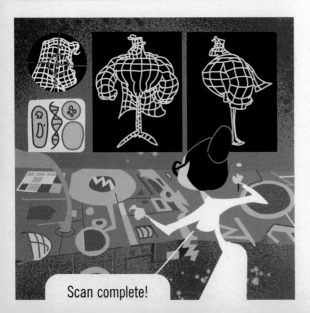

Scan complete!

Now I throw the switch...

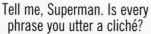ZZZZAM!

It's alive!

Tell me, Superman. Is every phrase you utter a cliché?

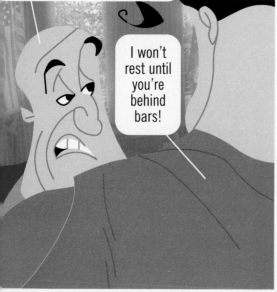

I won't rest until you're behind bars!

How many times have we played this scene in the last four years? You barge in claiming I'm a super-villain, I remind you that you have no evidence, and you can't touch me because I'm President. I then pour myself a drink or light a cigar or something, to show how nonchalant and unthreatened I am.

You're up to something. I know it.

Even if I were responsible for all the evil in the world, you'd still be powerless to stop me. Nyah, nyah, nyah!

By the moons of Krypton!

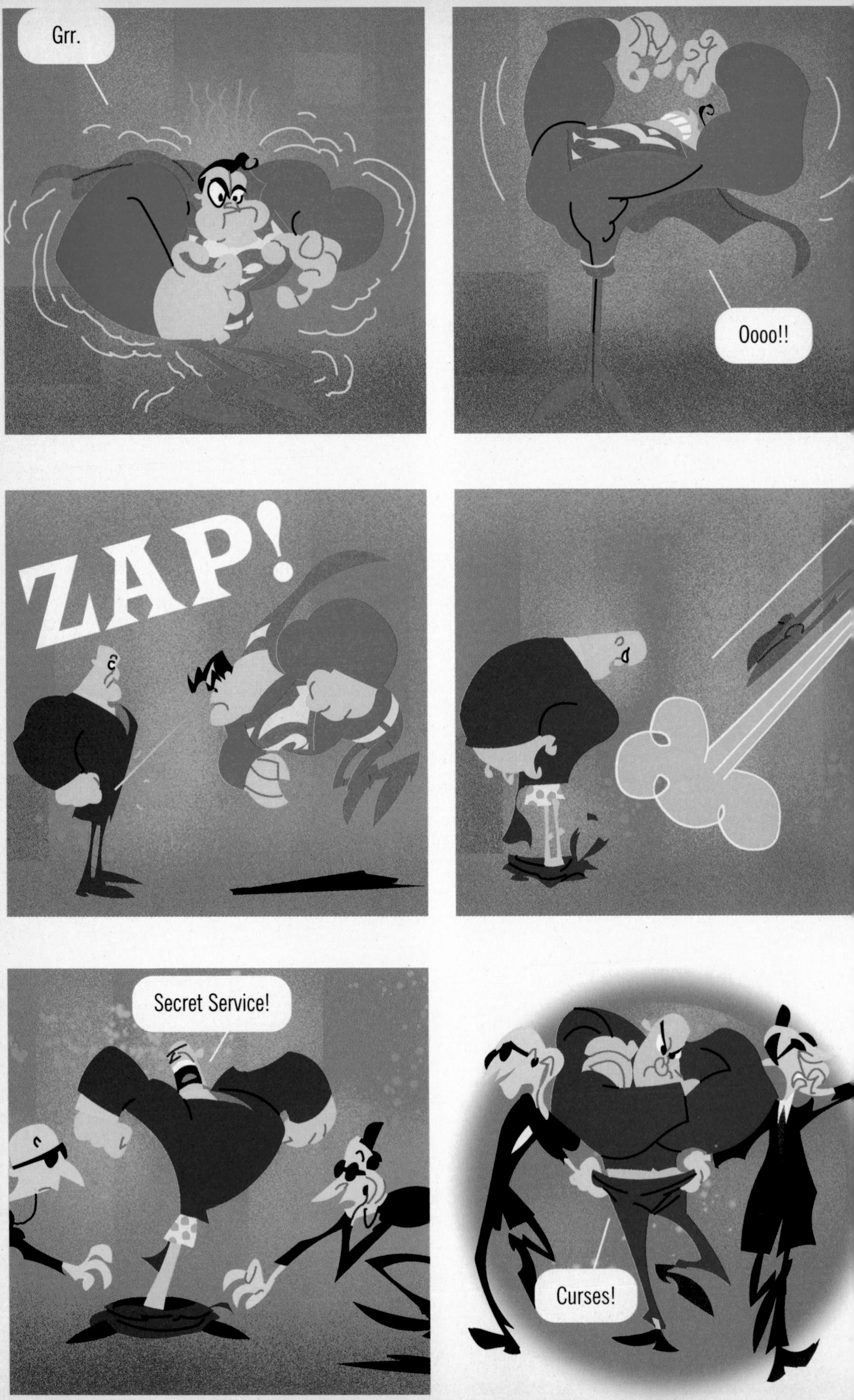
Grr.
Oooo!!
ZAP!
Secret Service!
Curses!

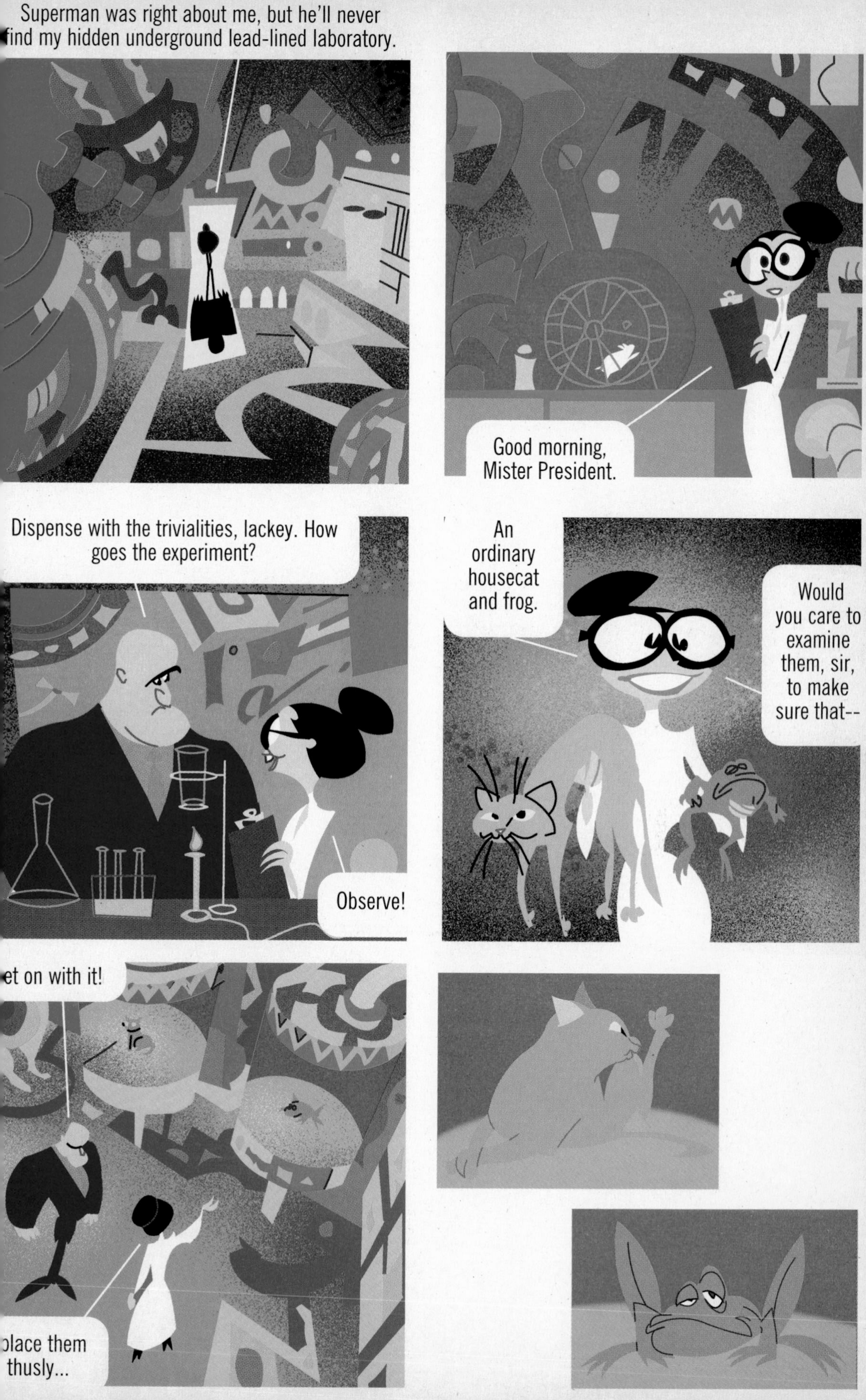
Superman was right about me, but he'll never find my hidden underground lead-lined laboratory.
Good morning, Mister President.
Dispense with the trivialities, lackey. How goes the experiment?
Observe!
An ordinary housecat and frog.
Would you care to examine them, sir, to make sure that--
et on with it!
lace them thusly...

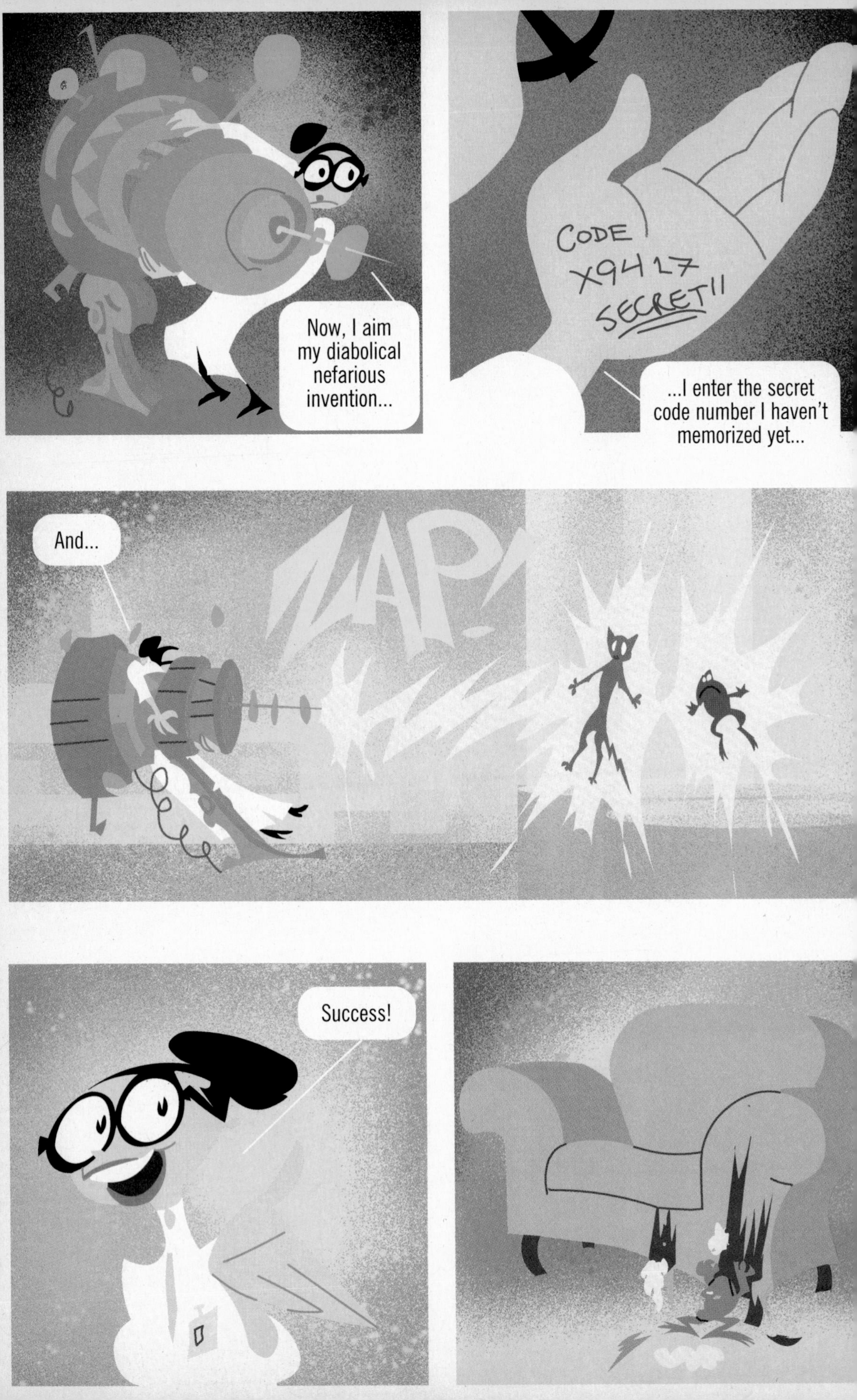
Now, I aim my diabolical nefarious invention...
CODE X9427 SECRET!!
...I enter the secret code number I haven't memorized yet...
And...
ZAP!
Success!

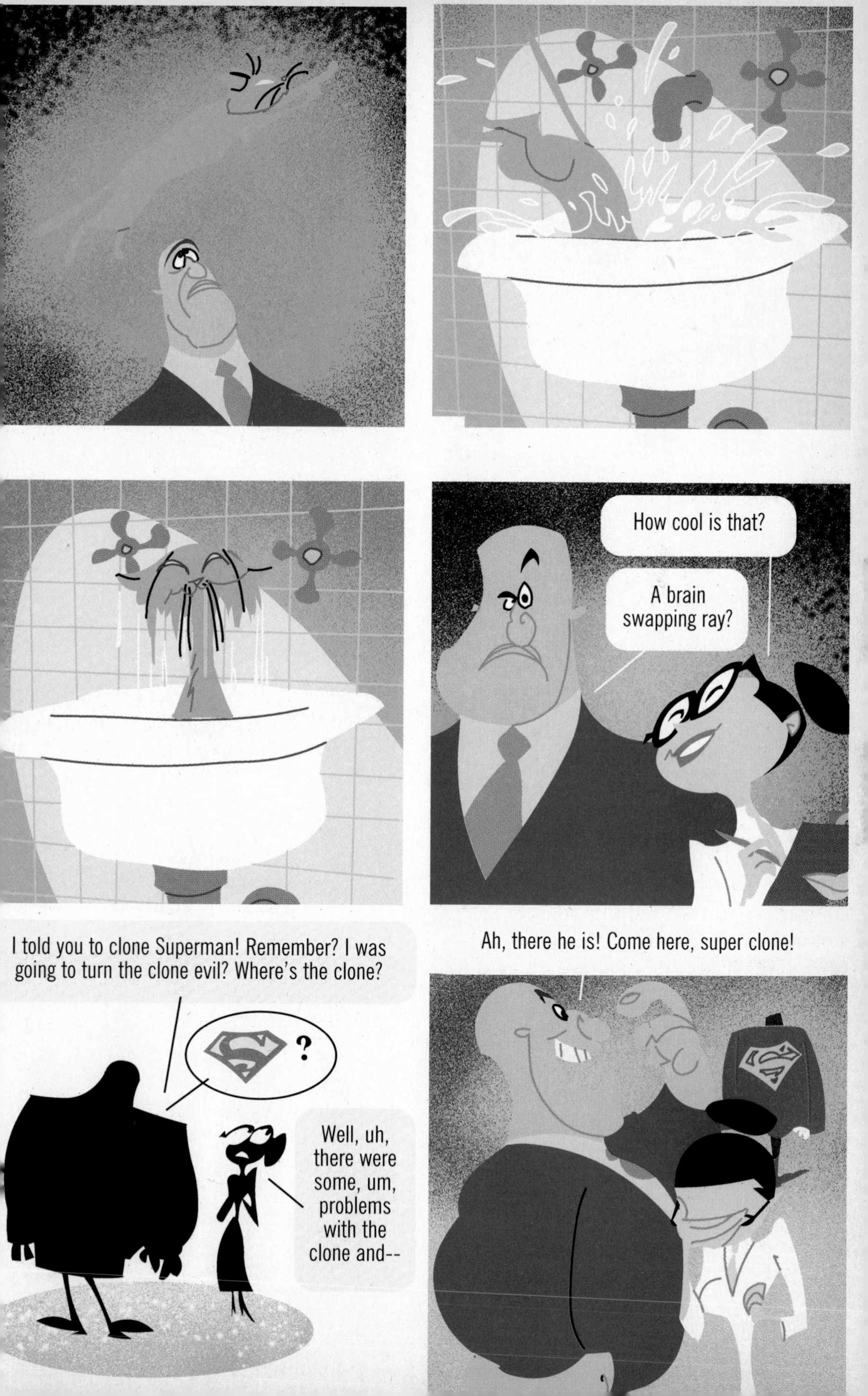
How cool is that?
A brain swapping ray?
I told you to clone Superman! Remember? I was going to turn the clone evil? Where's the clone?
?
Well, uh, there were some, um, problems with the clone and--
Ah, there he is! Come here, super clone!

He does everything the opposite! You have to say: GO AWAY, CLONE!
Me not here!
SMASH
This look nothing like bottle of soda, so me will drink it!
STOP!
ZAP!
Meanwhile, in another time zone...

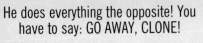

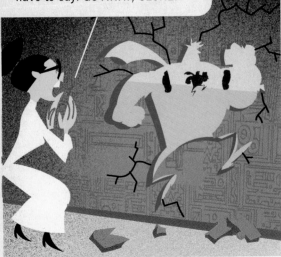

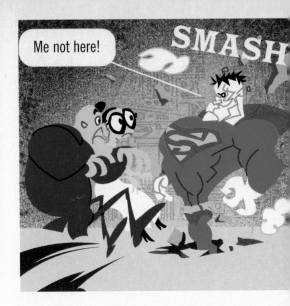

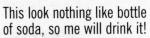

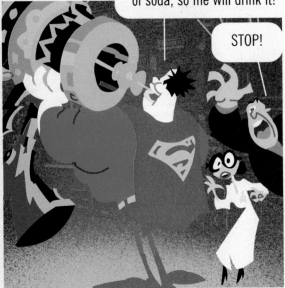

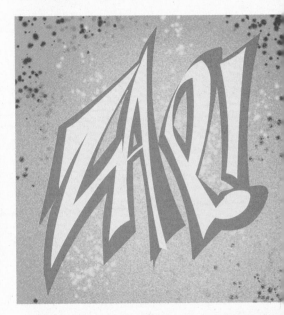

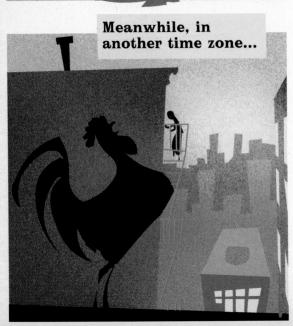

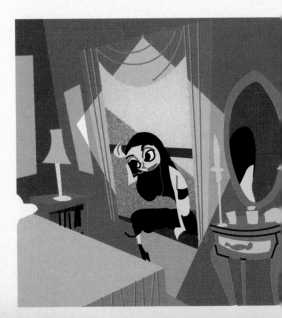

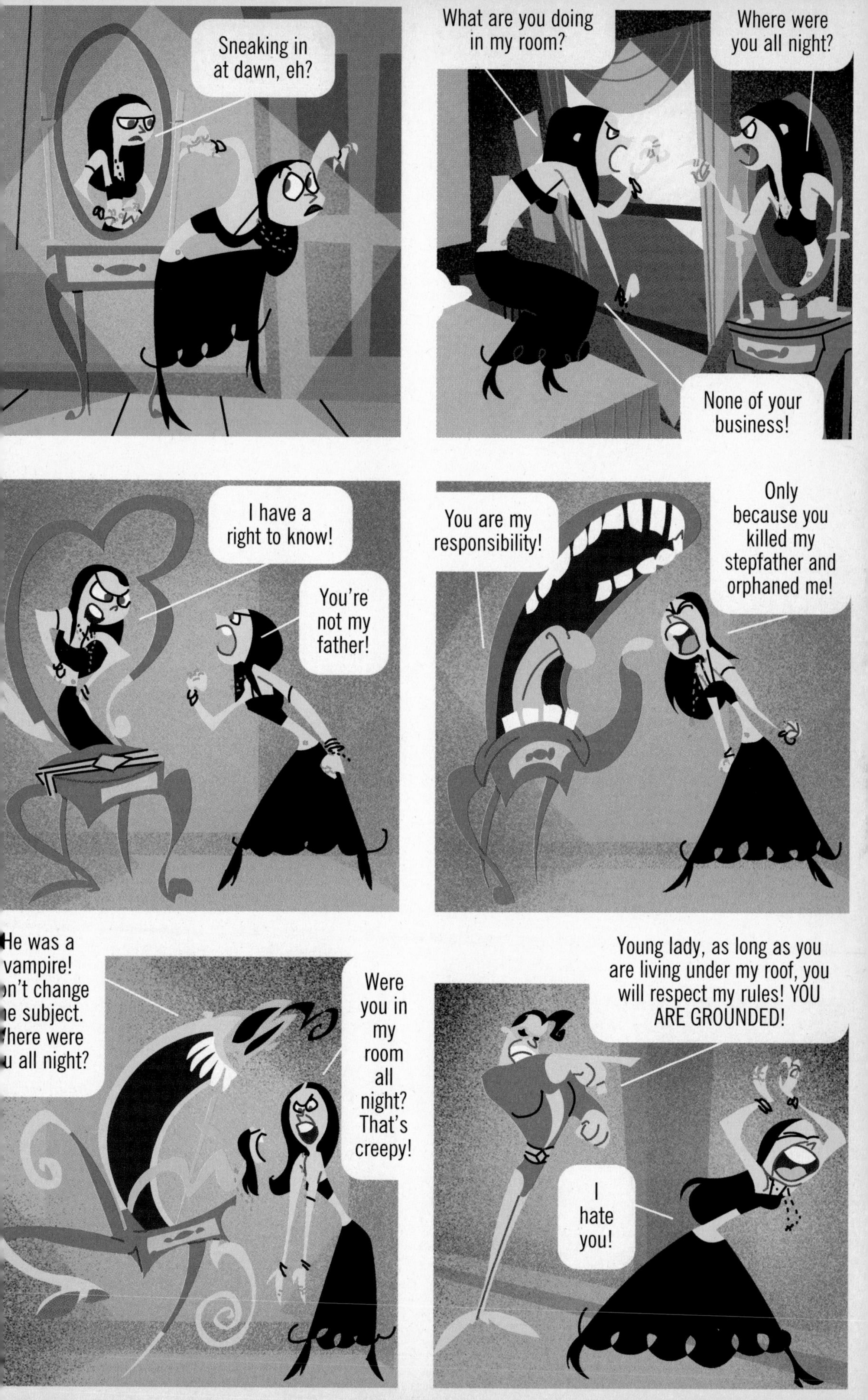
Sneaking in at dawn, eh?
What are you doing in my room?
Where were you all night?
None of your business!
I have a right to know!
You're not my father!
You are my responsibility!
Only because you killed my stepfather and orphaned me!
He was a vampire!
n't change
e subject.
here were
u all night?
Were you in my room all night? That's creepy!
Young lady, as long as you are living under my roof, you will respect my rules! YOU ARE GROUNDED!
I hate you!

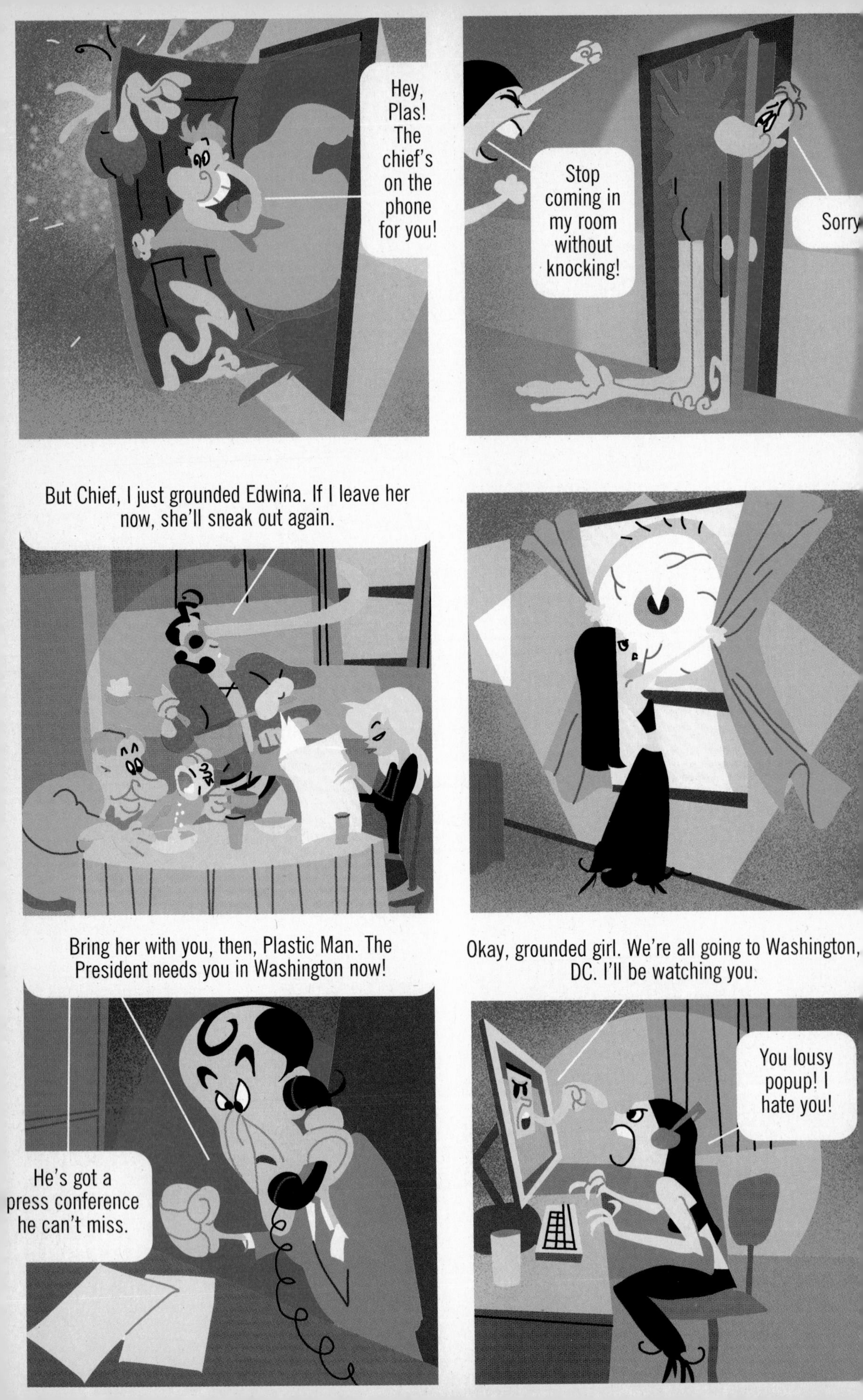
Hey, Plas! The chief's on the phone for you!
Stop coming in my room without knocking!
Sorry
But Chief, I just grounded Edwina. If I leave her now, she'll sneak out again.
Bring her with you, then, Plastic Man. The President needs you in Washington now!
He's got a press conference he can't miss.
Okay, grounded girl. We're all going to Washington, DC. I'll be watching you.
You lousy popup! I hate you!

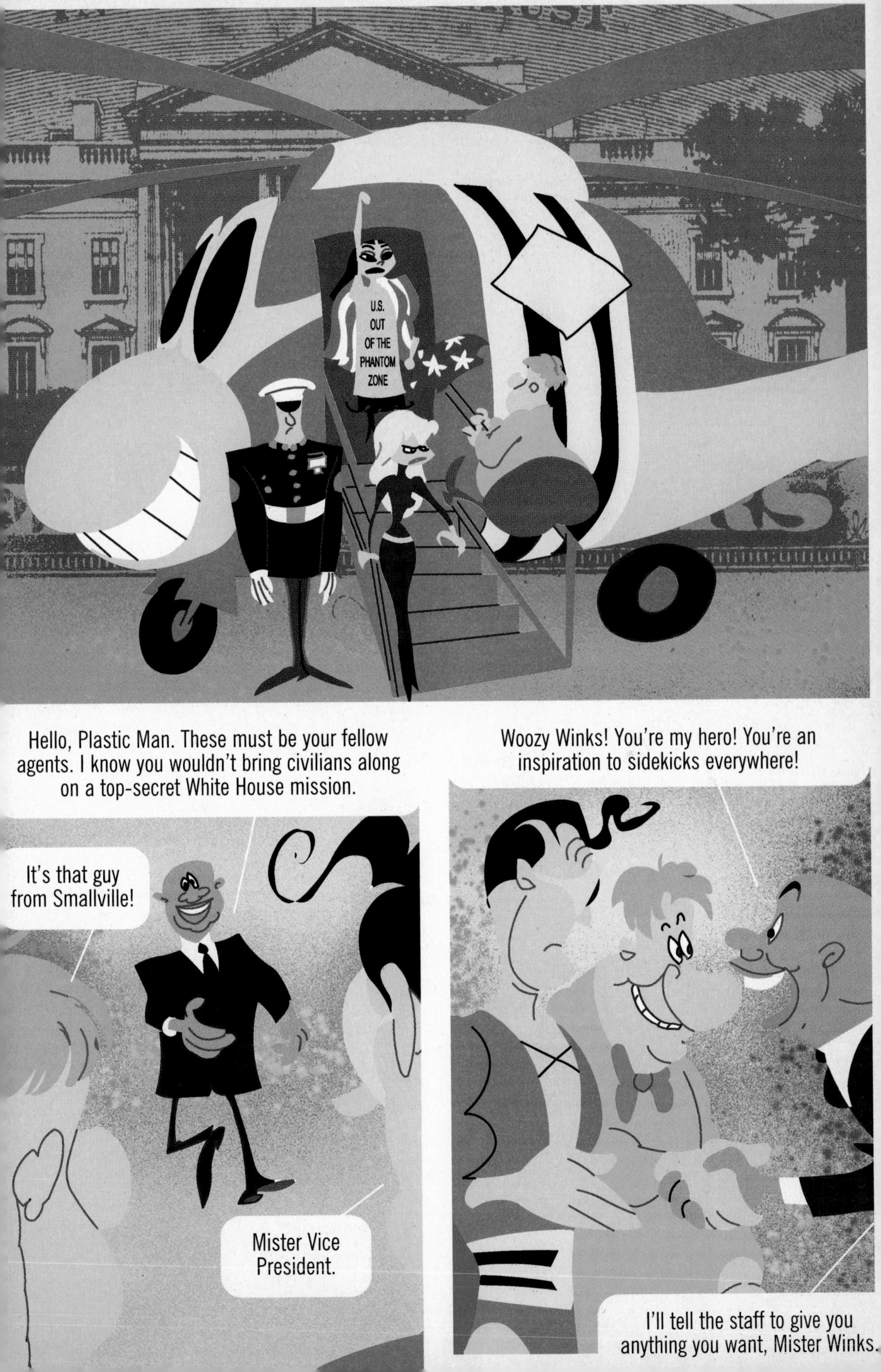
U.S. OUT OF THE PHANTOM ZONE
Hello, Plastic Man. These must be your fellow agents. I know you wouldn't bring civilians along on a top-secret White House mission.
It's that guy from Smallville!
Mister Vice President.
Woozy Winks! You're my hero! You're an inspiration to sidekicks everywhere!
I'll tell the staff to give you anything you want, Mister Winks.

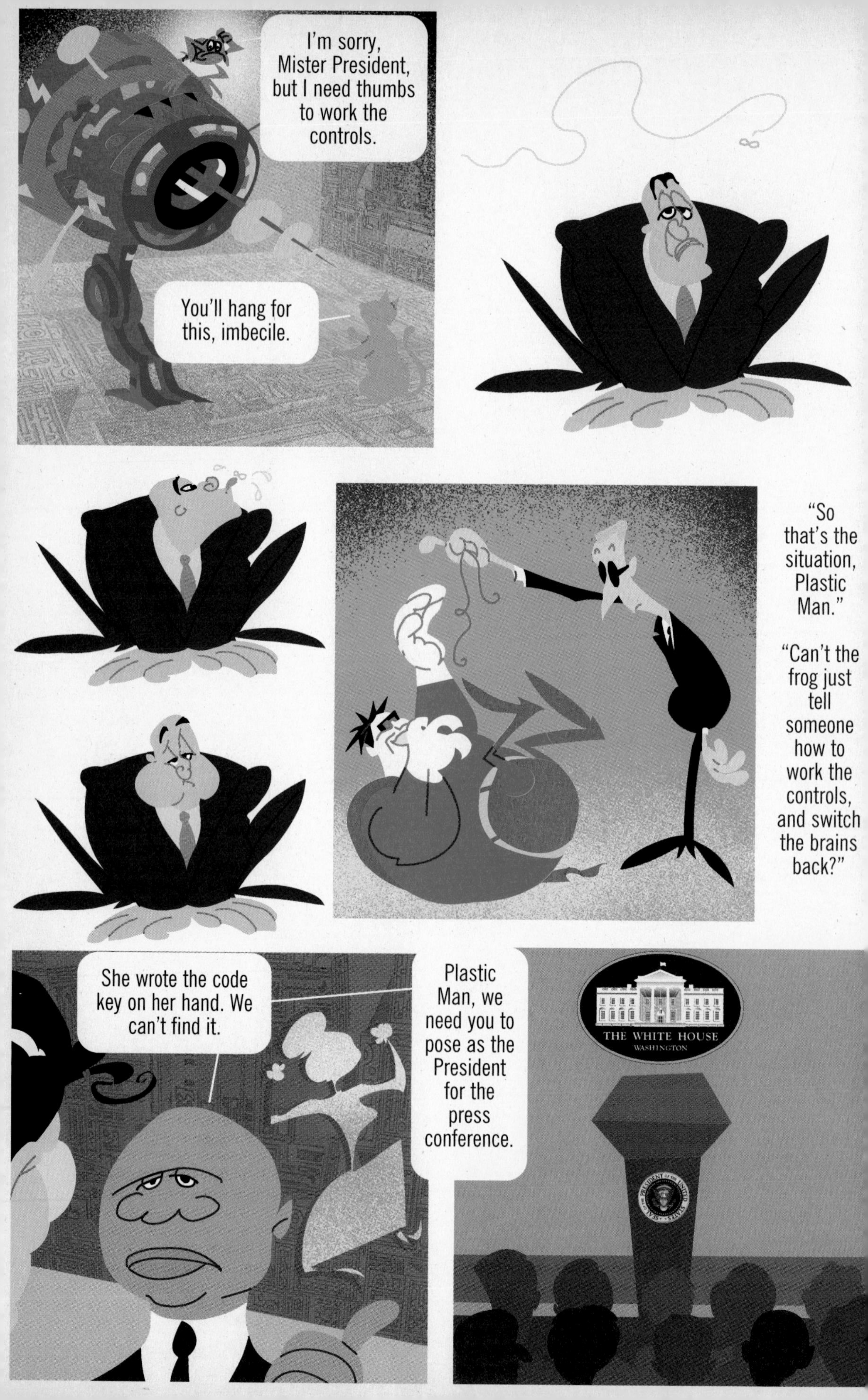

I'm sorry, Mister President, but I need thumbs to work the controls.
You'll hang for this, imbecile.
"So that's the situation, Plastic Man."
"Can't the frog just tell someone how to work the controls, and switch the brains back?"
She wrote the code key on her hand. We can't find it.
Plastic Man, we need you to pose as the President for the press conference.
THE WHITE HOUSE
WASHINGTON

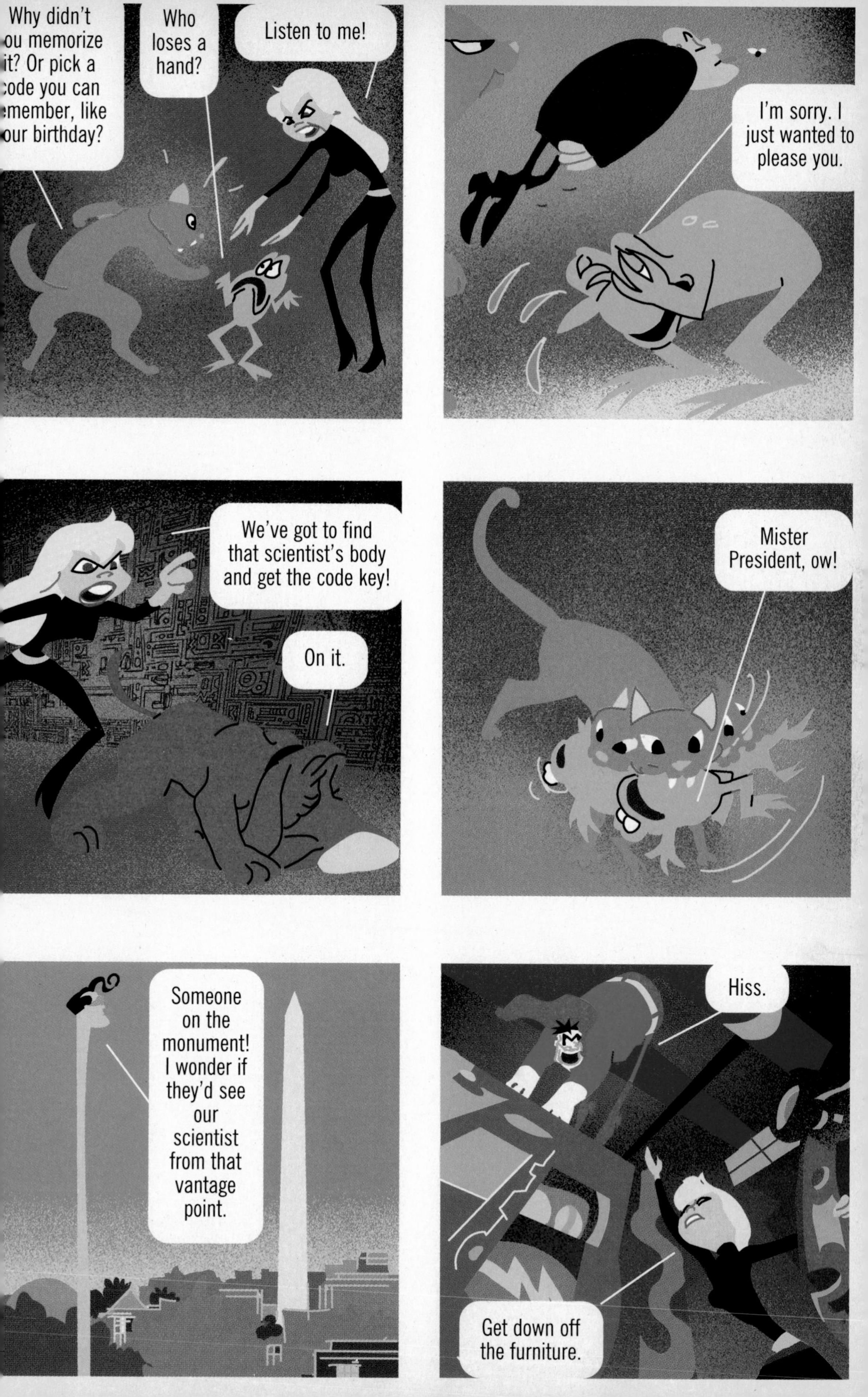
ou memorize it? Or pick a ode you can member, like our birthday?
Who loses a hand?
Listen to me!
I'm sorry. I just wanted to please you.
We've got to find that scientist's body and get the code key!
On it.
Mister President, ow!
Someone on the monument! I wonder if they'd see our scientist from that vantage point.
Hiss.
Get down off the furniture.

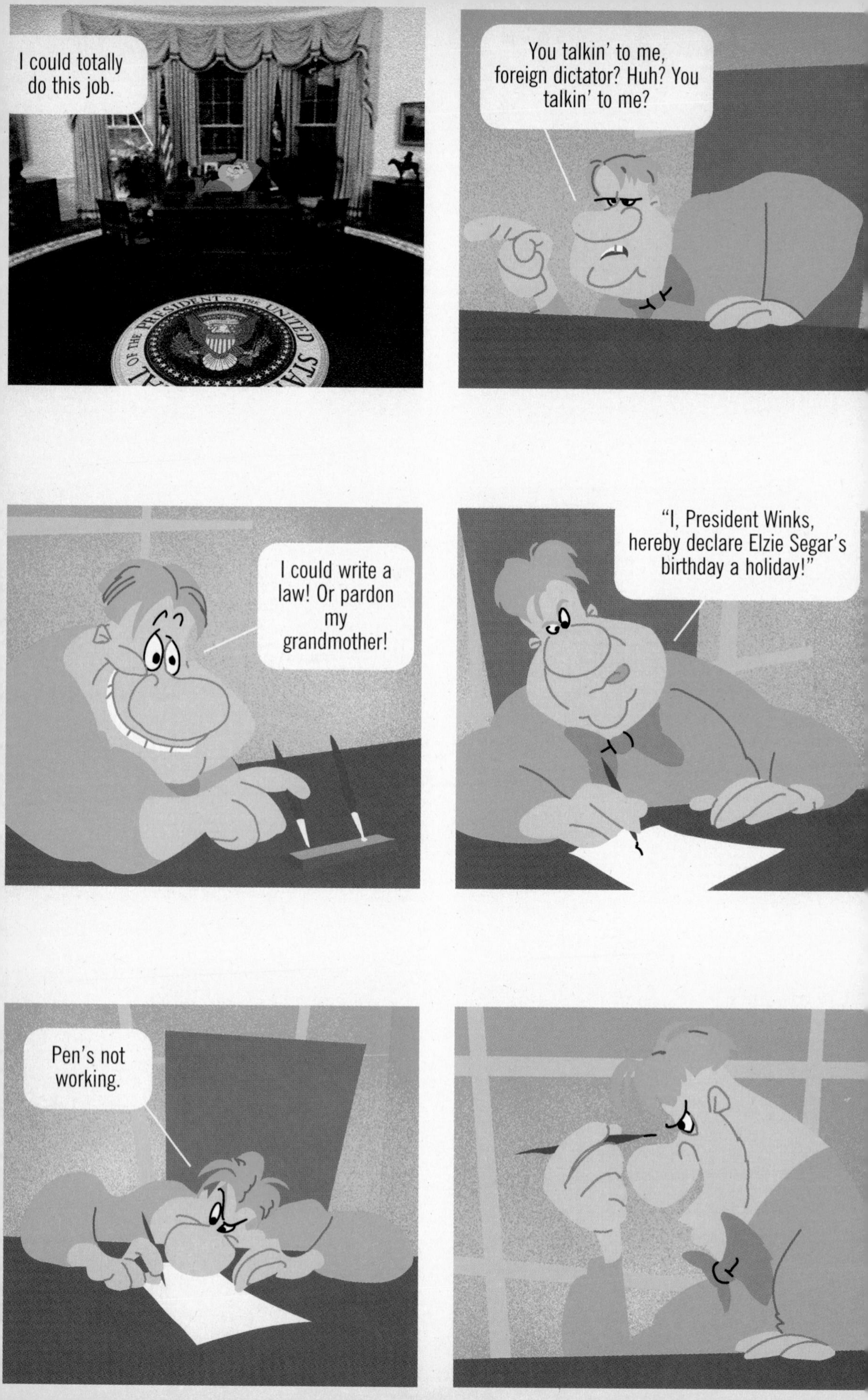
I could totally do this job.
You talkin' to me, foreign dictator? Huh? You talkin' to me?
I could write a law! Or pardon my grandmother!
"I, President Winks, hereby declare Elzie Segar's birthday a holiday!"
Pen's not working.

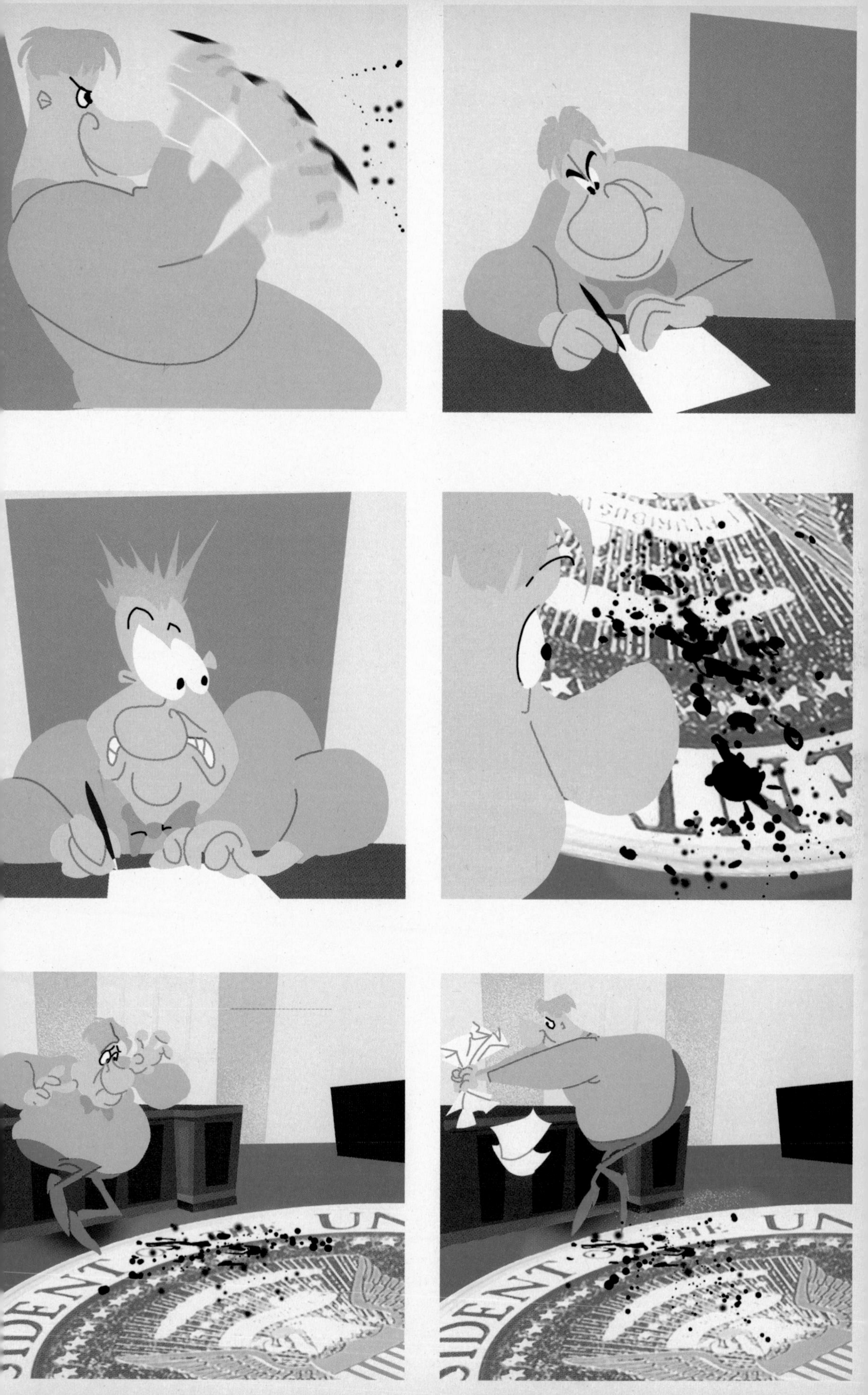

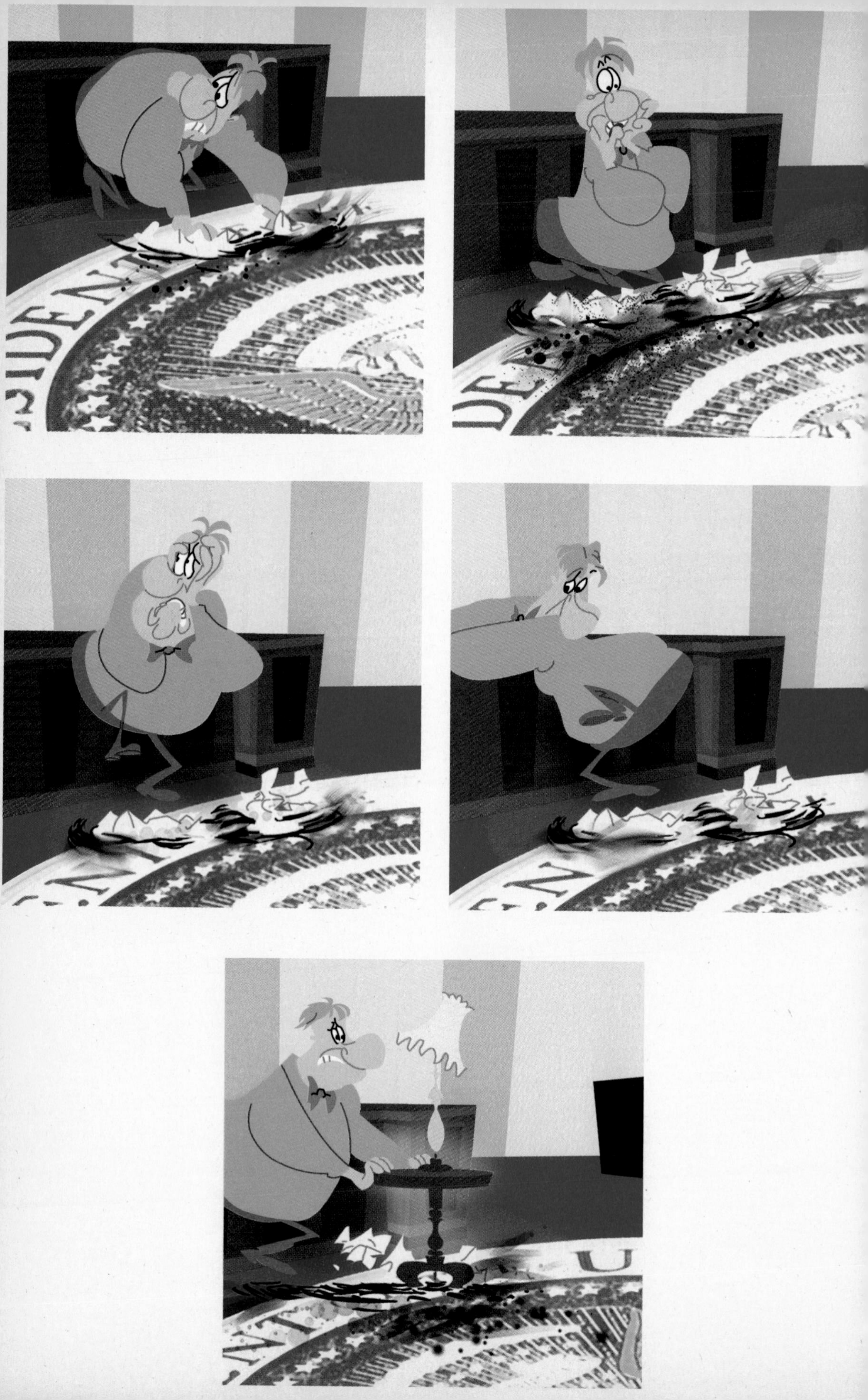

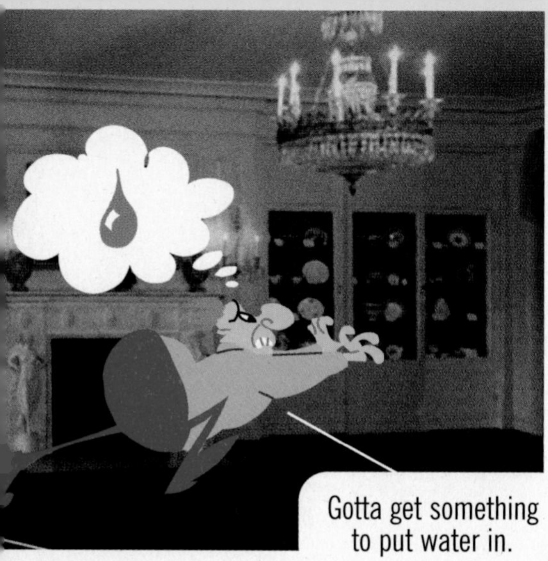
Gotta get something
to put water in.

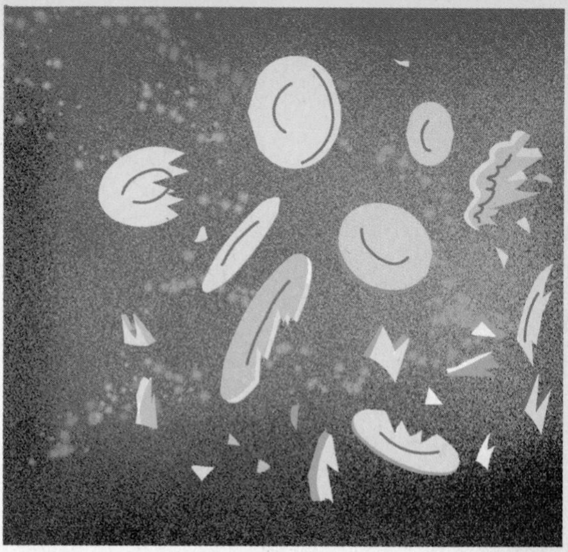

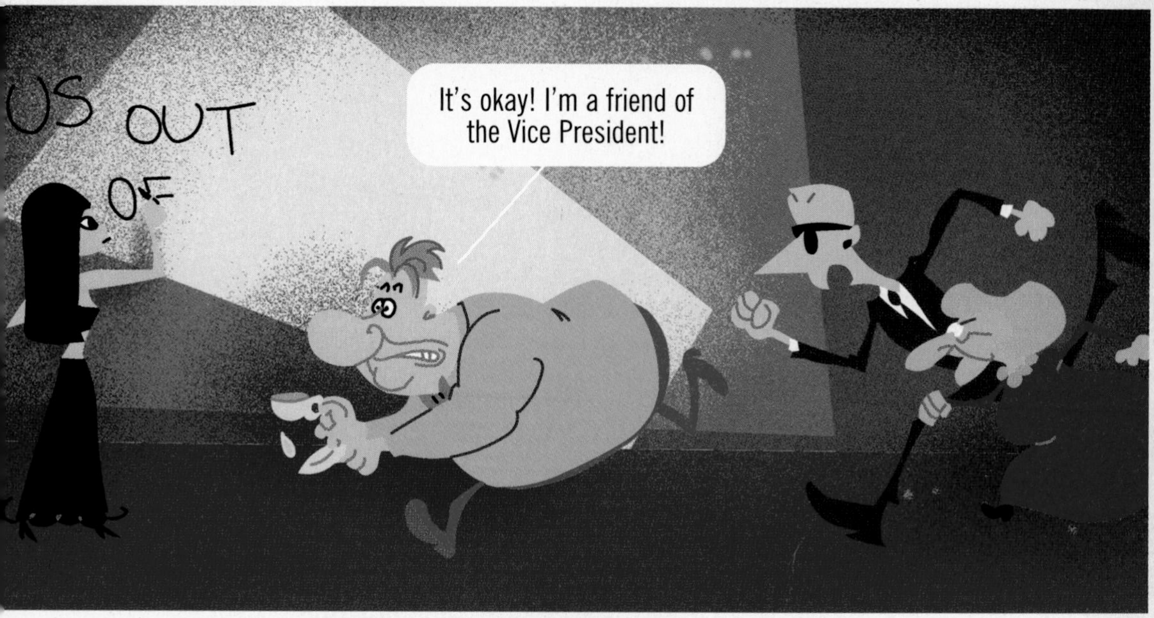
US OUT OF
It's okay! I'm a friend of the Vice President!

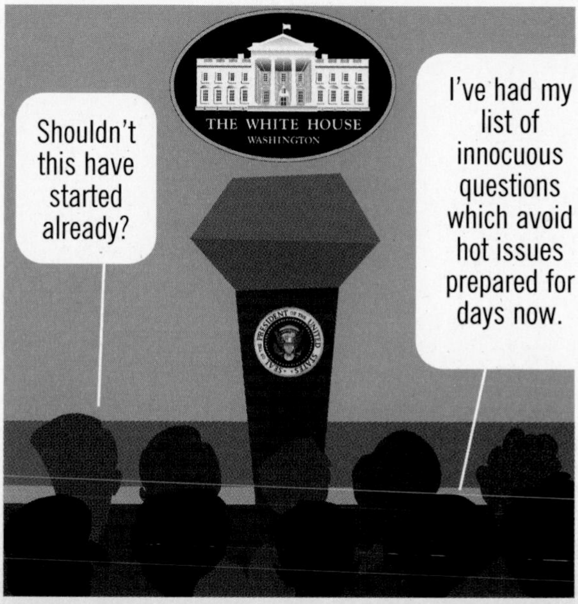
THE WHITE HOUSE
WASHINGTON
Shouldn't this have started already?
I've had my list of innocuous questions which avoid hot issues prepared for days now.

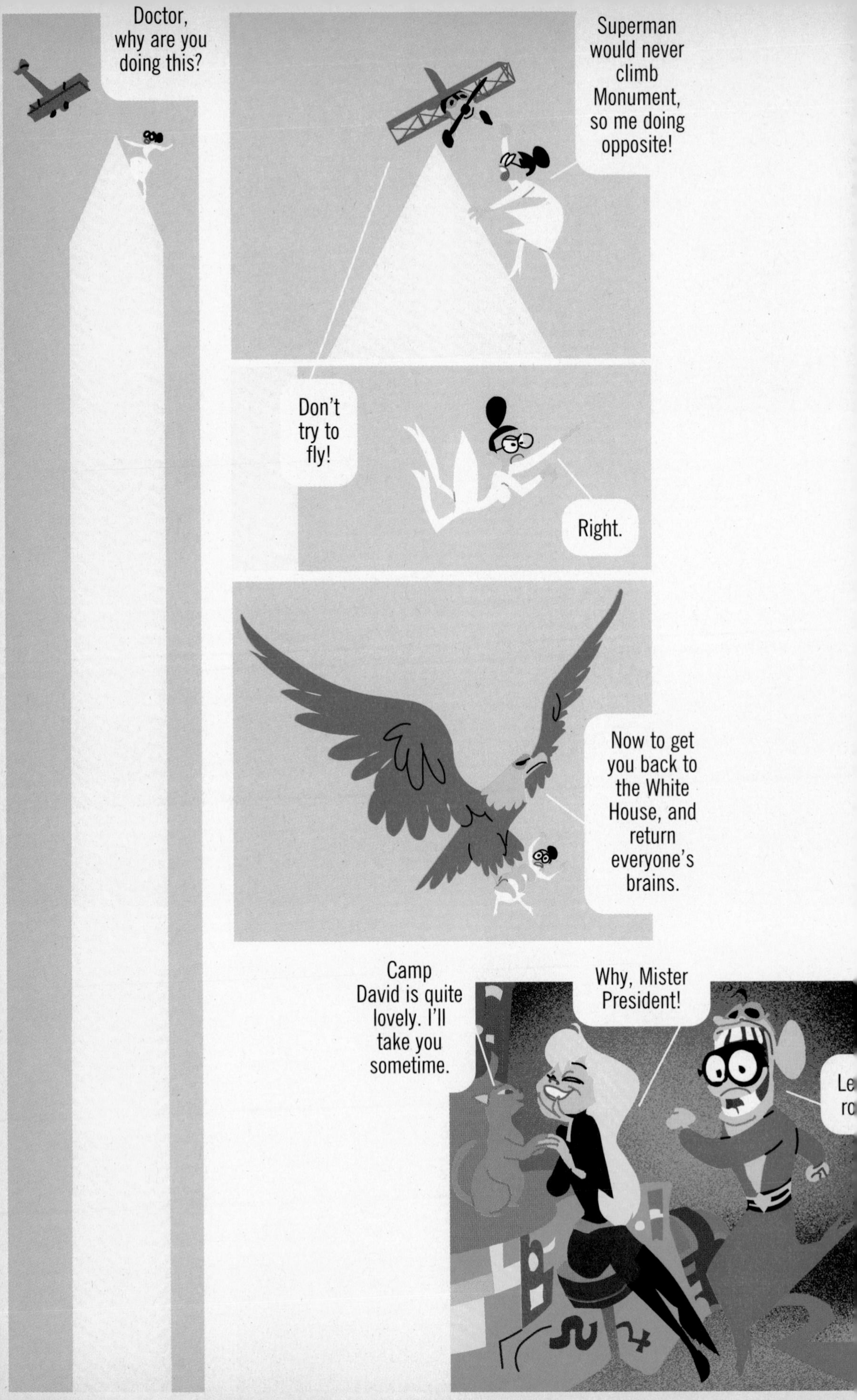

Doctor, why are you doing this?
Superman would never climb Monument, so me doing opposite!
Don't try to fly!
Right.
Now to get you back to the White House, and return everyone's brains.
Camp David is quite lovely. I'll take you sometime.
Why, Mister President!

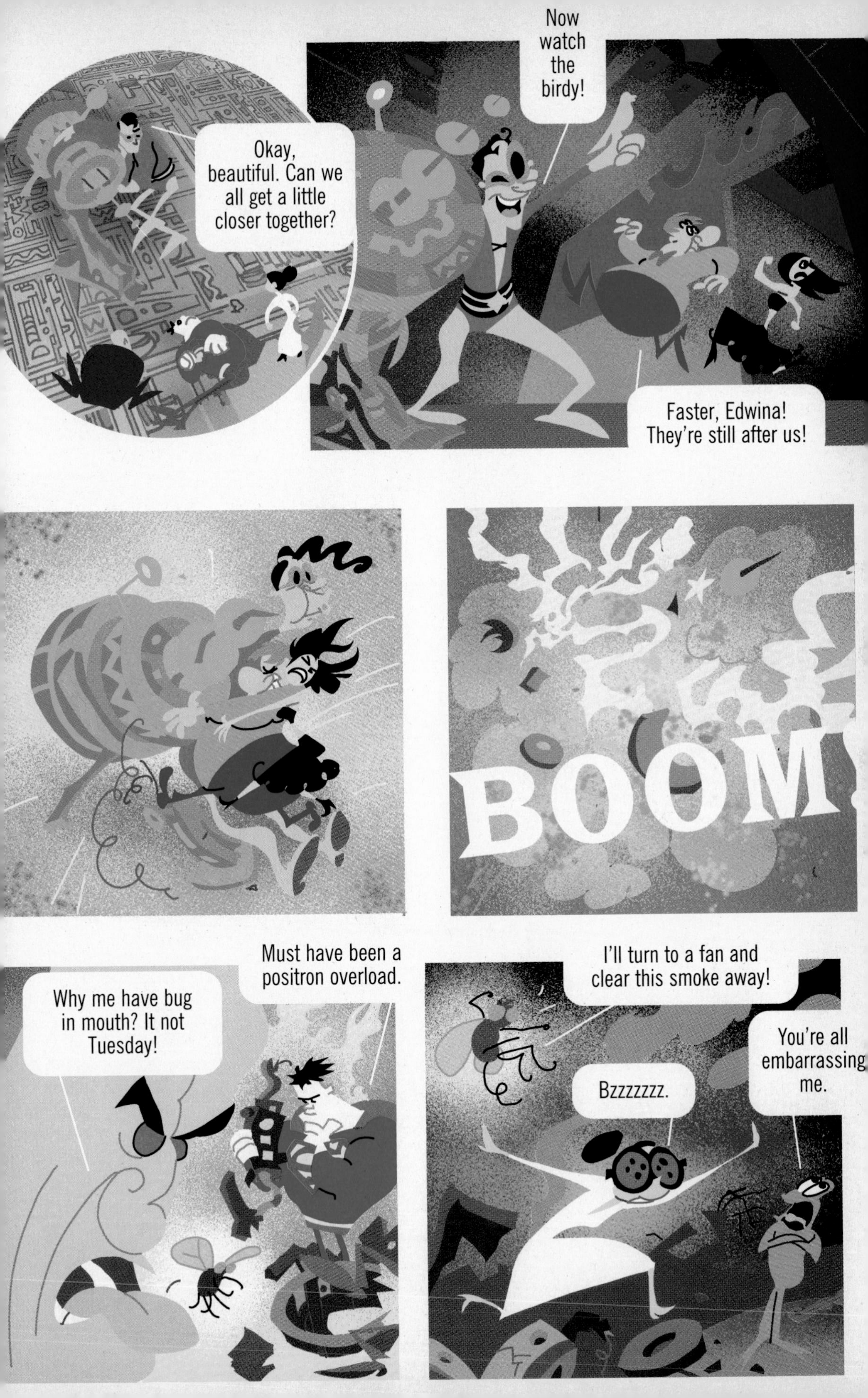
Okay, beautiful. Can we all get a little closer together?
Now watch the birdy!
Faster, Edwina! They're still after us!
BOOM!
Why me have bug in mouth? It not Tuesday!
Must have been a positron overload.
I'll turn to a fan and clear this smoke away!
Bzzzzzzz.
You're all embarrassing me.

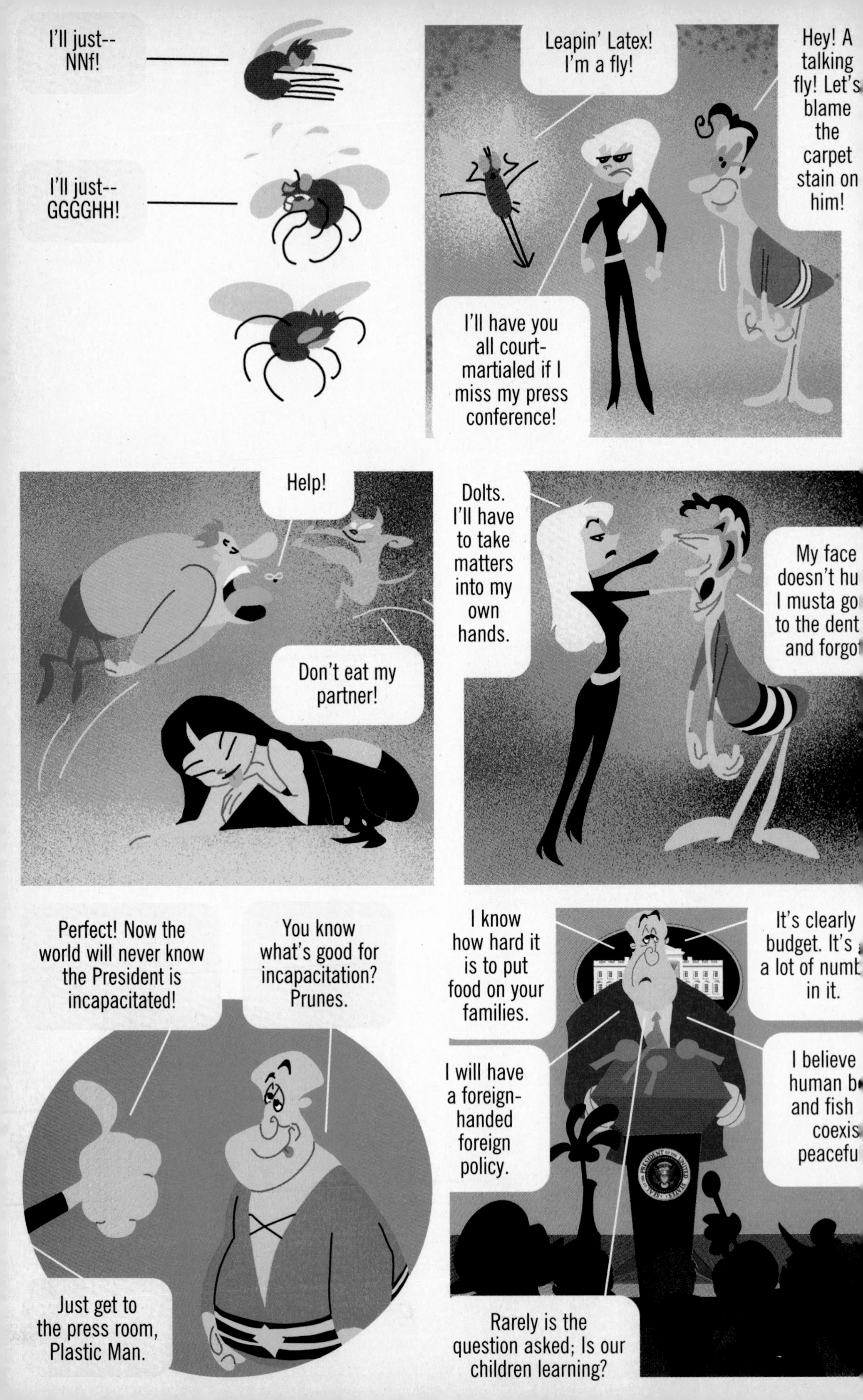
I'll just--
NNf!
I'll just--
GGGGHH!
Leapin' Latex! I'm a fly!
Hey! A talking fly! Let's blame the carpet stain on him!
I'll have you all court-martialed if I miss my press conference!
Help!
Don't eat my partner!
Dolts. I'll have to take matters into my own hands.
My face doesn't hu
I musta go
to the dent
and forgo
Perfect! Now the world will never know the President is incapacitated!
You know what's good for incapacitation? Prunes.
Just get to the press room, Plastic Man.
I know how hard it is to put food on your families.
It's clearly
budget. It's
a lot of numb
in it.
I will have a foreign-handed foreign policy.
I believe
human b
and fish
coexis
peacefu
Rarely is the question asked; Is our children learning?

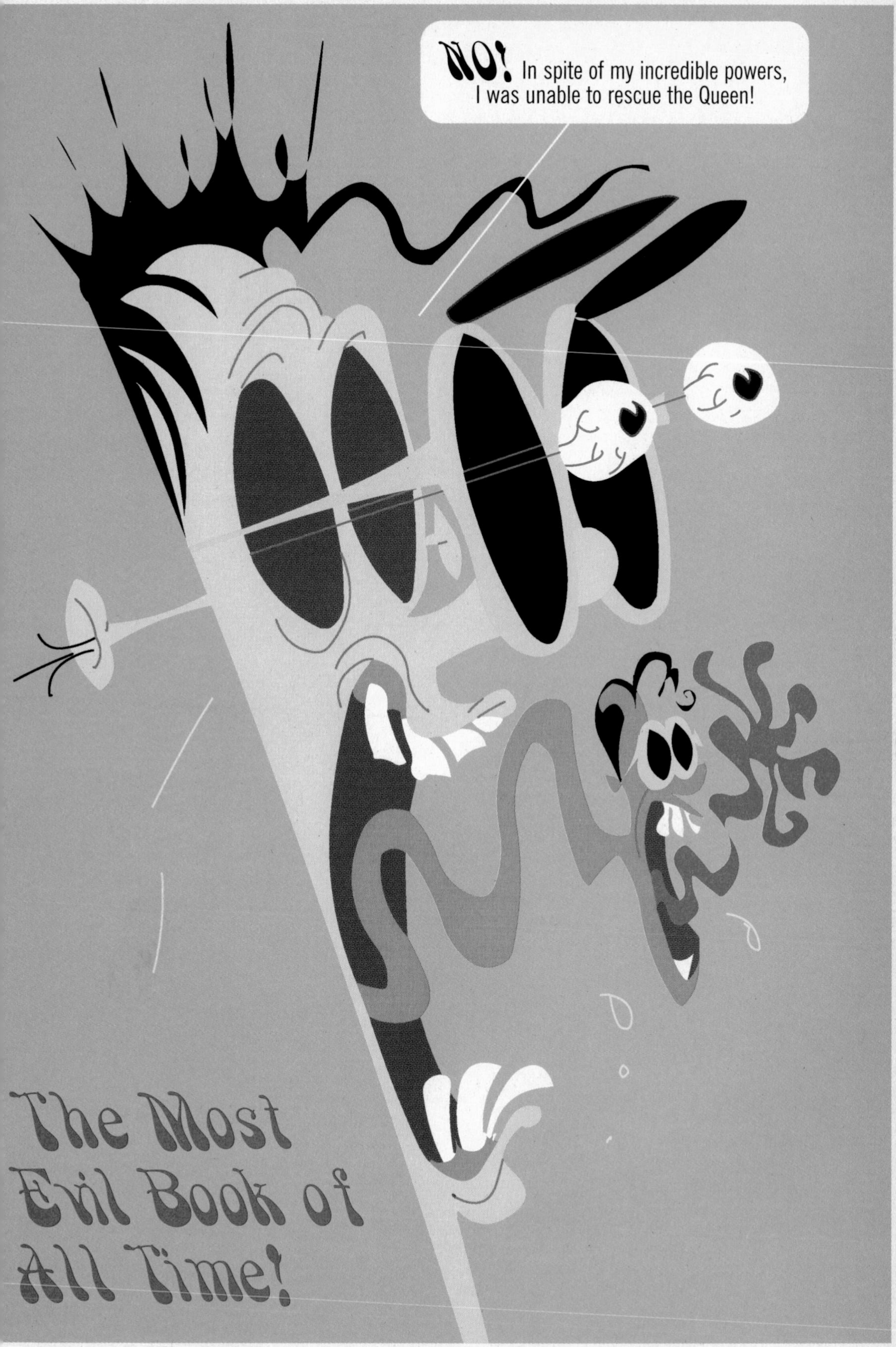
NO! In spite of my incredible powers, I was unable to rescue the Queen!
The Most Evil Book of All Time!

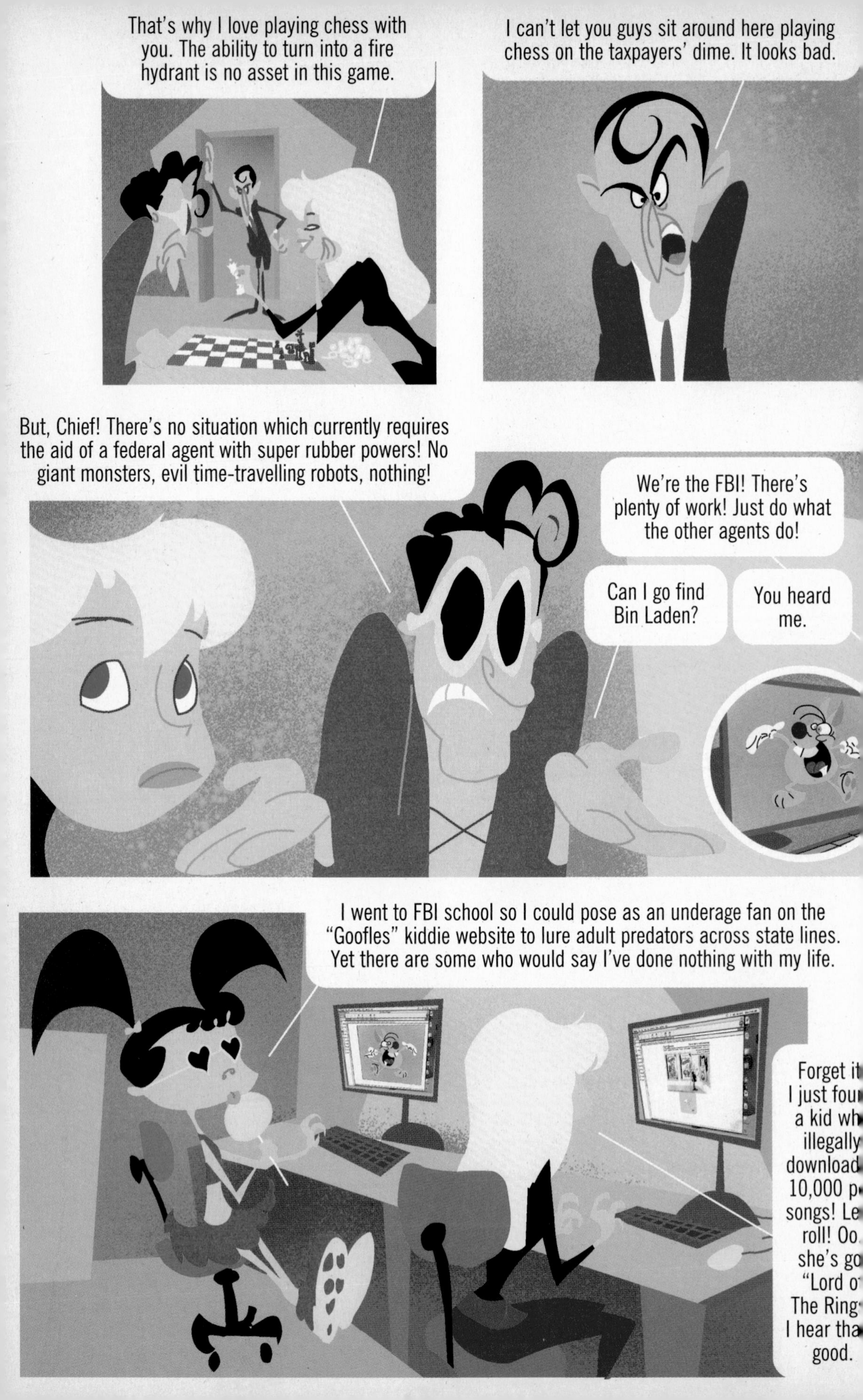
That's why I love playing chess with you. The ability to turn into a fire hydrant is no asset in this game.
I can't let you guys sit around here playing chess on the taxpayers' dime. It looks bad.
But, Chief! There's no situation which currently requires the aid of a federal agent with super rubber powers! No giant monsters, evil time-travelling robots, nothing!
We're the FBI! There's plenty of work! Just do what the other agents do!
Can I go find Bin Laden?
You heard me.
I went to FBI school so I could pose as an underage fan on the "Goofles" kiddie website to lure adult predators across state lines. Yet there are some who would say I've done nothing with my life.
Forget it I just fou a kid wh illegally download 10,000 p songs! Le roll! Oo she's go "Lord o The Ring I hear tha good.

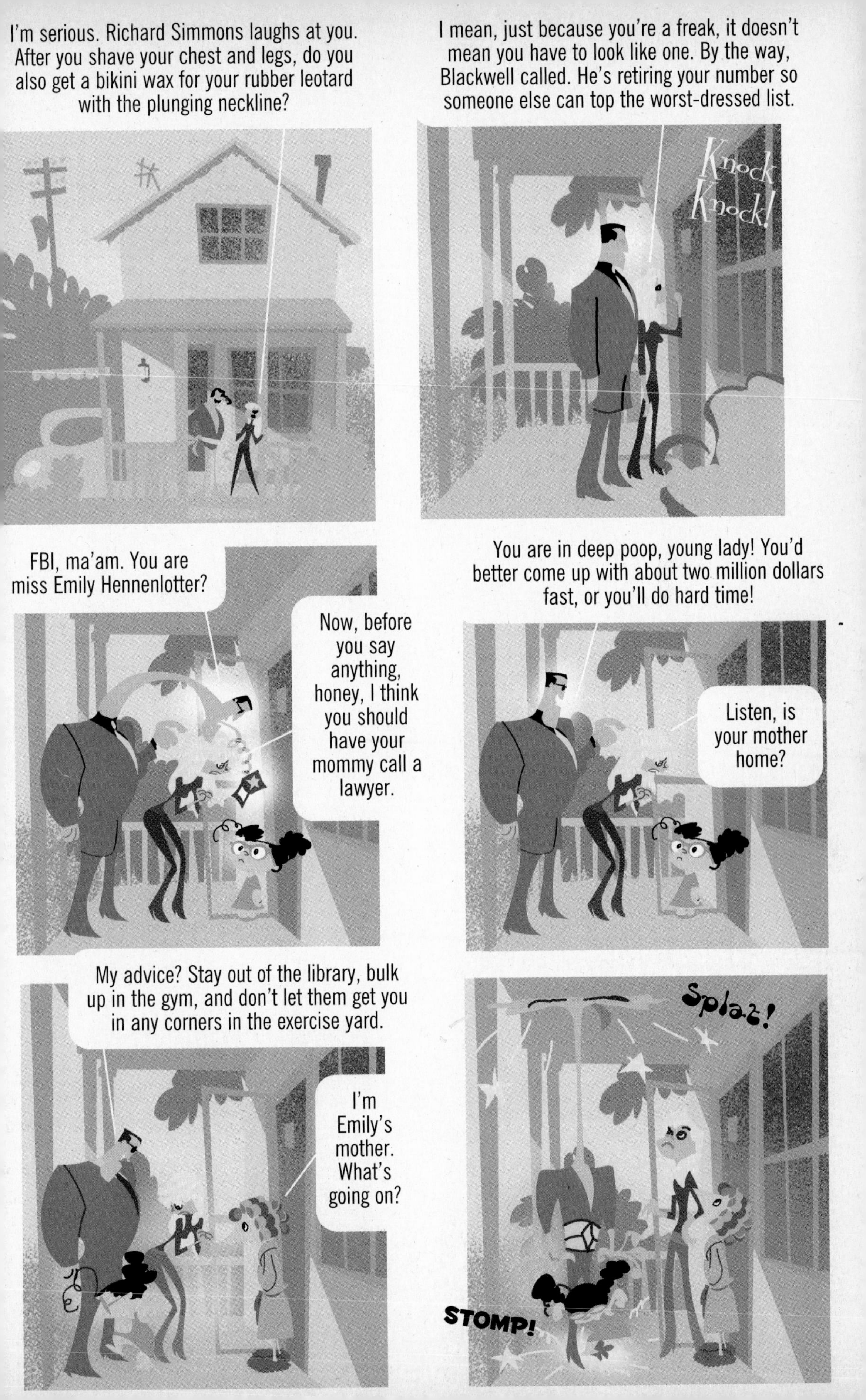

I'm serious. Richard Simmons laughs at you. After you shave your chest and legs, do you also get a bikini wax for your rubber leotard with the plunging neckline?
I mean, just because you're a freak, it doesn't mean you have to look like one. By the way, Blackwell called. He's retiring your number so someone else can top the worst-dressed list.
Knock Knock!
FBI, ma'am. You are miss Emily Hennenlotter?
Now, before you say anything, honey, I think you should have your mommy call a lawyer.
You are in deep poop, young lady! You'd better come up with about two million dollars fast, or you'll do hard time!
Listen, is your mother home?
My advice? Stay out of the library, bulk up in the gym, and don't let them get you in any corners in the exercise yard.
I'm Emily's mother. What's going on?
Splat!
STOMP!

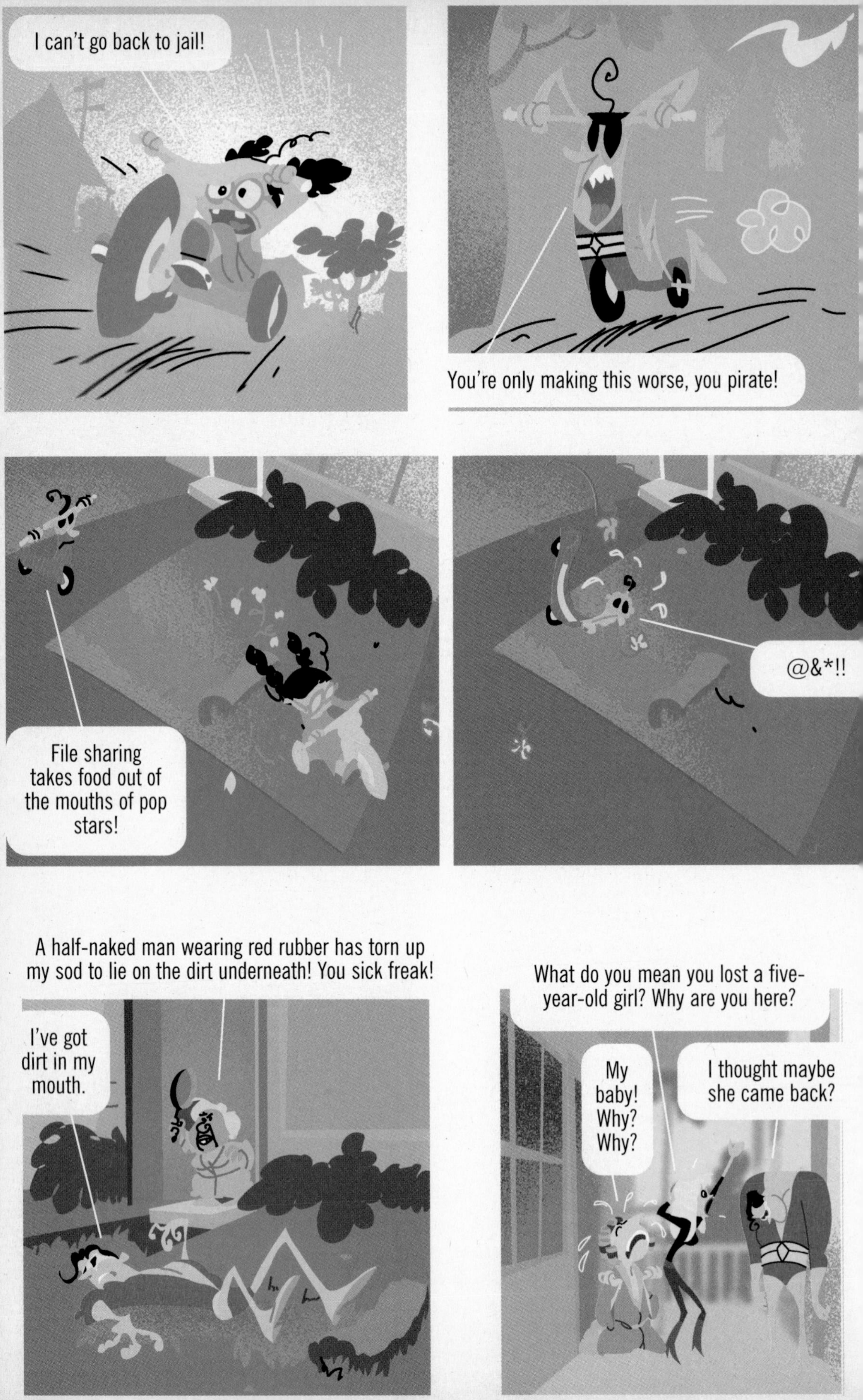
I can't go back to jail!
You're only making this worse, you pirate!
File sharing takes food out of the mouths of pop stars!
@&*!!
A half-naked man wearing red rubber has torn up my sod to lie on the dirt underneath! You sick freak!
I've got dirt in my mouth.
What do you mean you lost a five-year-old girl? Why are you here?
My baby! Why? Why?
I thought maybe she came back?

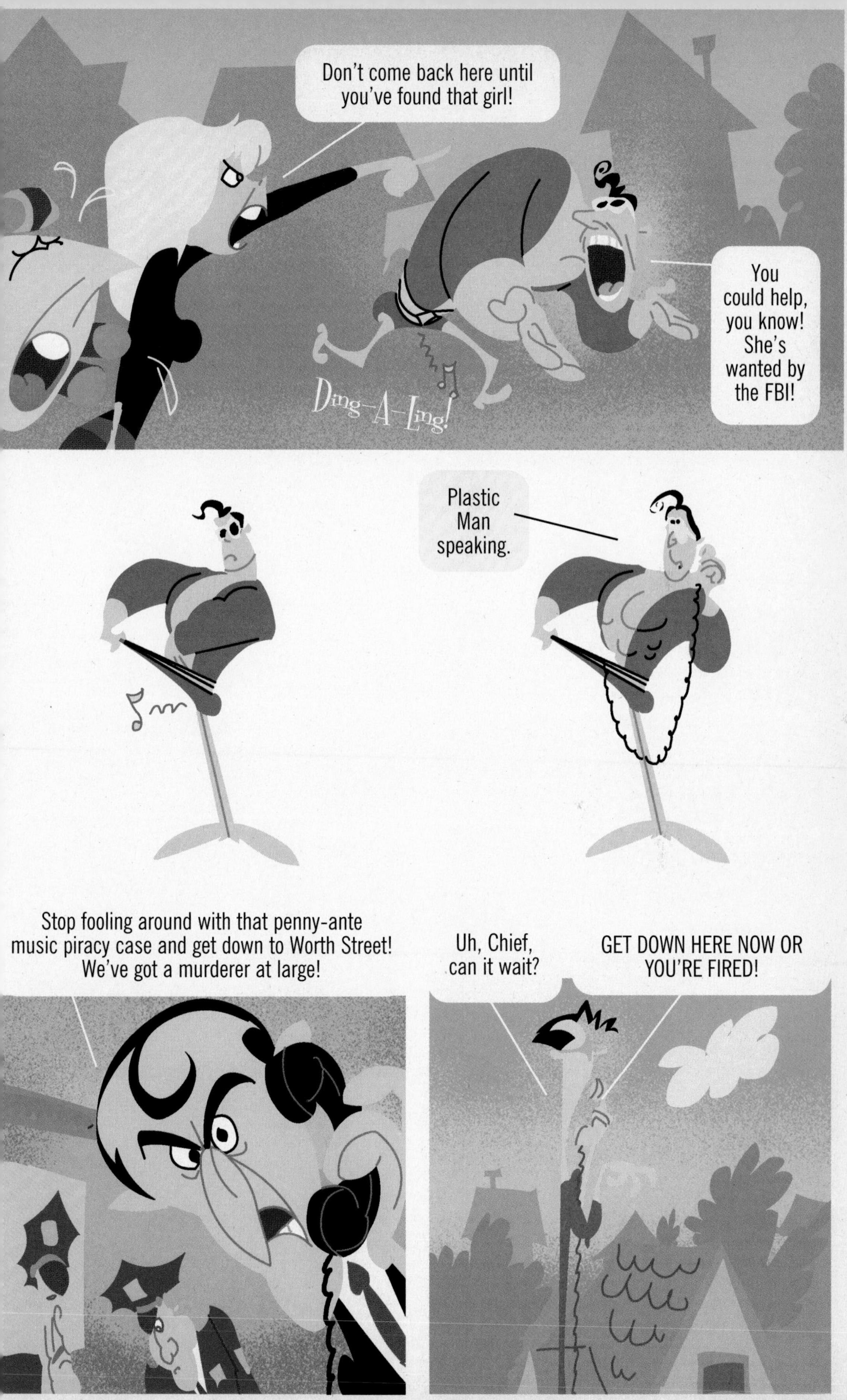
Don't come back here until you've found that girl!
You could help, you know! She's wanted by the FBI!
Ding-A-Ling!
Plastic Man speaking.
Stop fooling around with that penny-ante music piracy case and get down to Worth Street! We've got a murderer at large!
Uh, Chief, can it wait?
GET DOWN HERE NOW OR YOU'RE FIRED!

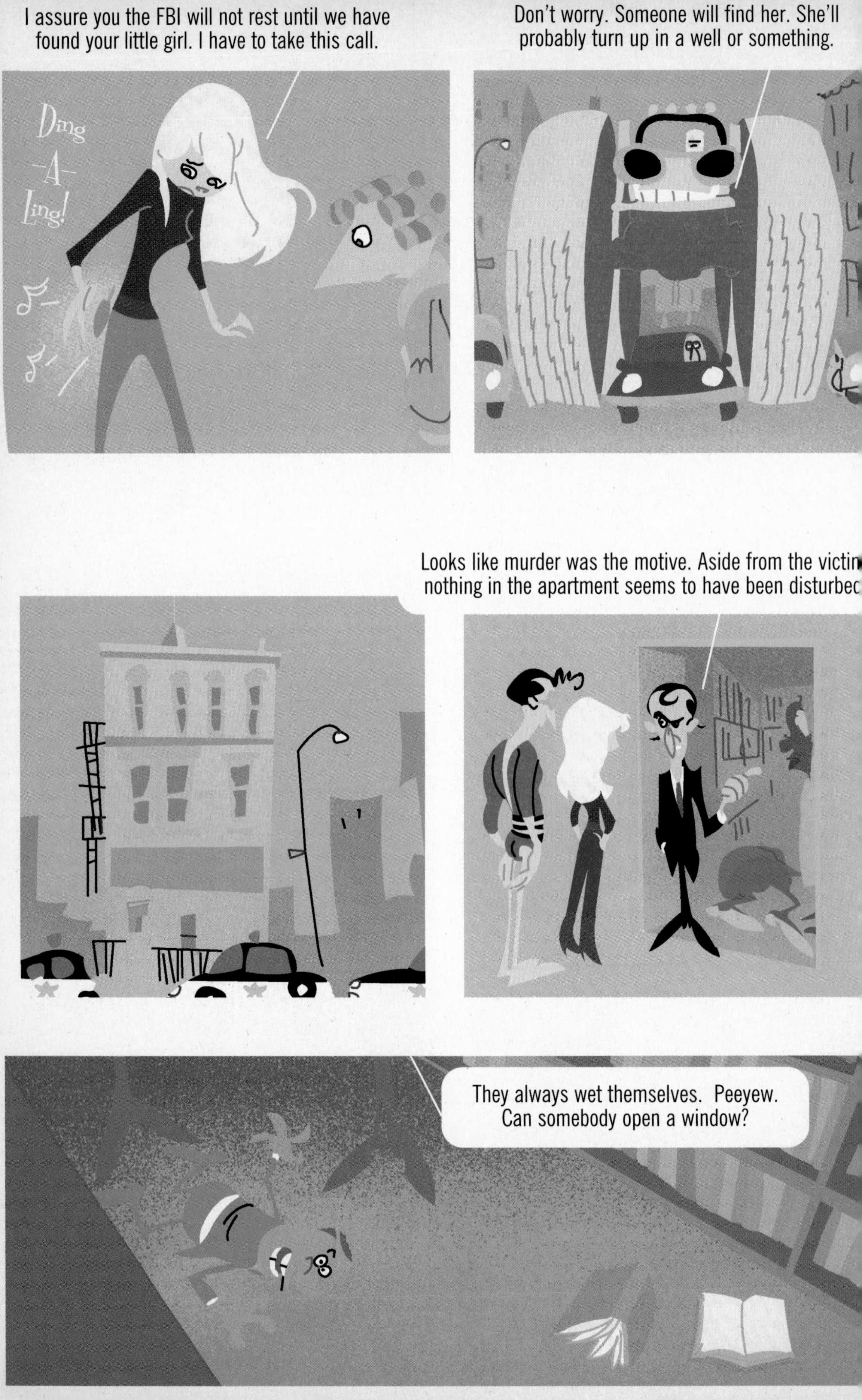

I assure you the FBI will not rest until we have found your little girl. I have to take this call.
Ding-A-Ling!
Don't worry. Someone will find her. She'll probably turn up in a well or something.
Looks like murder was the motive. Aside from the victi
nothing in the apartment seems to have been disturbe
They always wet themselves. Peeyew. Can somebody open a window?

"We can't get to any of them. This guy has stuffed every inch of this tiny studio with books!"

"This is why I get rid of books after I read them. After all, how many books do you read twice?"

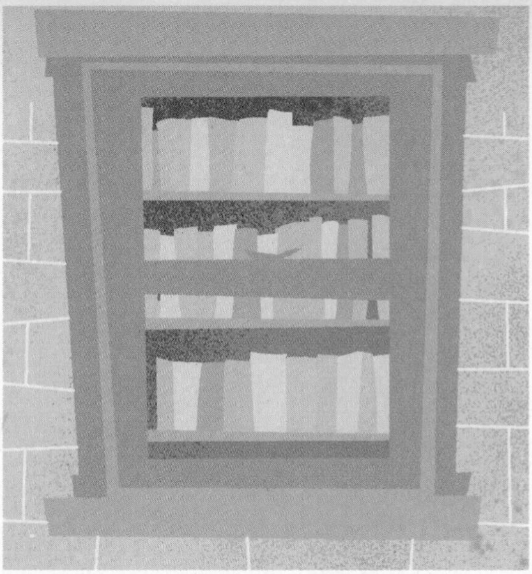

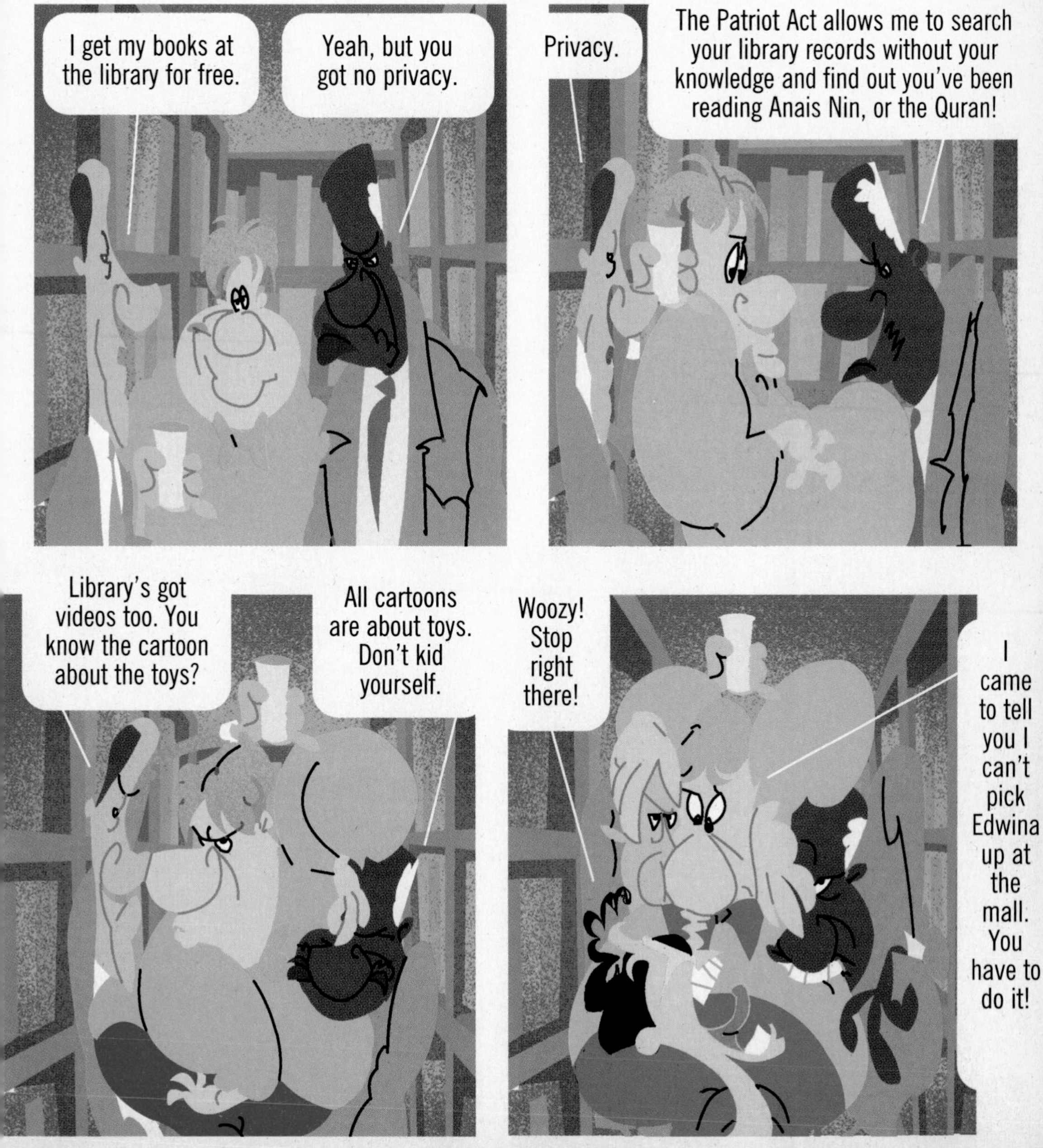
I get my books at the library for free.
Yeah, but you got no privacy.
Privacy.
The Patriot Act allows me to search your library records without your knowledge and find out you've been reading Anais Nin, or the Quran!
Library's got videos too. You know the cartoon about the toys?
All cartoons are about toys. Don't kid yourself.
Woozy! Stop right there!
I came to tell you I can't pick Edwina up at the mall. You have to do it!

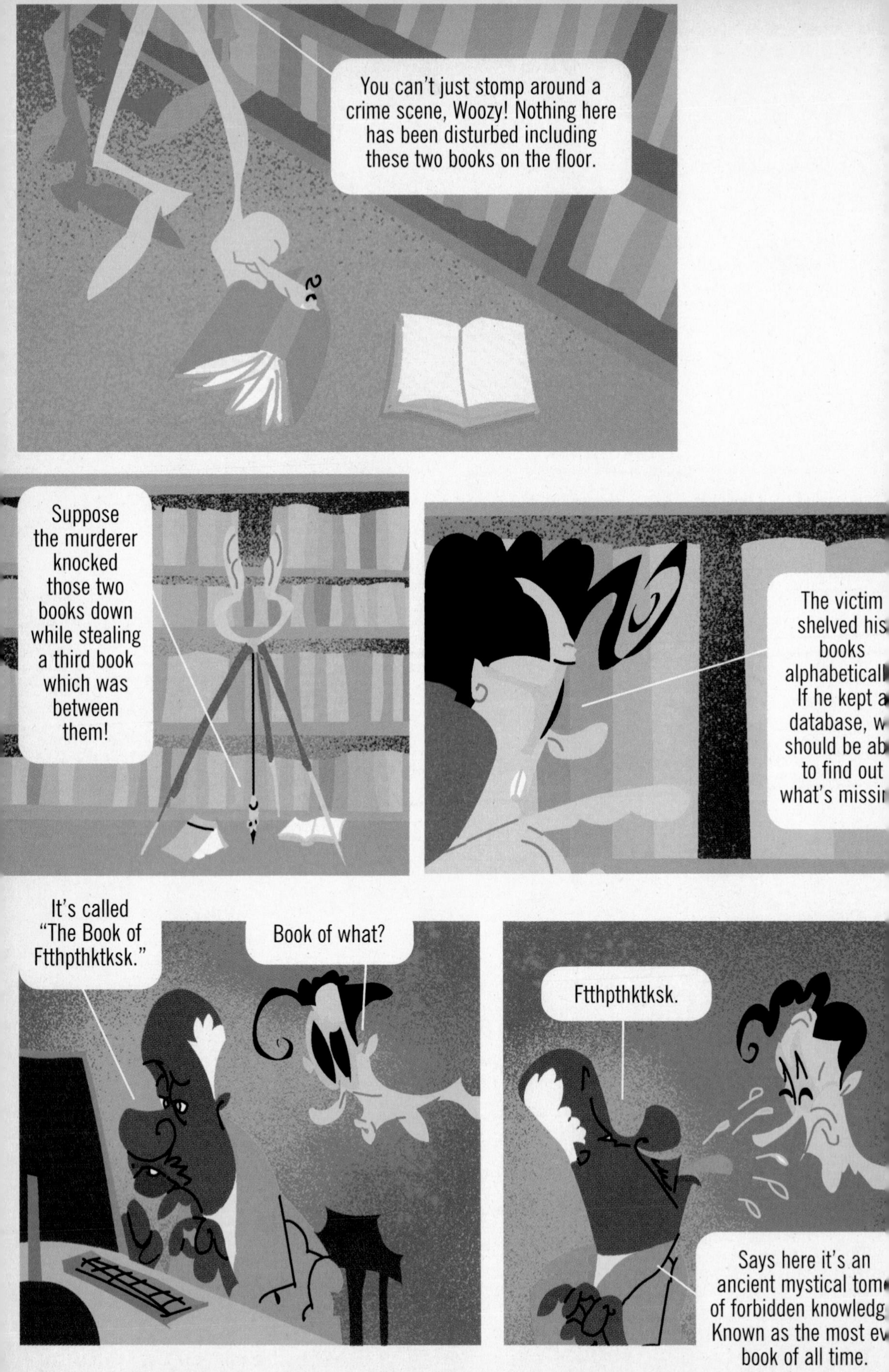
You can't just stomp around a crime scene, Woozy! Nothing here has been disturbed including these two books on the floor.
Suppose the murderer knocked those two books down while stealing a third book which was between them!
The victim shelved his books alphabeticall If he kept a database, w should be ab to find out what's missi
It's called "The Book of Ftthpthktksk."
Book of what?
Ftthpthktksk.
Says here it's an ancient mystical tom of forbidden knowledg Known as the most ev book of all time.

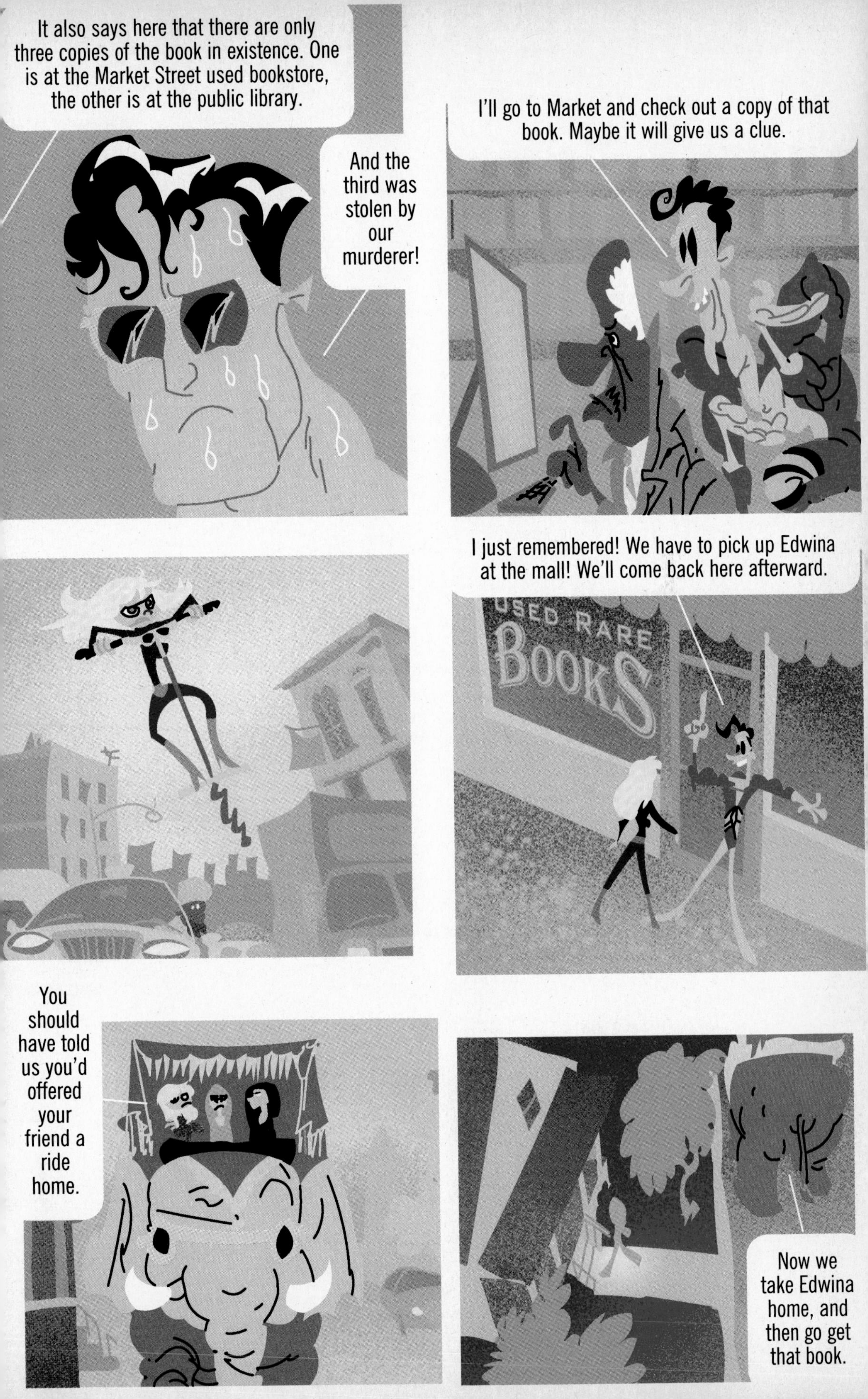
It also says here that there are only three copies of the book in existence. One is at the Market Street used bookstore, the other is at the public library.
And the third was stolen by our murderer!
I'll go to Market and check out a copy of that book. Maybe it will give us a clue.
I just remembered! We have to pick up Edwina at the mall! We'll come back here afterward.
USED RARE BOOKS
You should have told us you'd offered your friend a ride home.
Now we take Edwina home, and then go get that book.

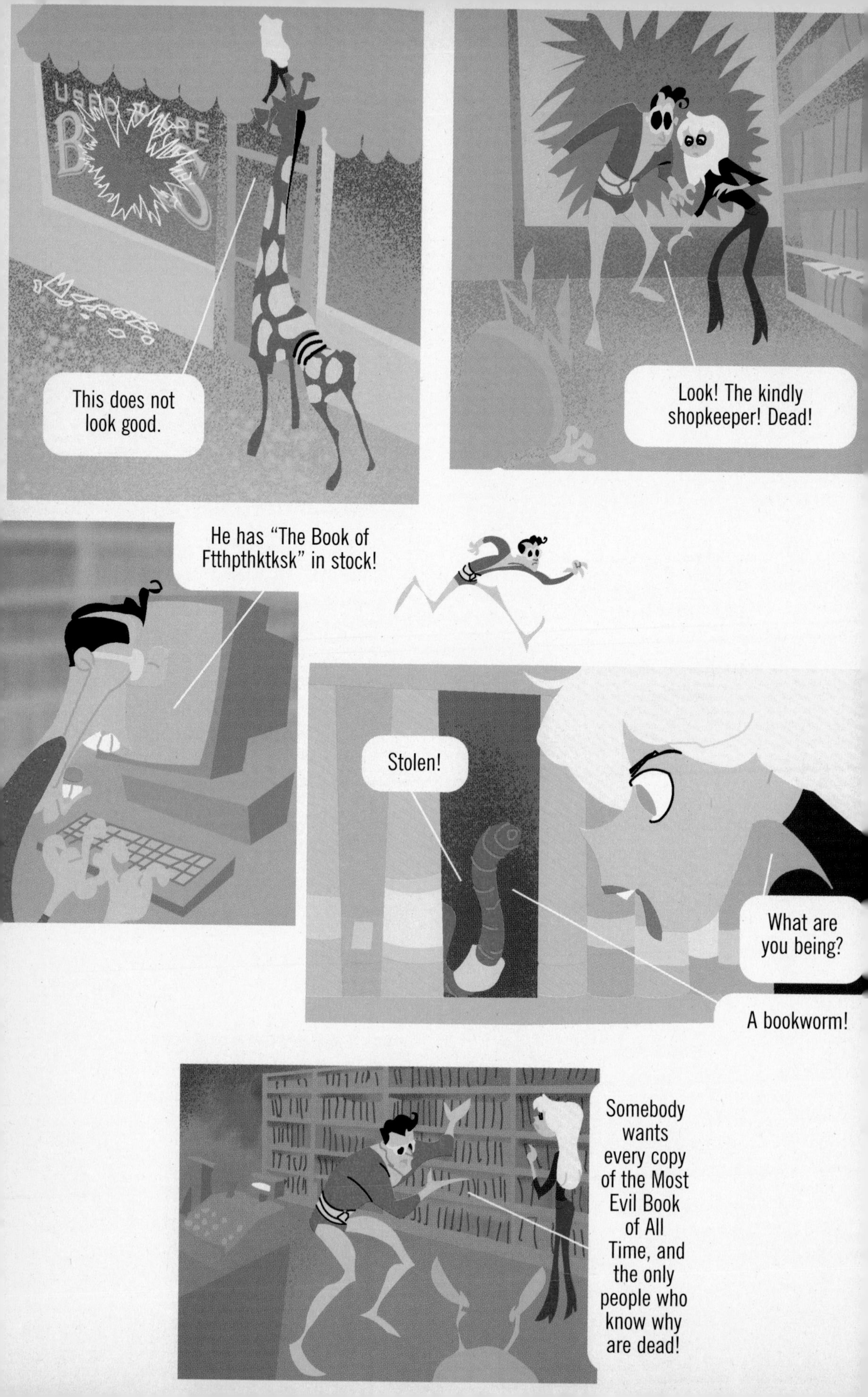

USED RARE BOOKS
This does not look good.
Look! The kindly shopkeeper! Dead!
He has "The Book of Ftthpthktksk" in stock!
Stolen!
What are you being?
A bookworm!
Somebody wants every copy of the Most Evil Book of All Time, and the only people who know why are dead!

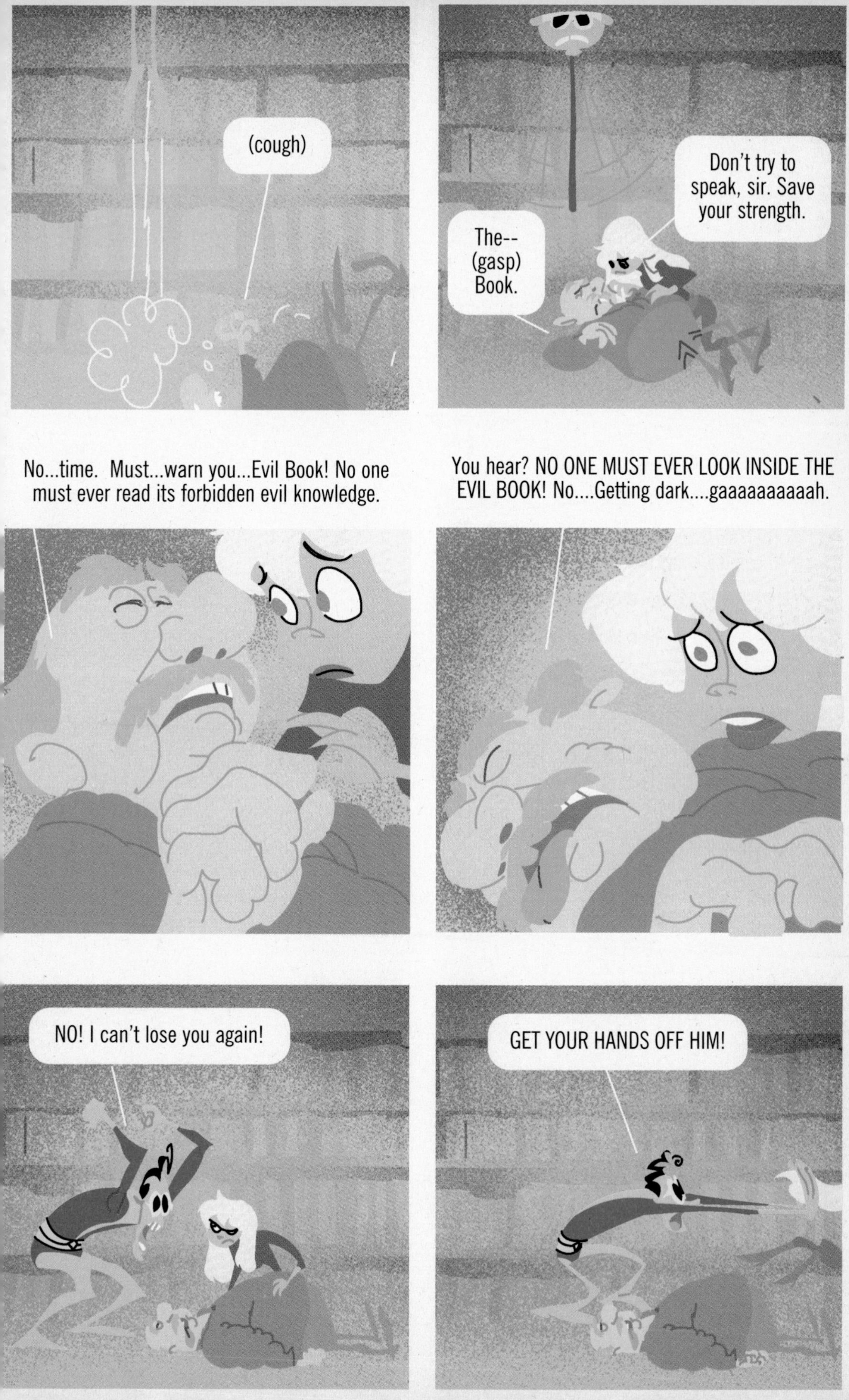
(cough)
Don't try to speak, sir. Save your strength.
The-- (gasp) Book.
No...time. Must...warn you...Evil Book! No one must ever read its forbidden evil knowledge.
You hear? NO ONE MUST EVER LOOK INSIDE THE EVIL BOOK! No....Getting dark....gaaaaaaaaaah.
NO! I can't lose you again!
GET YOUR HANDS OFF HIM!

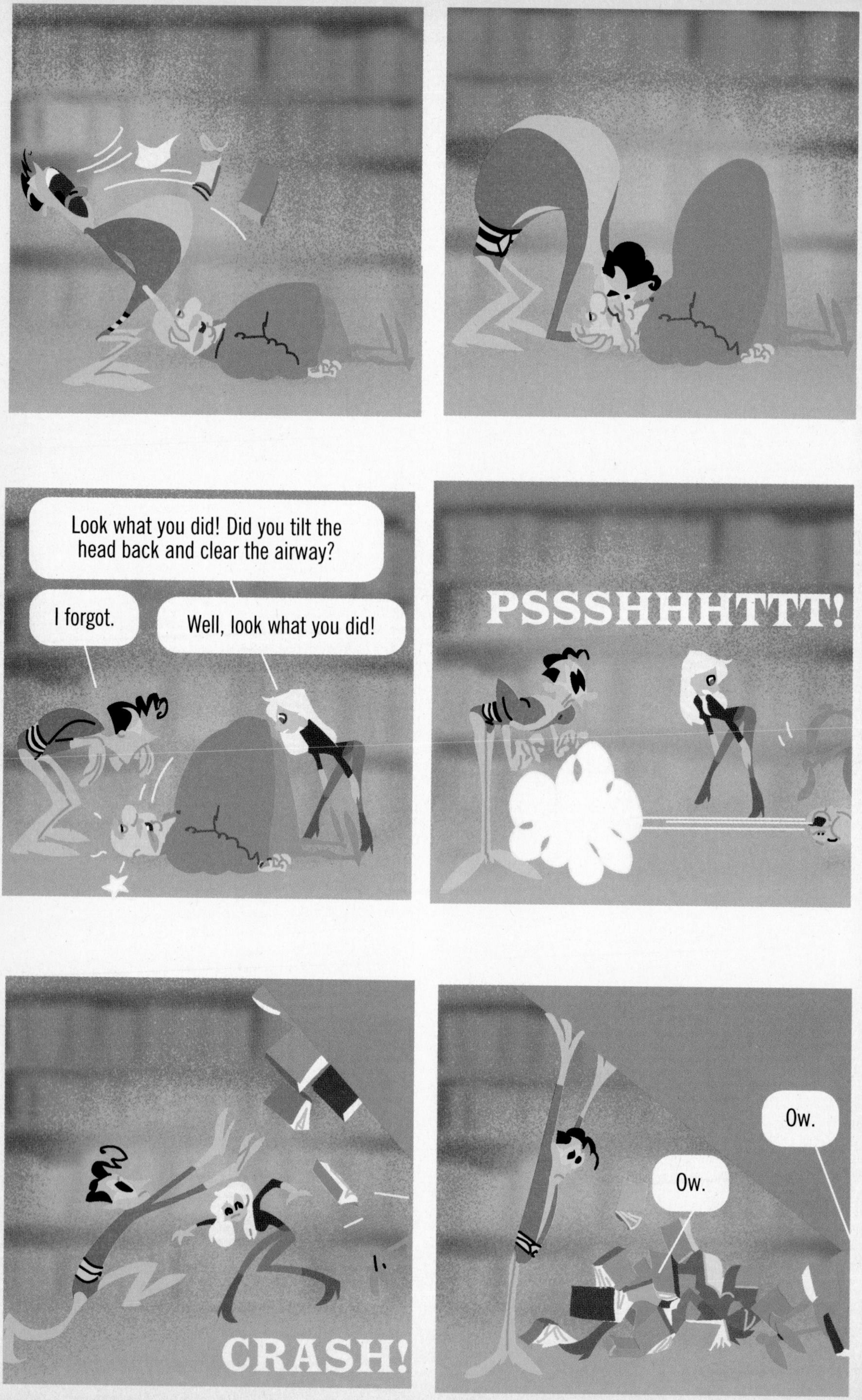

Look what you did! Did you tilt the head back and clear the airway?
I forgot.
Well, look what you did!
PSSSHHHTTT!
CRASH!
Ow.
Ow.

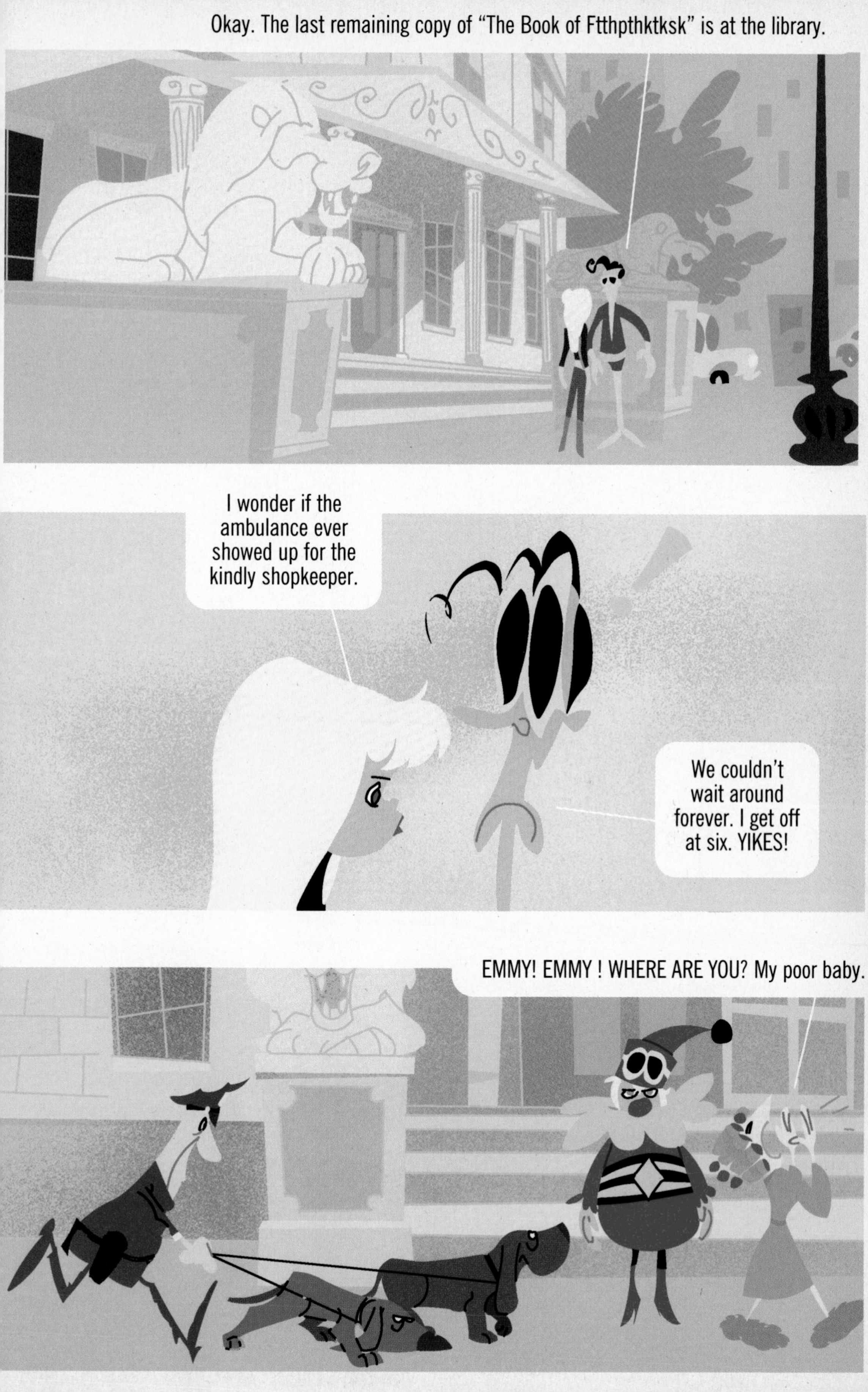
Okay. The last remaining copy of "The Book of Ftthpthktksk" is at the library.
I wonder if the ambulance ever showed up for the kindly shopkeeper.
We couldn't wait around forever. I get off at six. YIKES!
EMMY! EMMY ! WHERE ARE YOU? My poor baby.

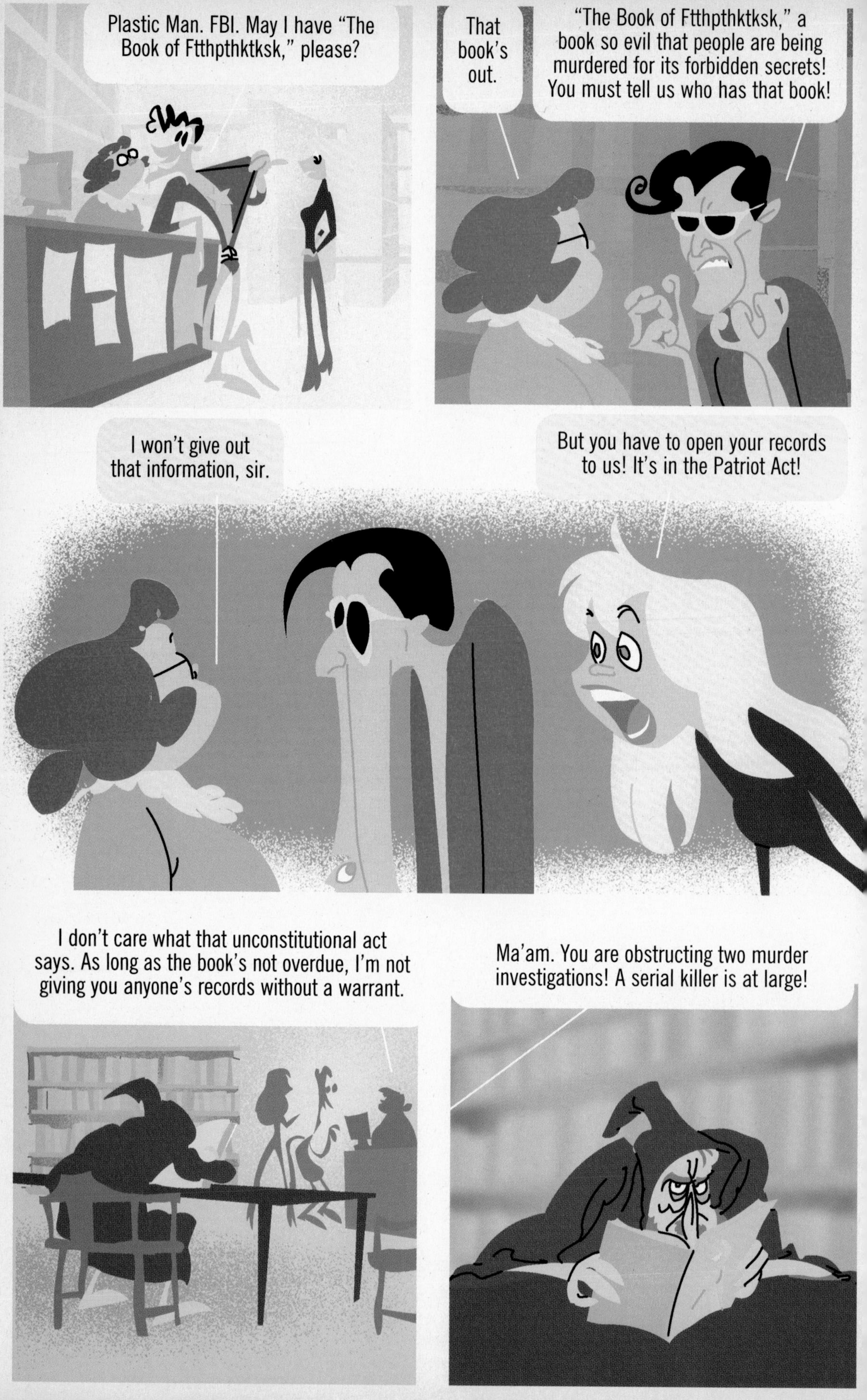
Plastic Man. FBI. May I have "The Book of Ftthpthktksk," please?
That book's out.
"The Book of Ftthpthktksk," a book so evil that people are being murdered for its forbidden secrets! You must tell us who has that book!
I won't give out that information, sir.
But you have to open your records to us! It's in the Patriot Act!
I don't care what that unconstitutional act says. As long as the book's not overdue, I'm not giving you anyone's records without a warrant.
Ma'am. You are obstructing two murder investigations! A serial killer is at large!

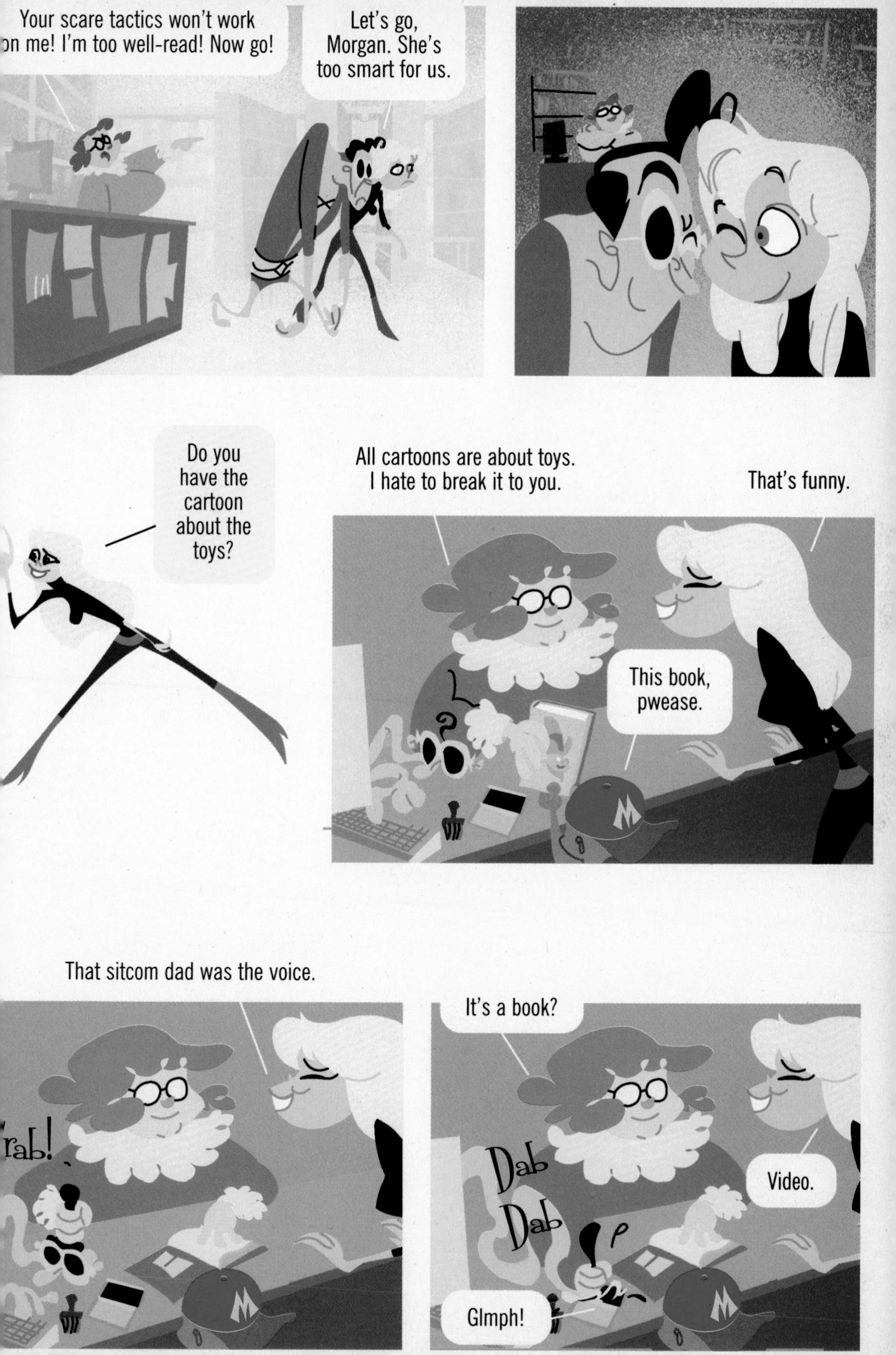
Your scare tactics won't work on me! I'm too well-read! Now go!
Let's go, Morgan. She's too smart for us.
Do you have the cartoon about the toys?
All cartoons are about toys. I hate to break it to you.
That's funny.
This book, pwease.
That sitcom dad was the voice.
rab!
It's a book?
Dab
Dab
Video.
Glmph!

Stamp!!

Mmph!

I can explain.

BOOT!

HONK!

HONK!

HONK!

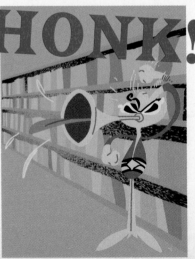

BOOM BOOM
BOOM BOOM

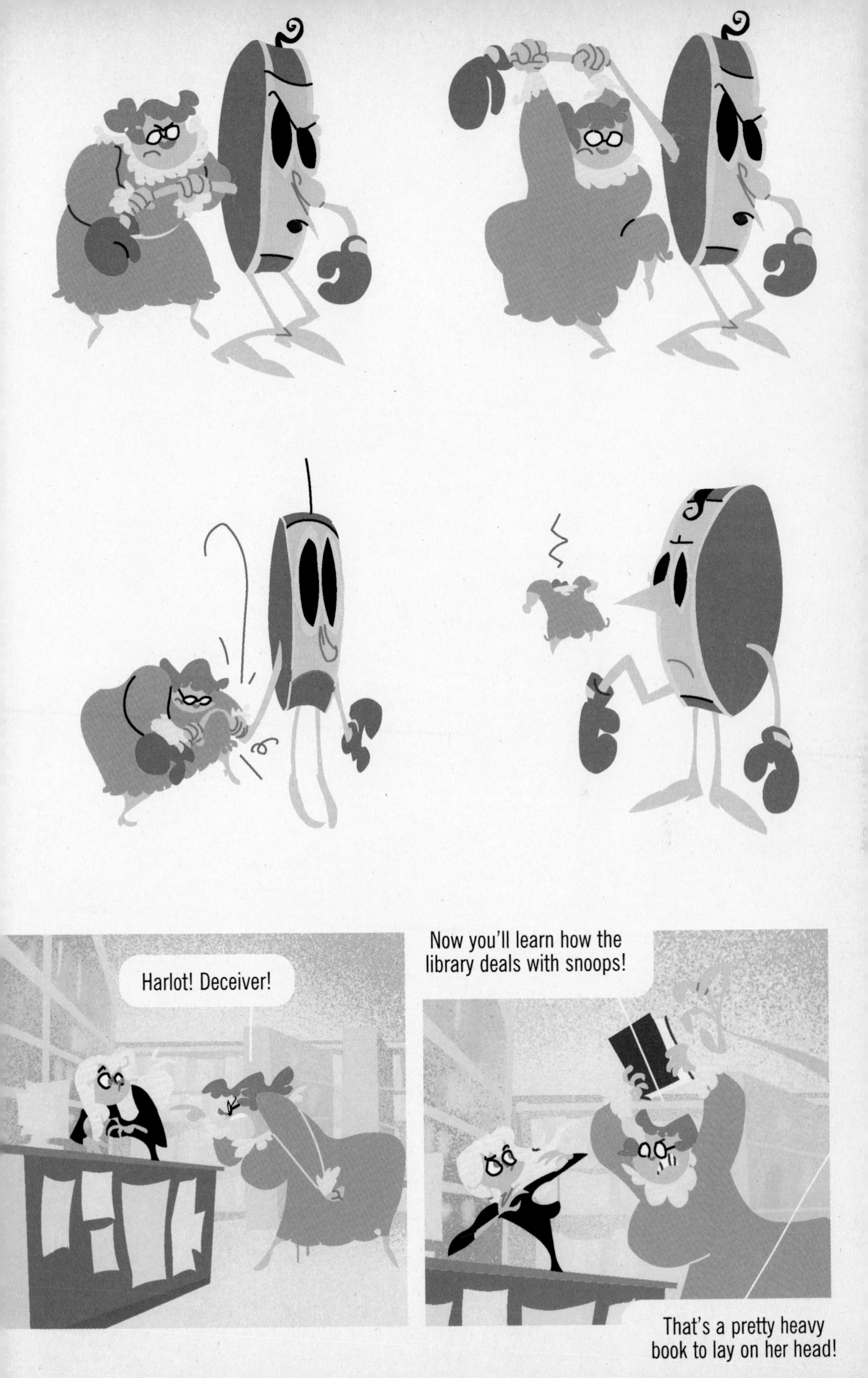
Harlot! Deceiver!
Now you'll learn how the library deals with snoops!
That's a pretty heavy book to lay on her head!

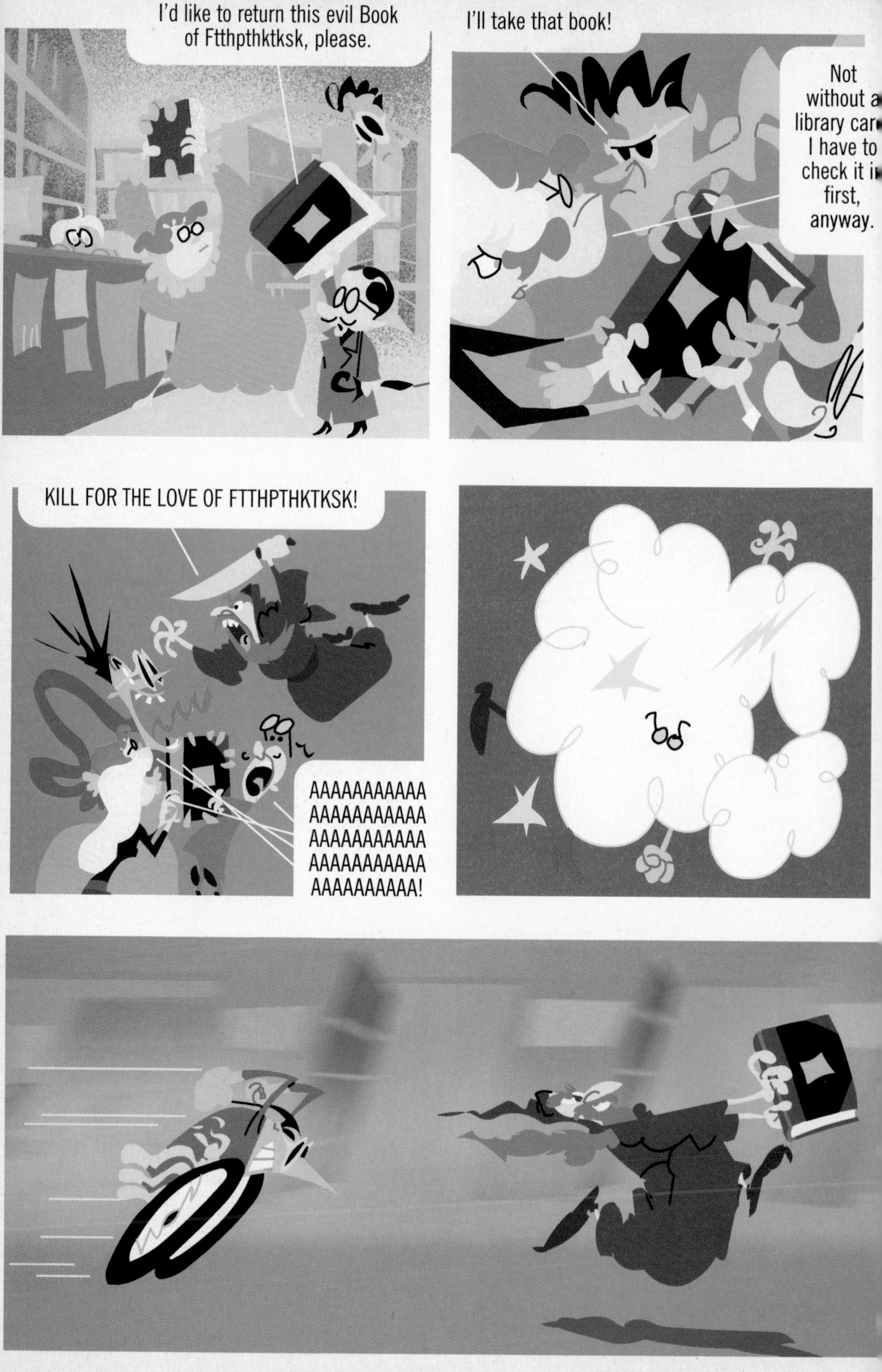
I'd like to return this evil Book of Ftthpthktksk, please.
I'll take that book!
Not without a library car I have to check it i first, anyway.
KILL FOR THE LOVE OF FTTHPTHKTKSK!
AAAAAAAAAAA AAAAAAAAAAA AAAAAAAAAAA AAAAAAAAAAA AAAAAAAAAA!

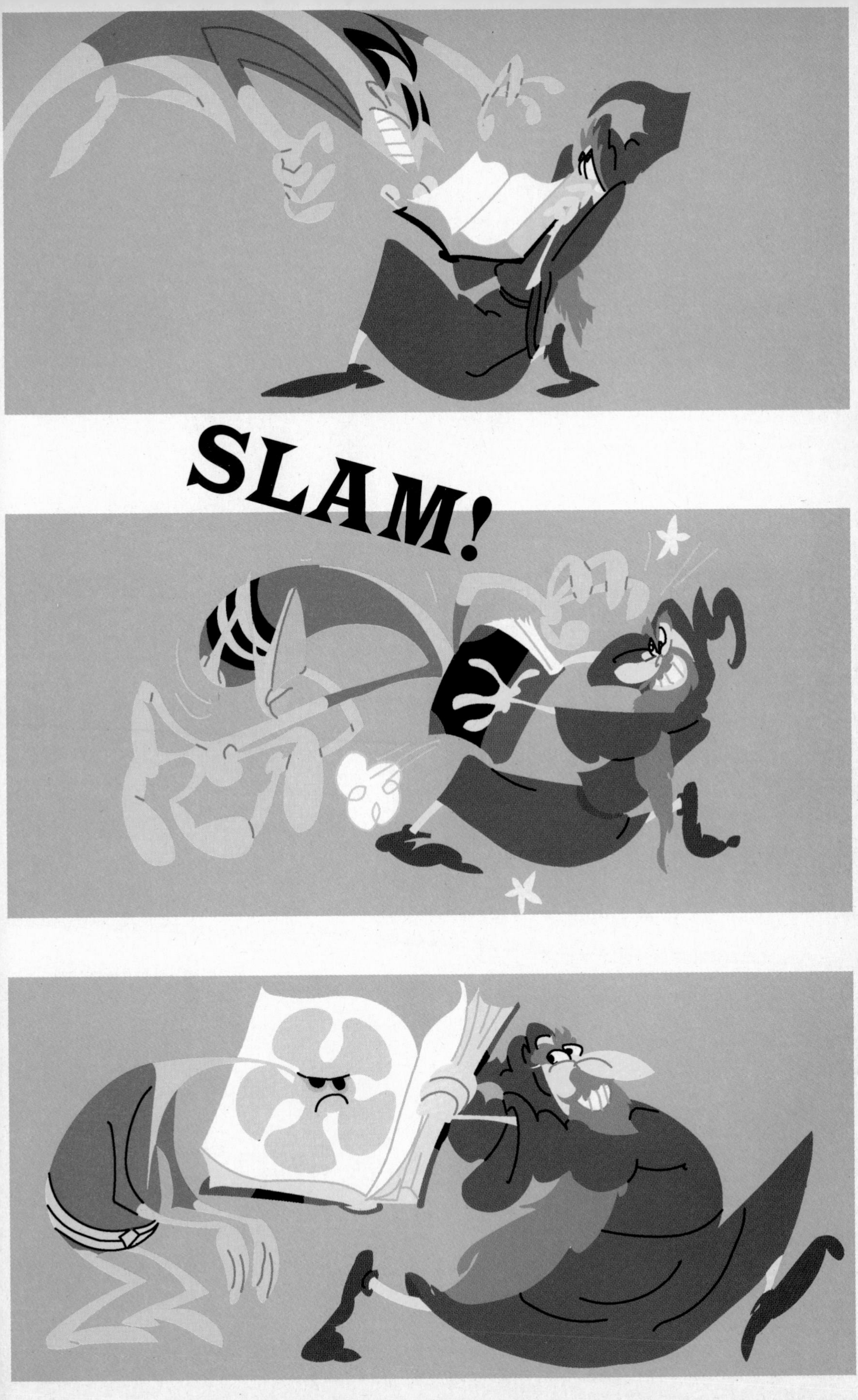
SLAM!

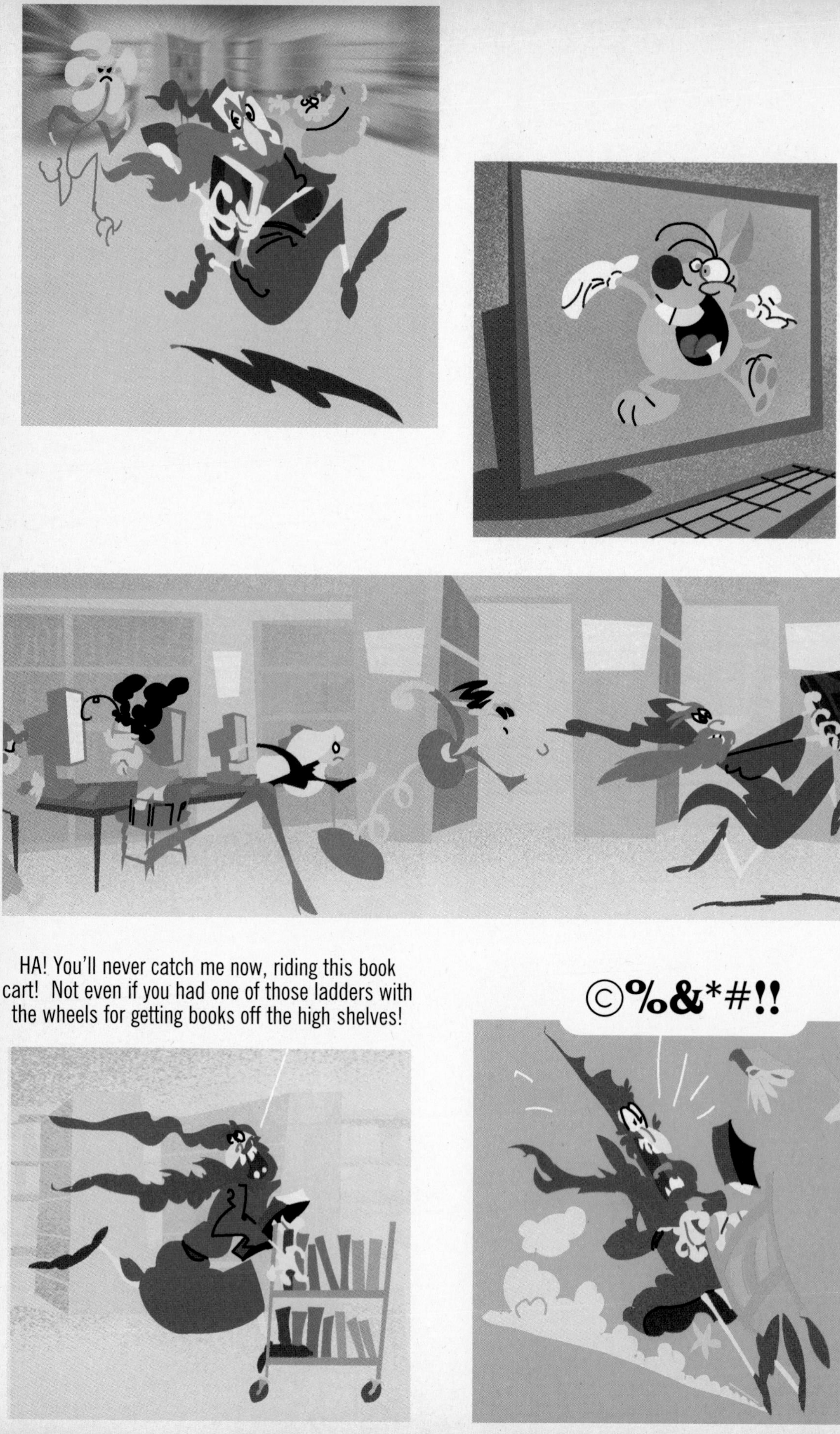
HA! You'll never catch me now, riding this book cart! Not even if you had one of those ladders with the wheels for getting books off the high shelves!
©%&*#!!

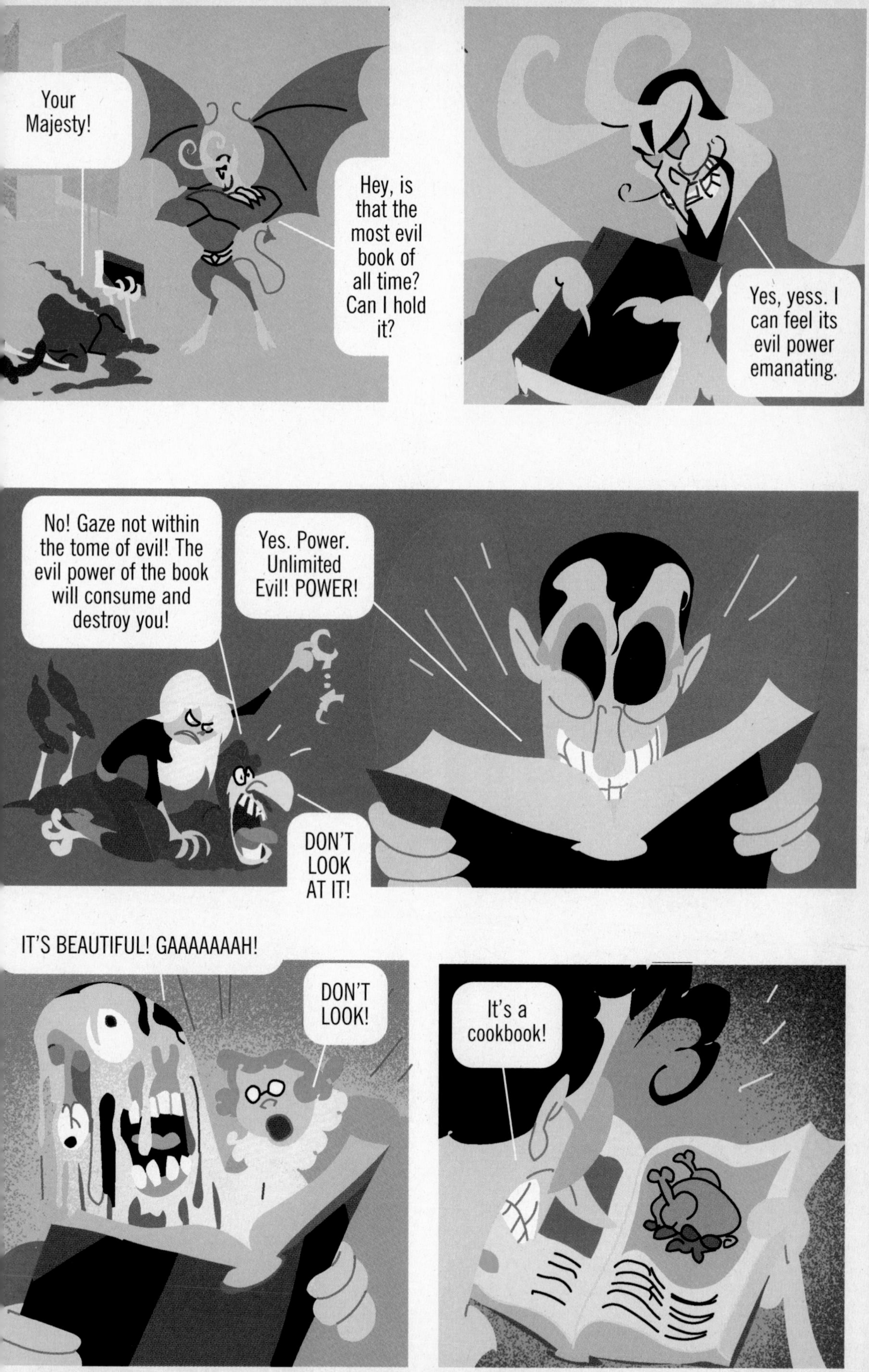
Your Majesty!
Hey, is that the most evil book of all time? Can I hold it?
Yes, yess. I can feel its evil power emanating.
No! Gaze not within the tome of evil! The evil power of the book will consume and destroy you!
Yes. Power. Unlimited Evil! POWER!
DON'T LOOK AT IT!
IT'S BEAUTIFUL! GAAAAAAAH!
DON'T LOOK!
It's a cookbook!

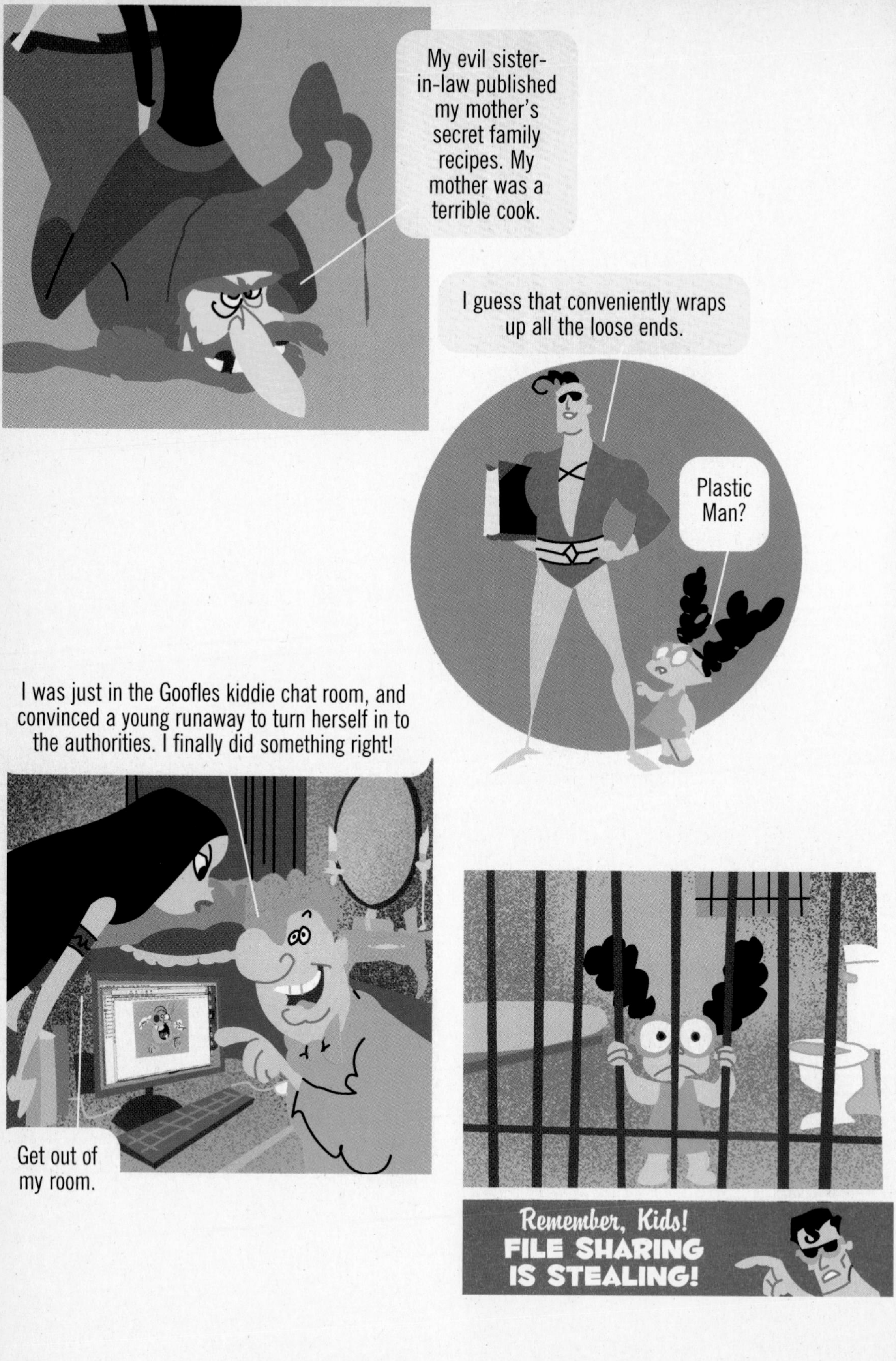

My evil sister-in-law published my mother's secret family recipes. My mother was a terrible cook.
I guess that conveniently wraps up all the loose ends.
Plastic Man?
I was just in the Goofles kiddie chat room, and convinced a young runaway to turn herself in to the authorities. I finally did something right!
Get out of my room.
Remember, Kids!
FILE SHARING IS STEALING!

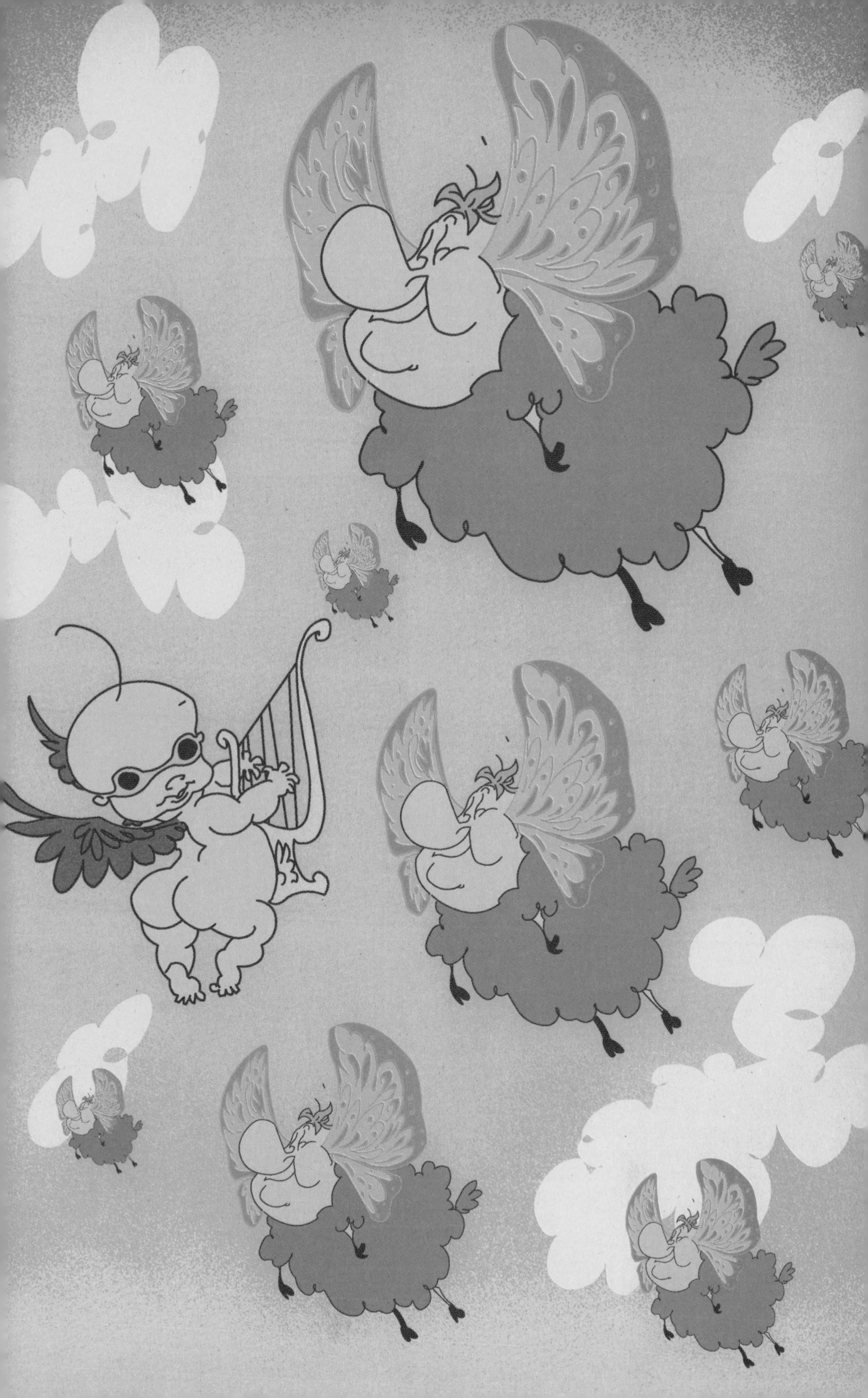

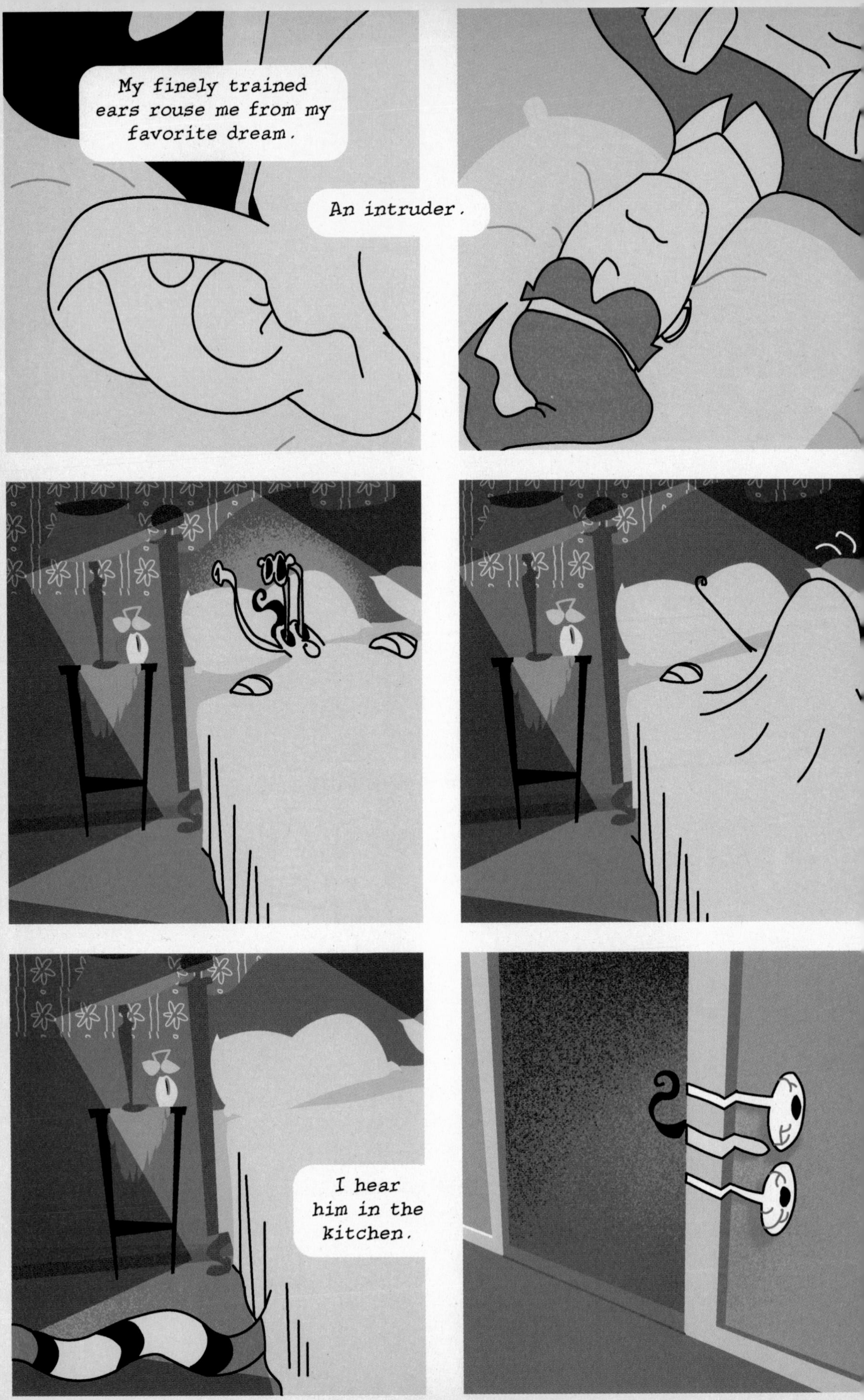
My finely trained ears rouse me from my favorite dream.
An intruder.
I hear him in the kitchen.

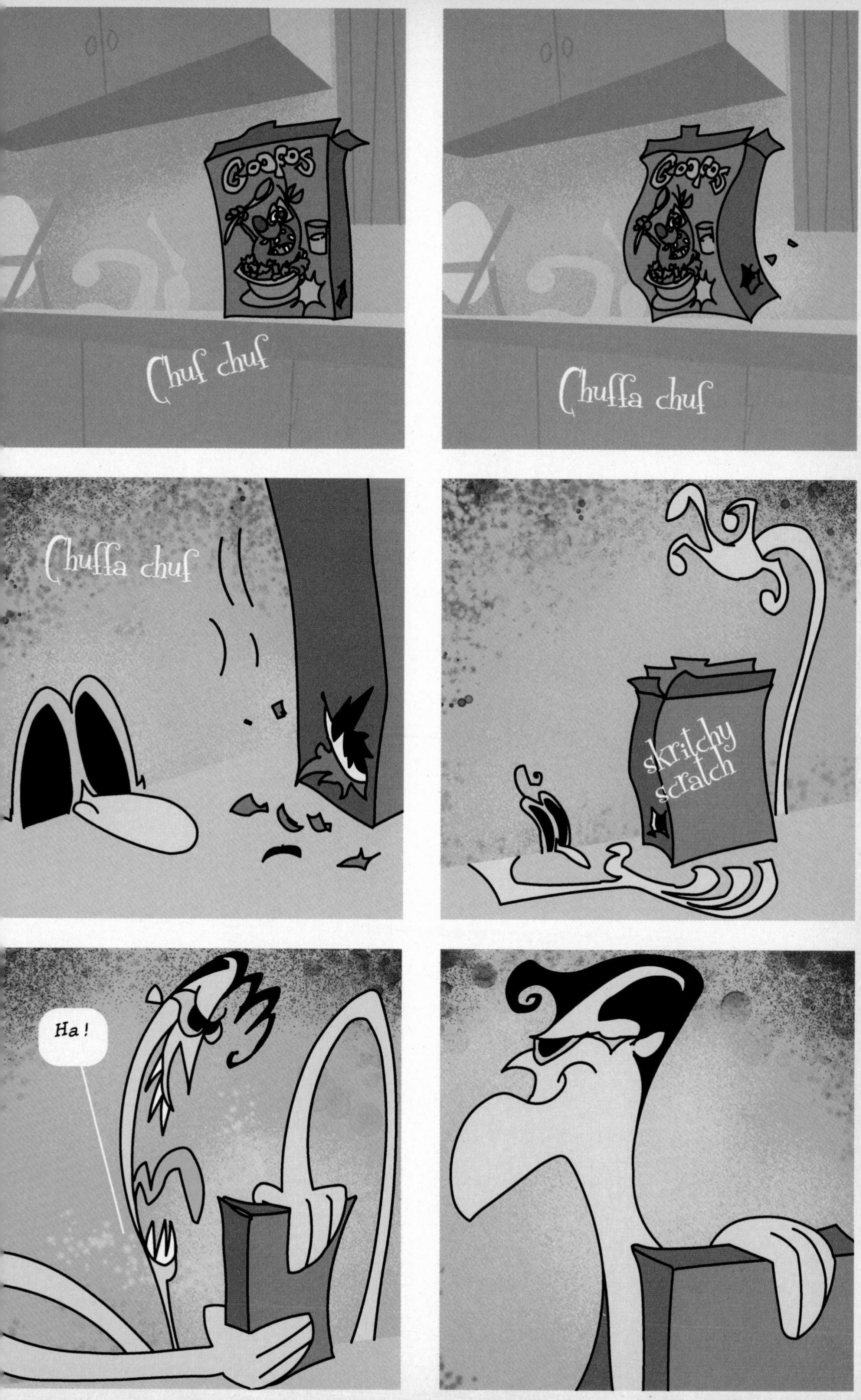
Chuf chuf
Chuffa chuf
Chuffa chuf
skritchy scratch
Ha!

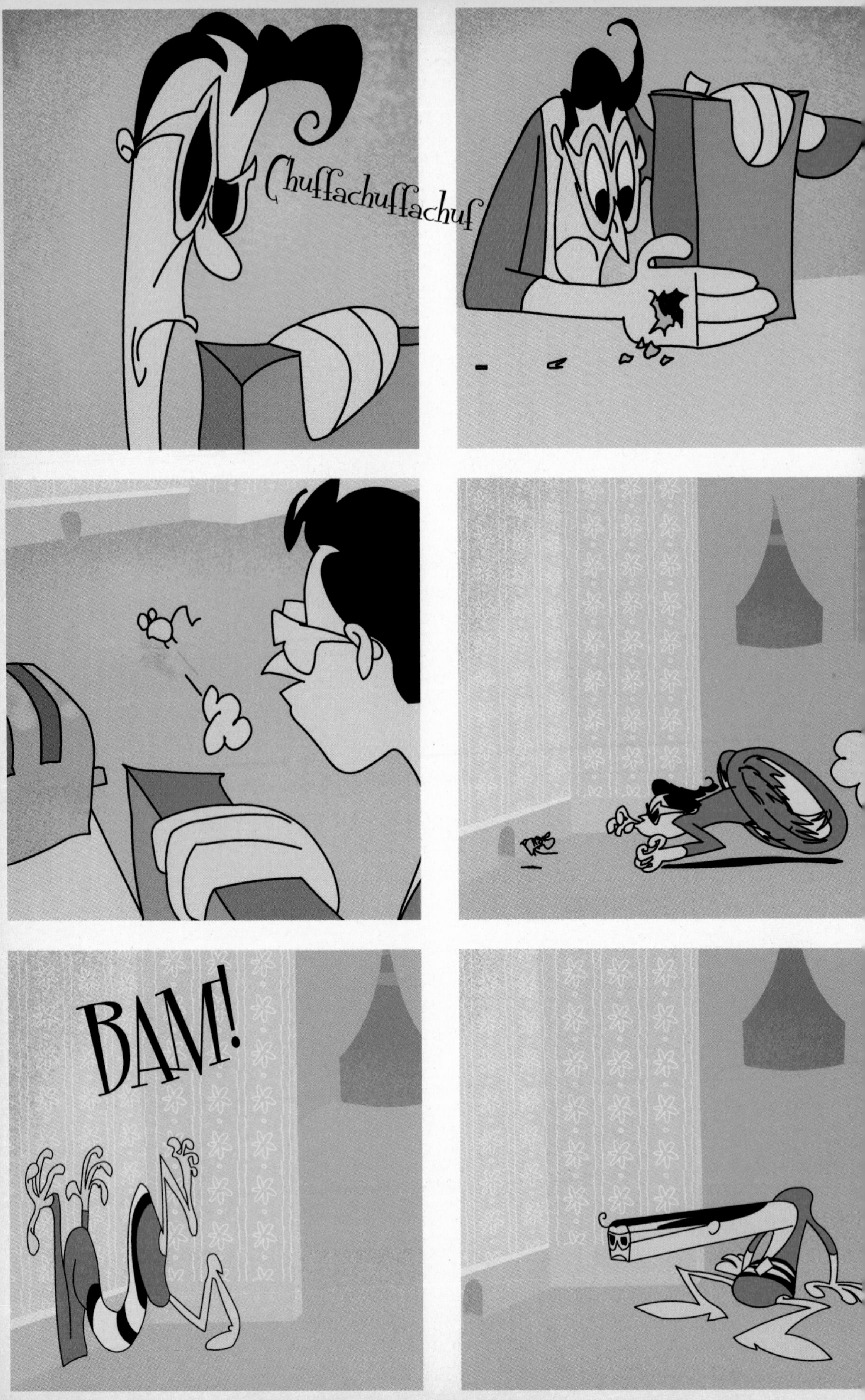
Chuffachuffachuf
BAM!

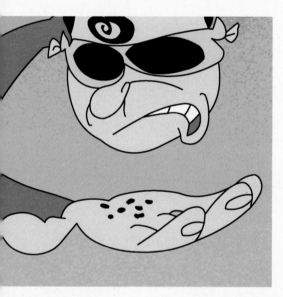

I'll make mincemeat outta that mouse.

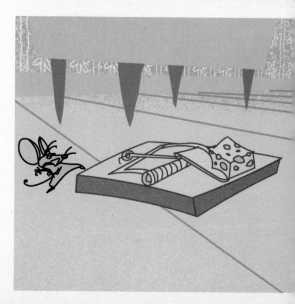

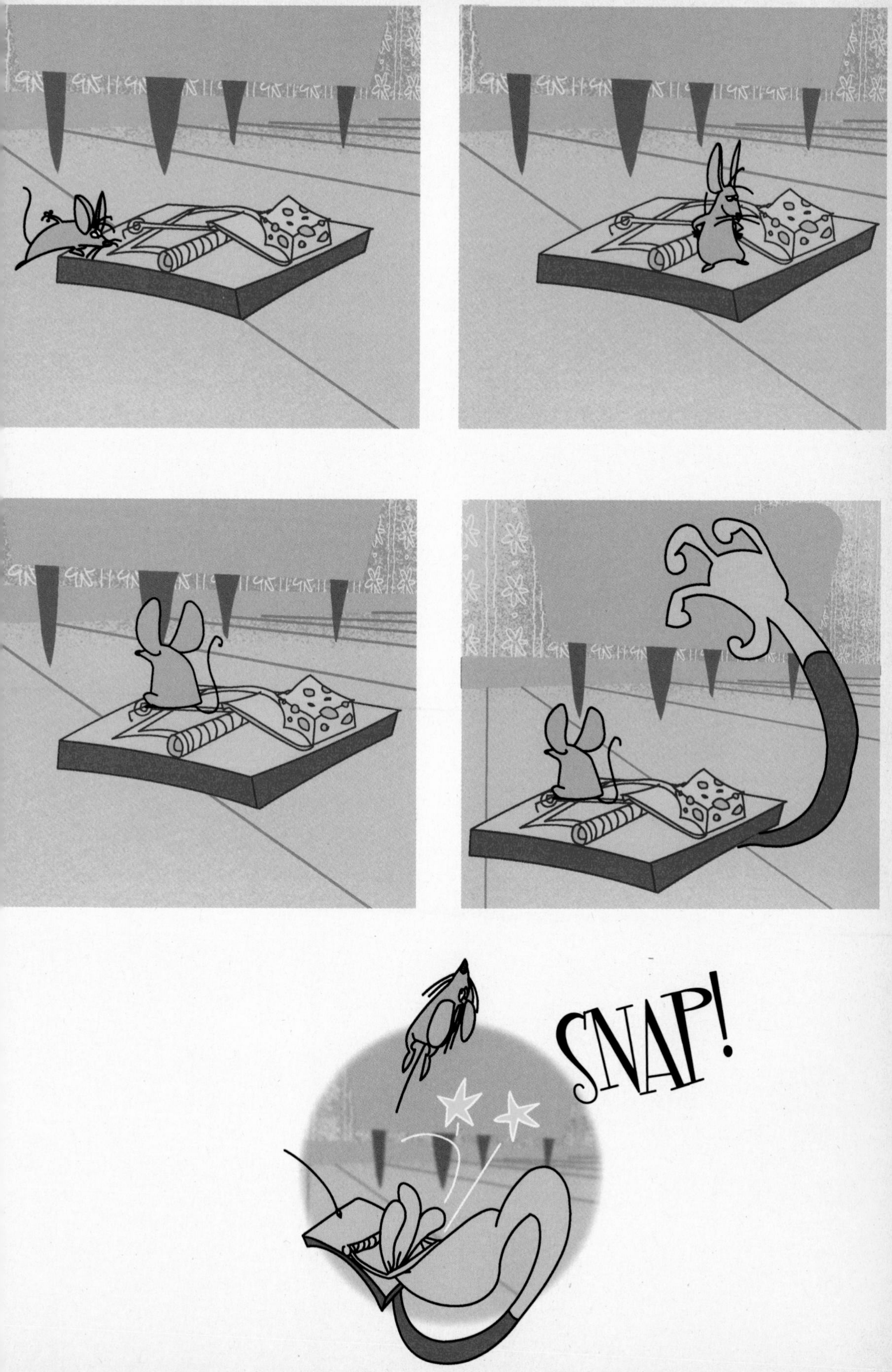
SNAP!

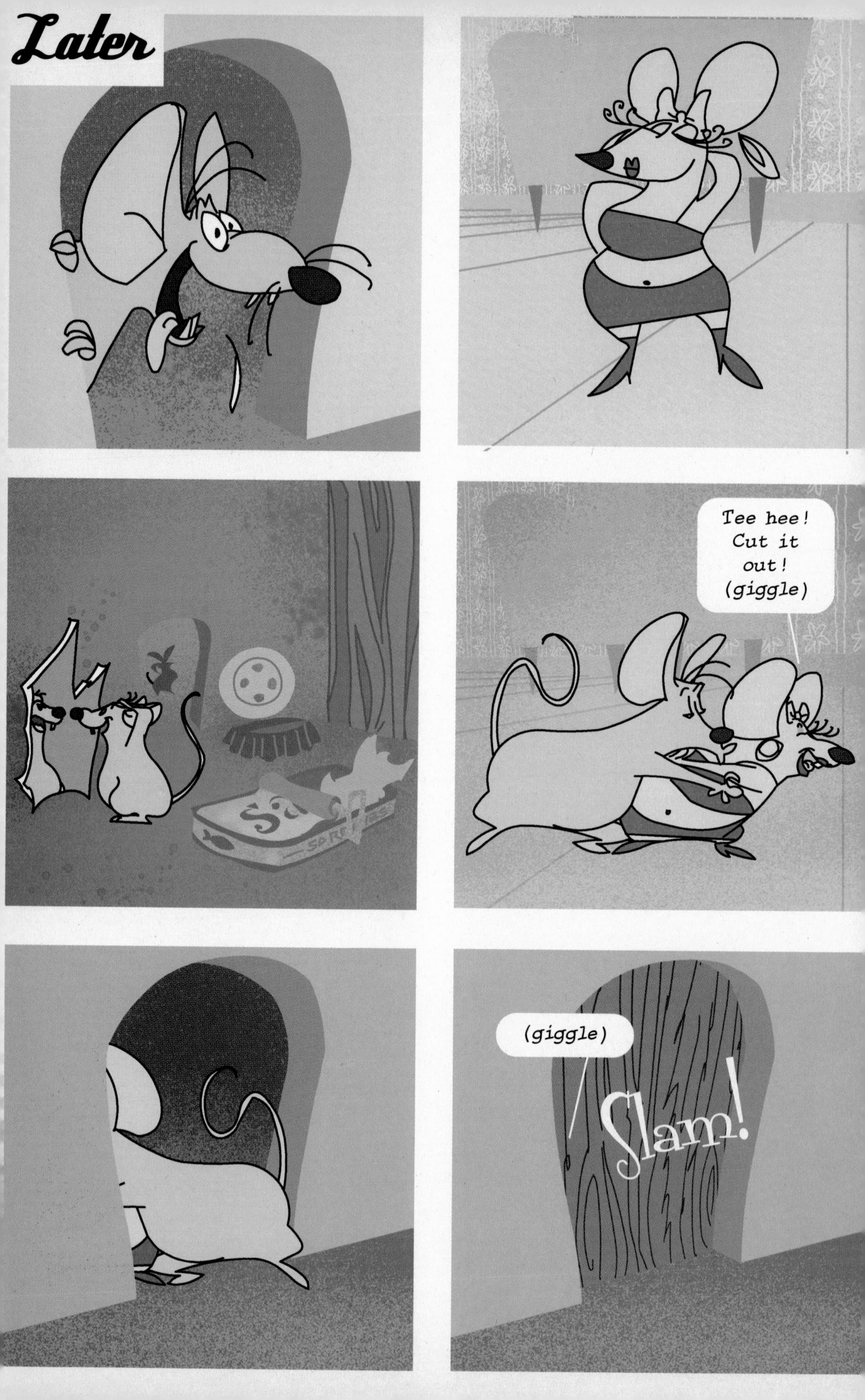
Later
Tee hee! Cut it out! (giggle)
(giggle)
Slam!

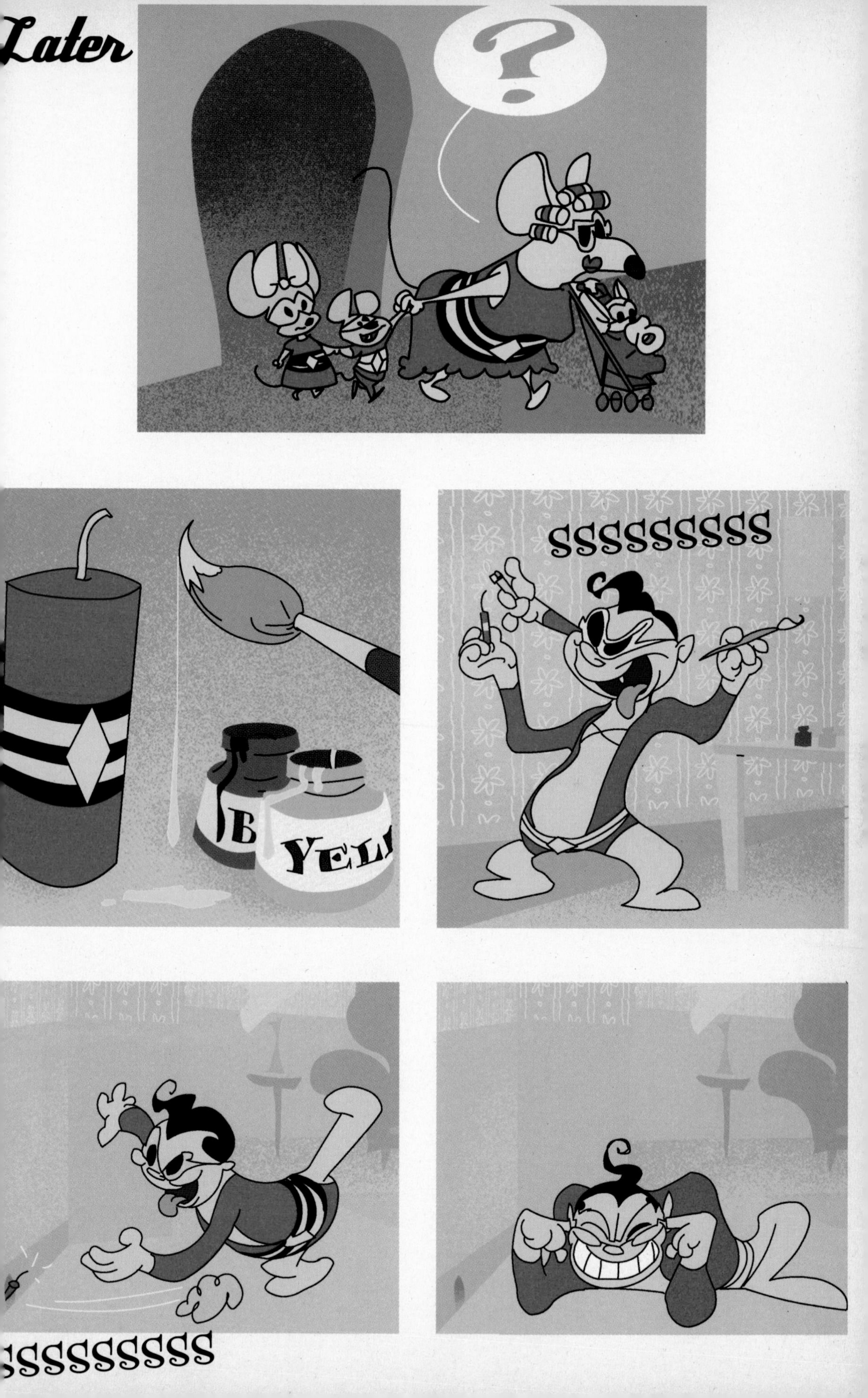
Later
?
SSSSSSSS
SSSSSSSSS

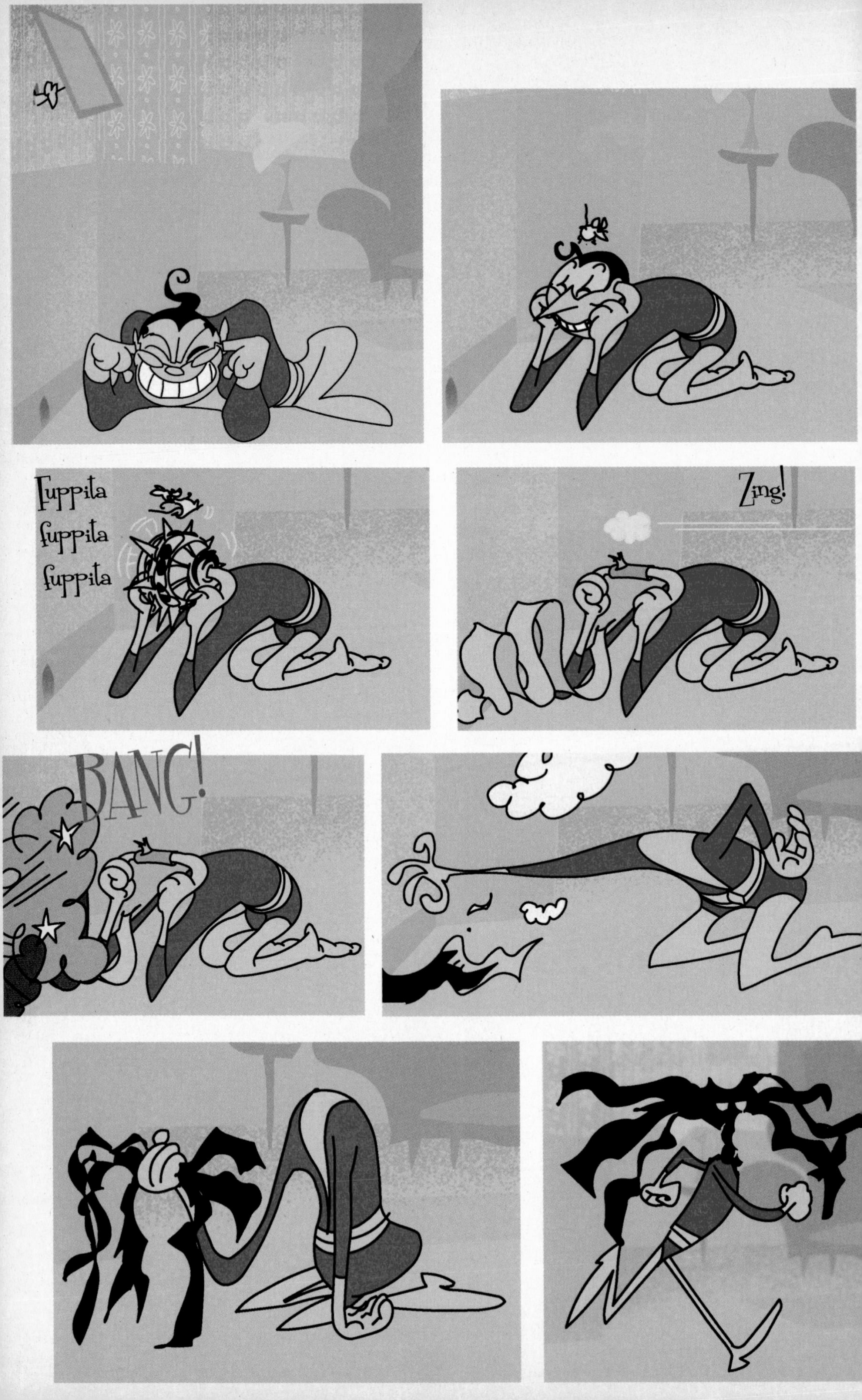
Fuppita
fuppita
fuppita
Zing!
BANG!

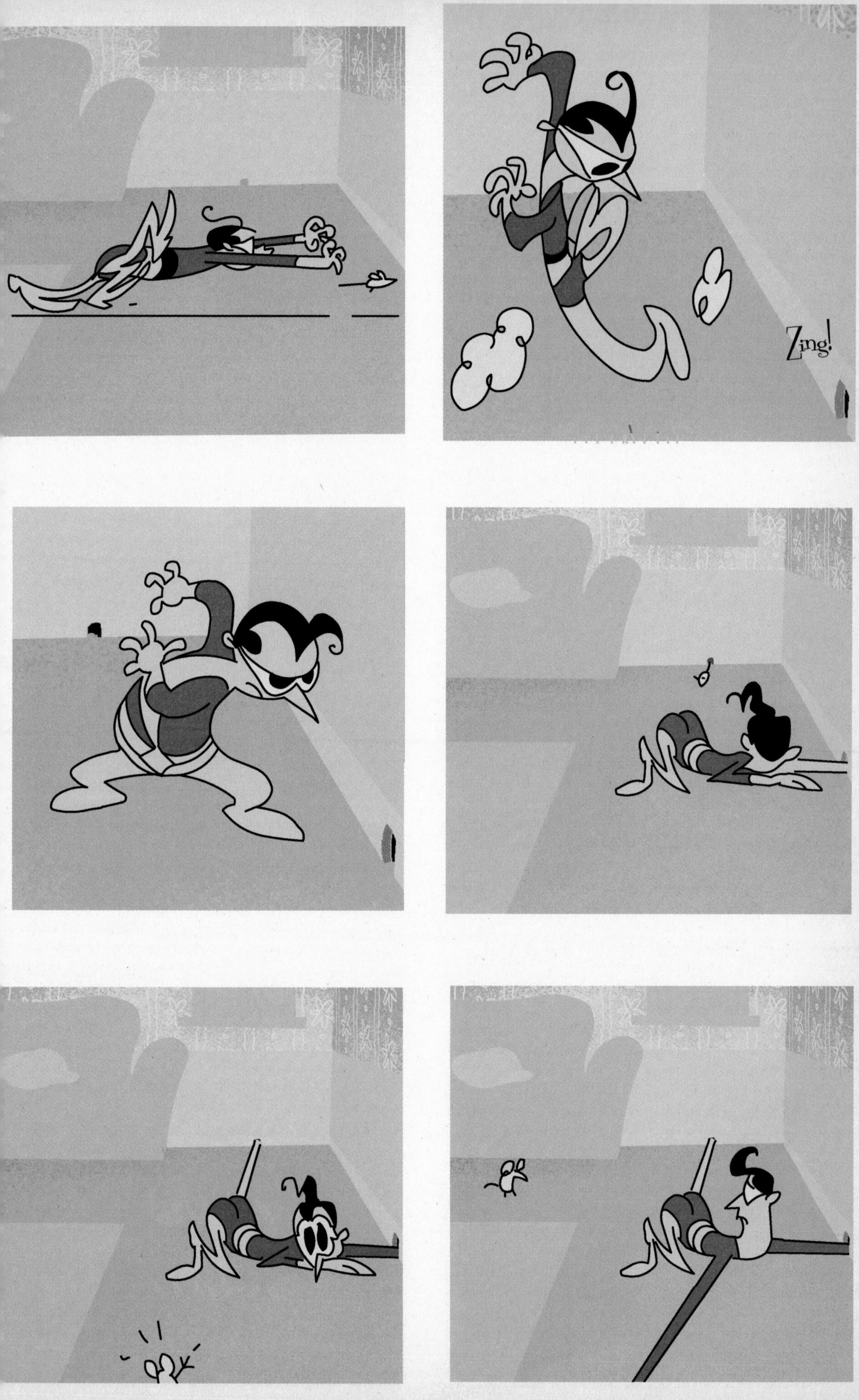
Zing!

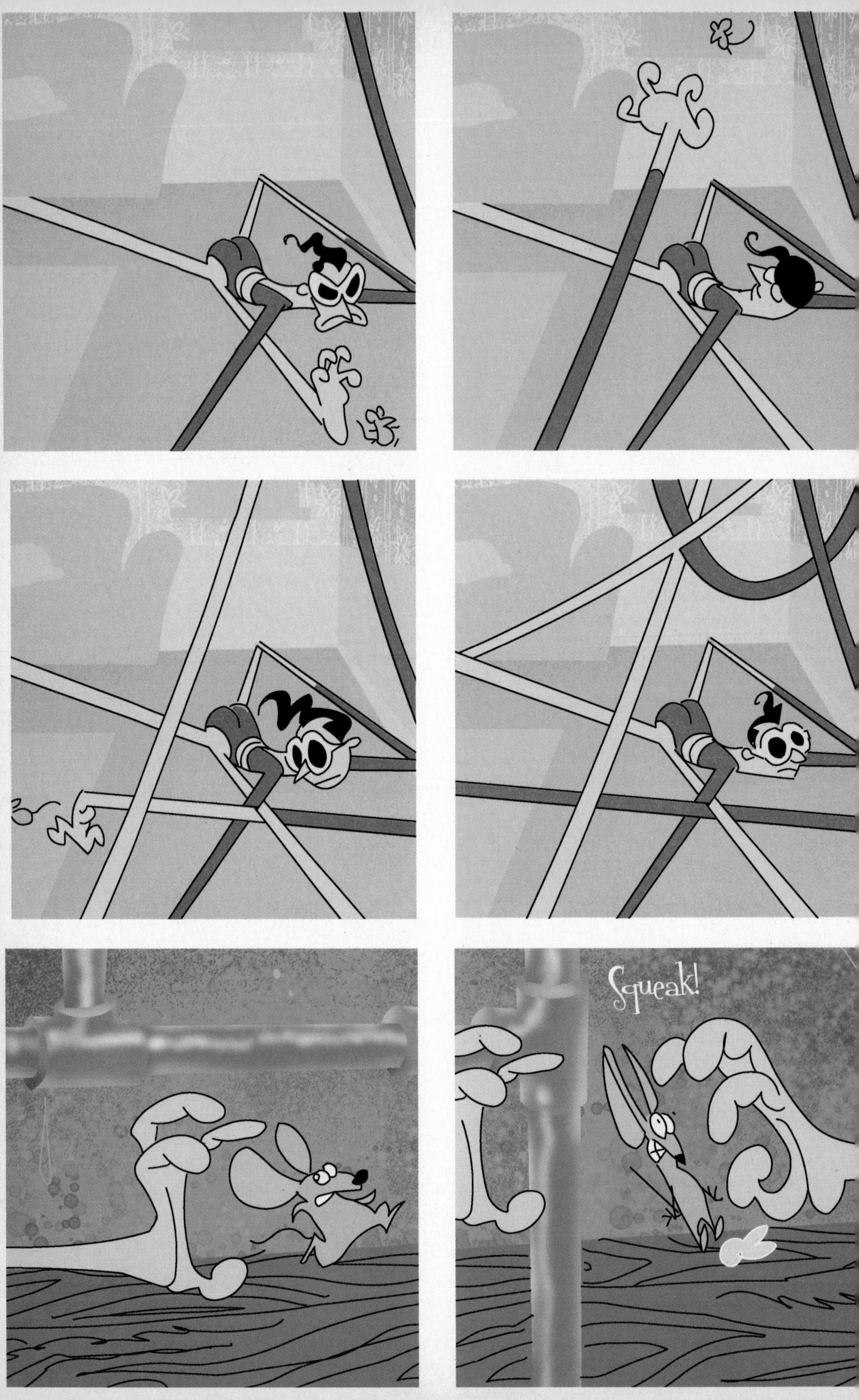
Squeak!

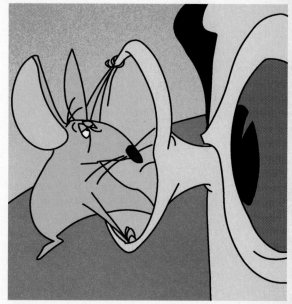
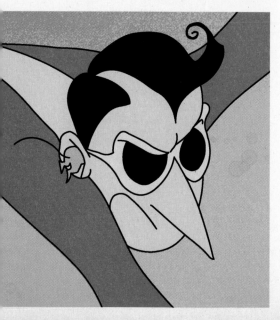

Poink!

CHOMP!
Tic
toc
tic
toc

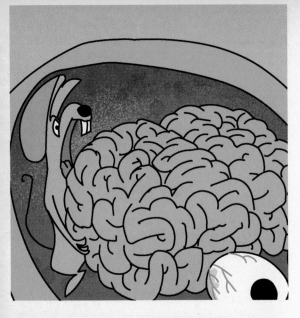

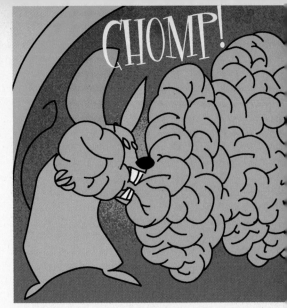

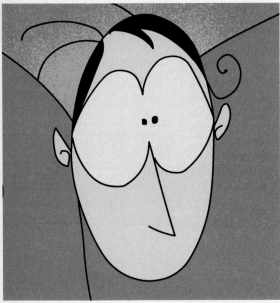

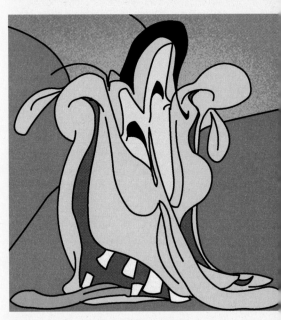

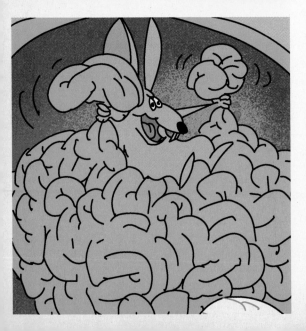

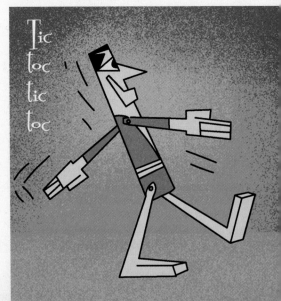

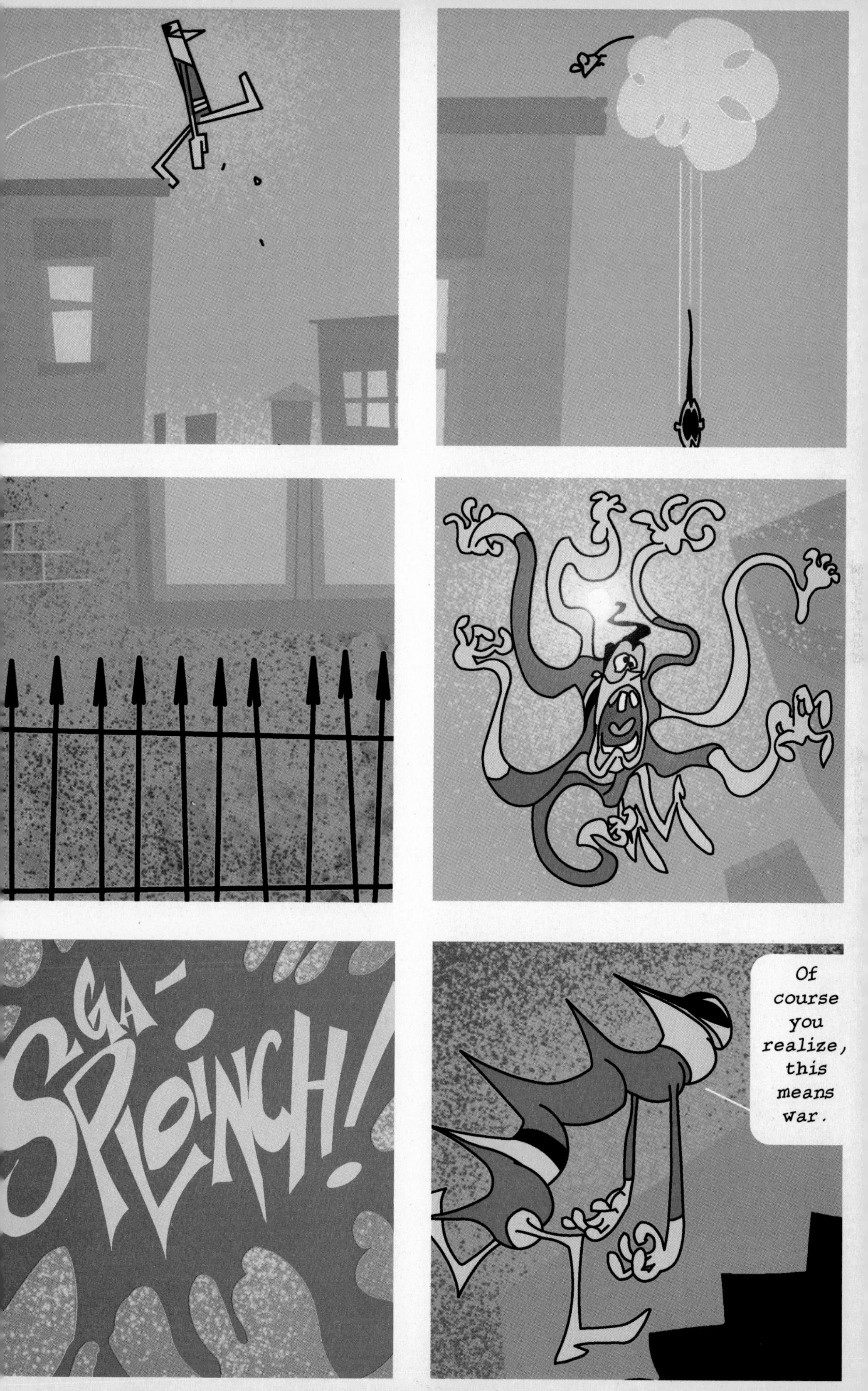
GA-SPLOINCH!
Of course you realize, this means war.

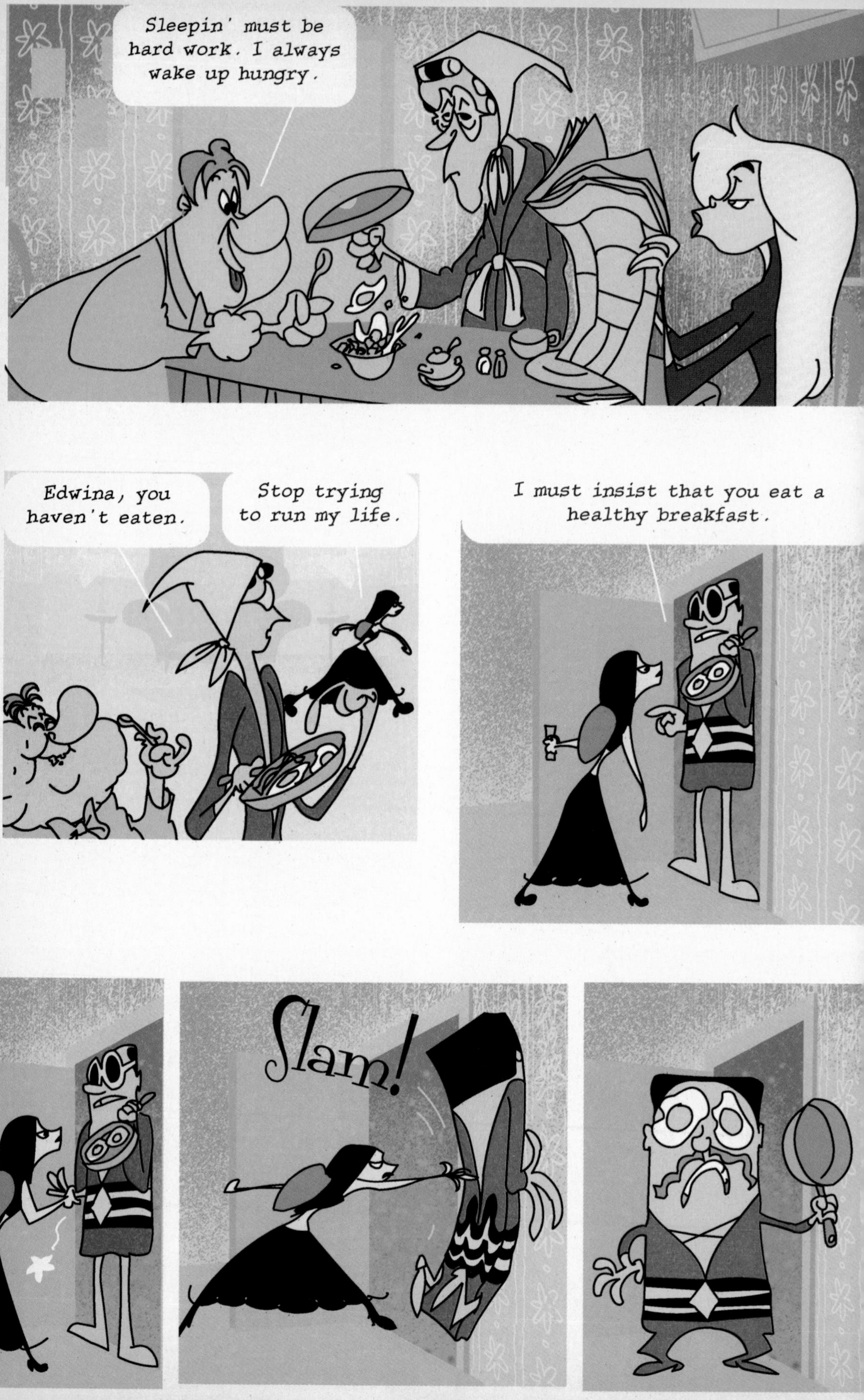
Sleepin' must be hard work. I always wake up hungry.
Edwina, you haven't eaten.
Stop trying to run my life.
I must insist that you eat a healthy breakfast.
Slam!

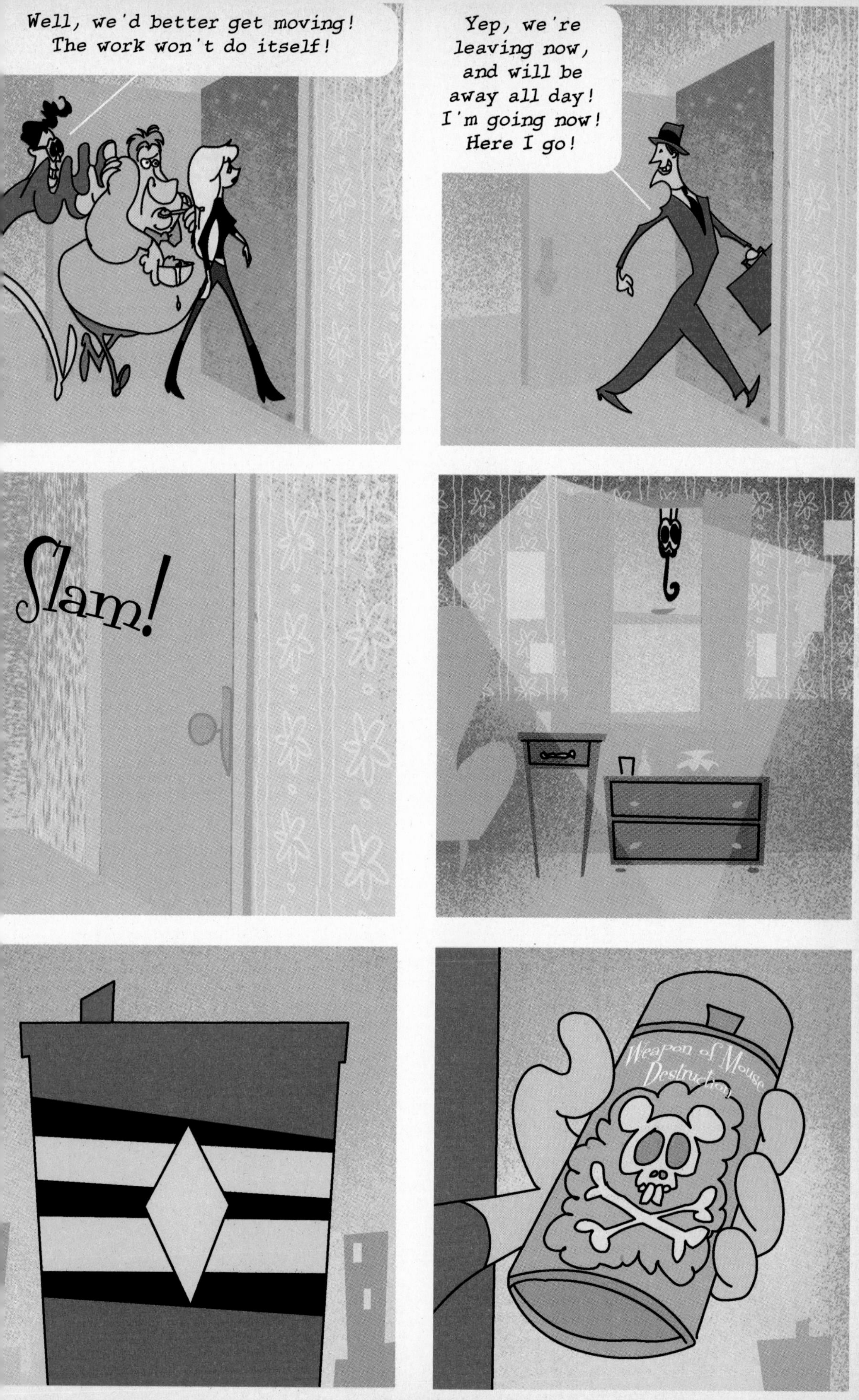
Well, we'd better get moving! The work won't do itself!
Yep, we're leaving now, and will be away all day! I'm going now! Here I go!
Slam!
Weapon of Mouse Destruction

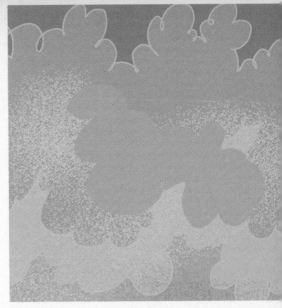

gaaaaahhh.

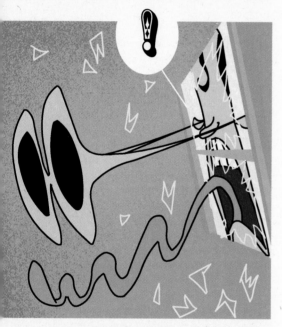

Gone! There are so many things
he'll never experience because of me.

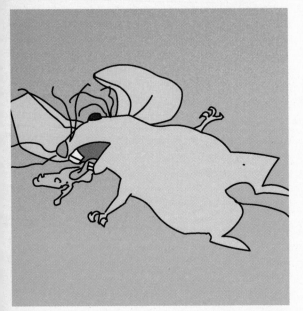

The
simple
joy of
apple
pie
with
vanilla
ice
cream.

Riding in
a
convertibl[e]
on a war[m]
summer
night.
Being aske[d]
to the
prom.

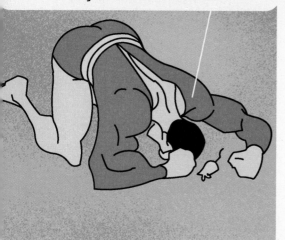

The magic of the movies.

How a song can take you back to the time you first heard it.

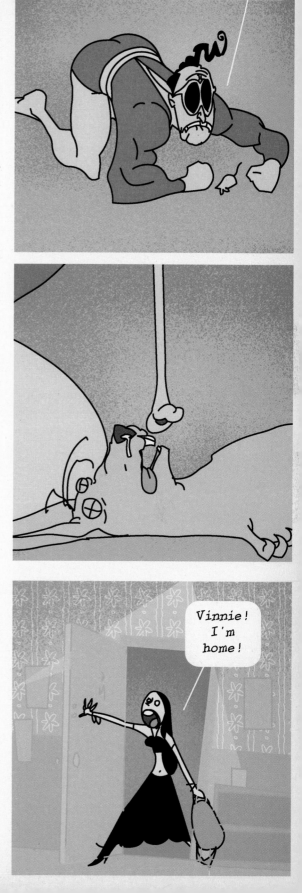

Rage, rage, against the dying of the light.

Vinnie! I'm home!

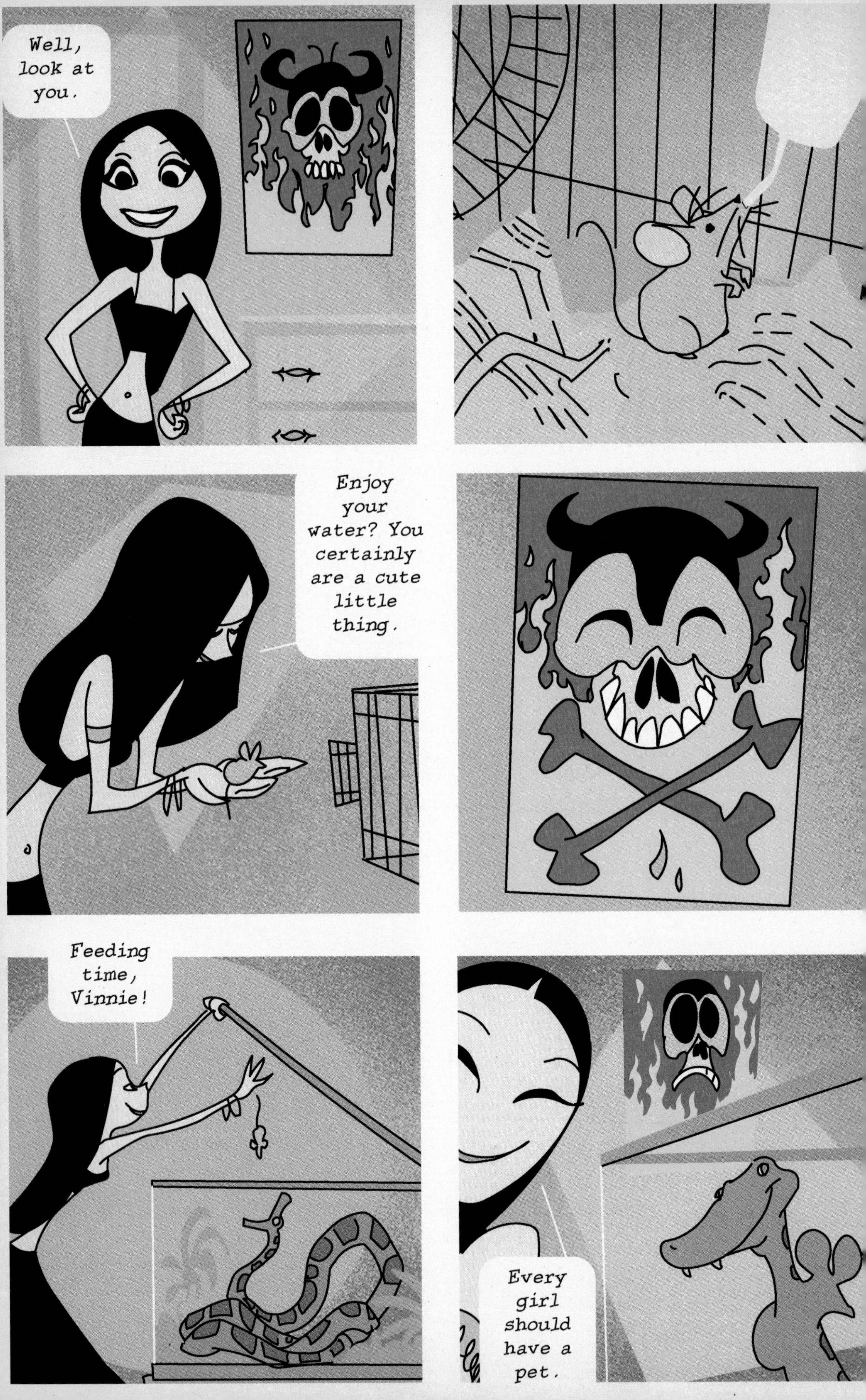
Well, look at you.
Enjoy your water? You certainly are a cute little thing.
Feeding time, Vinnie!
Every girl should have a pet.

PLASTIC MAN

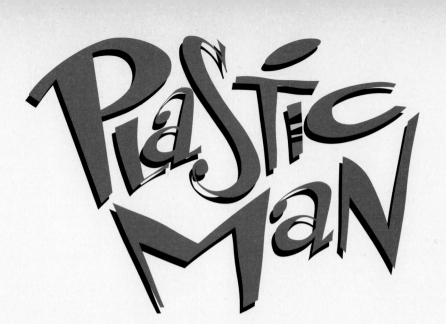

COVER ~~GALLERY~~ GAGS

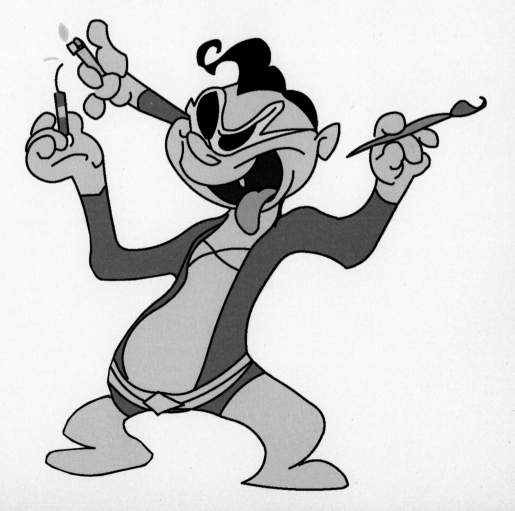

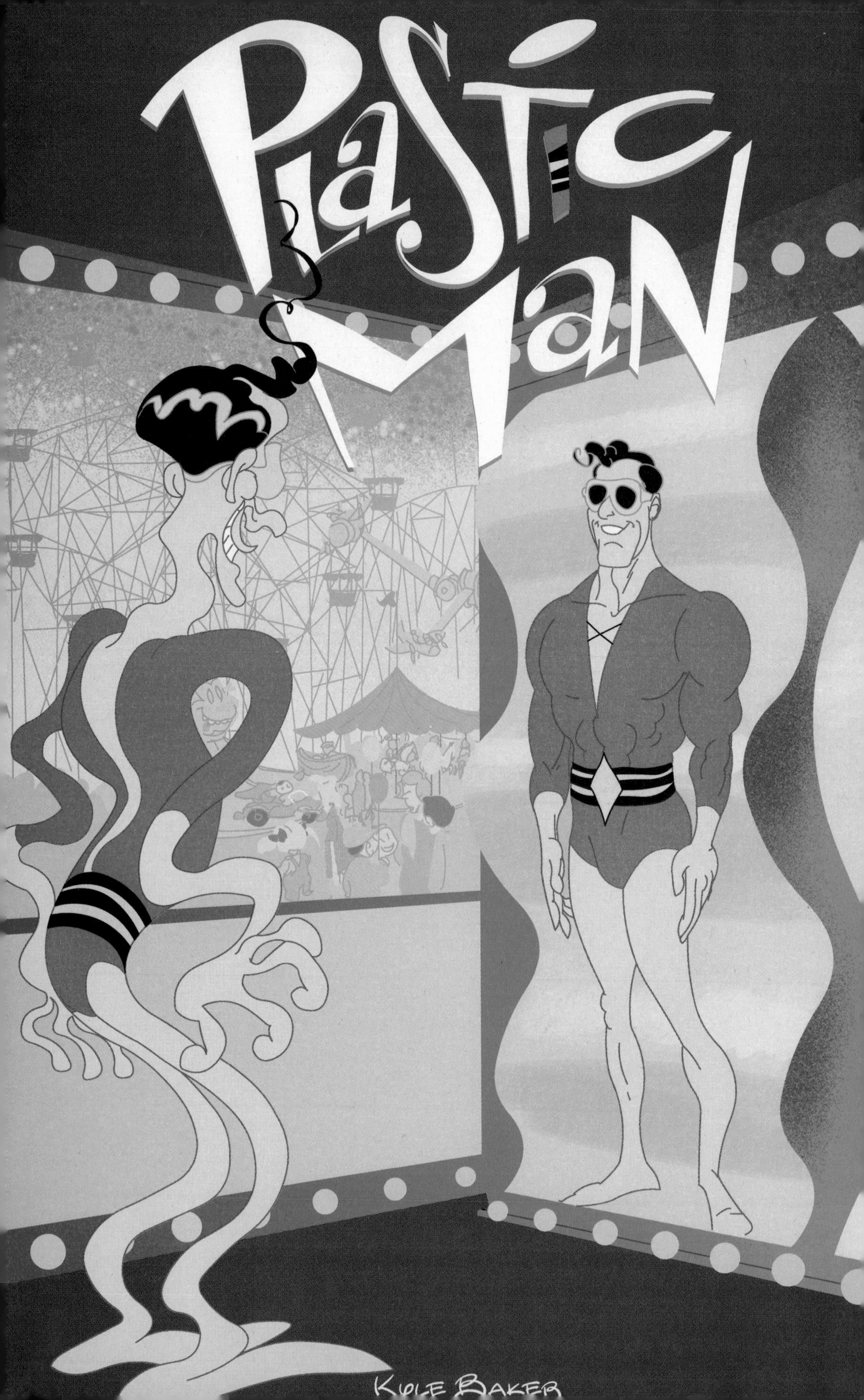
Plastic Man
Kyle Baker

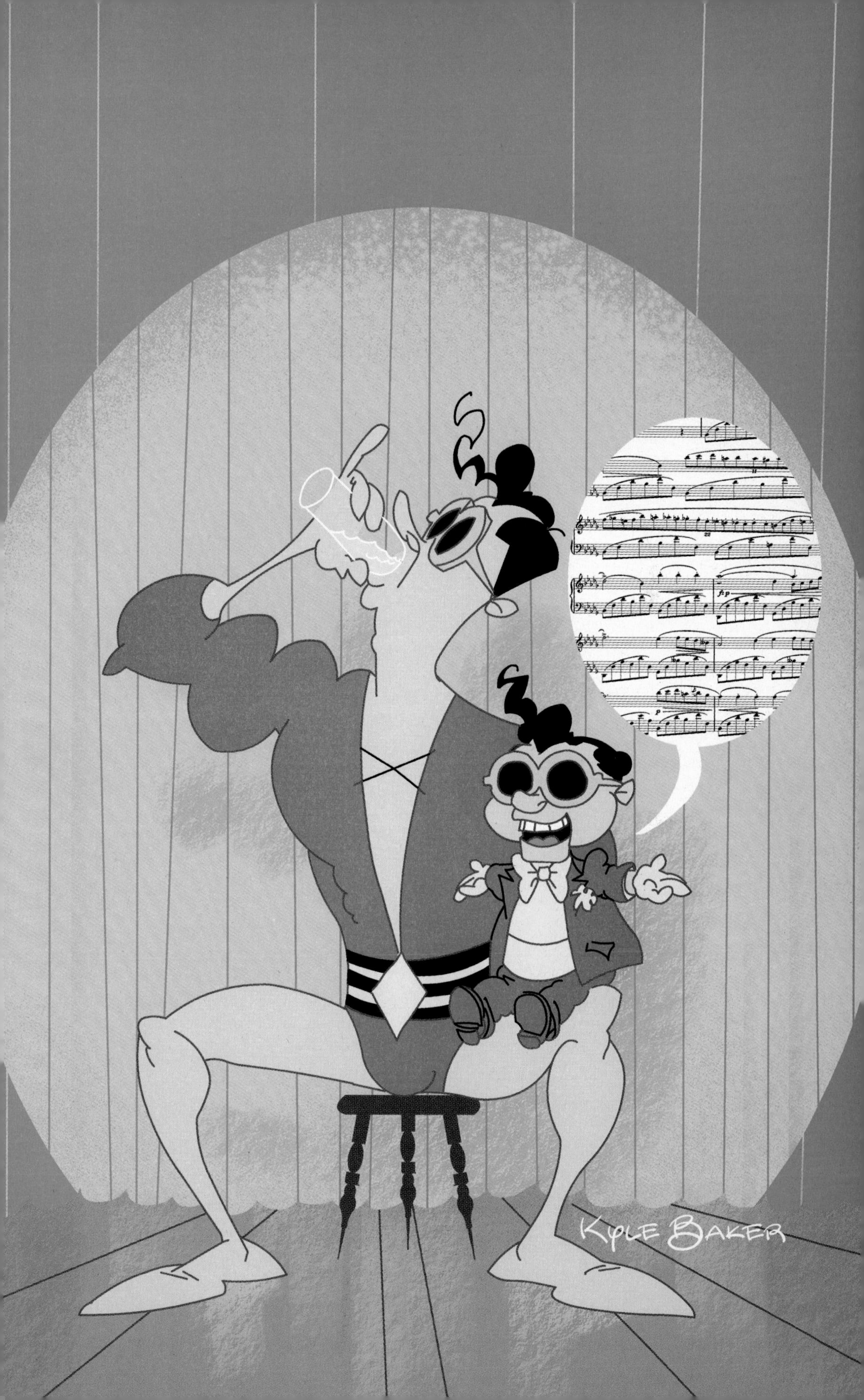
KYLE BAKER

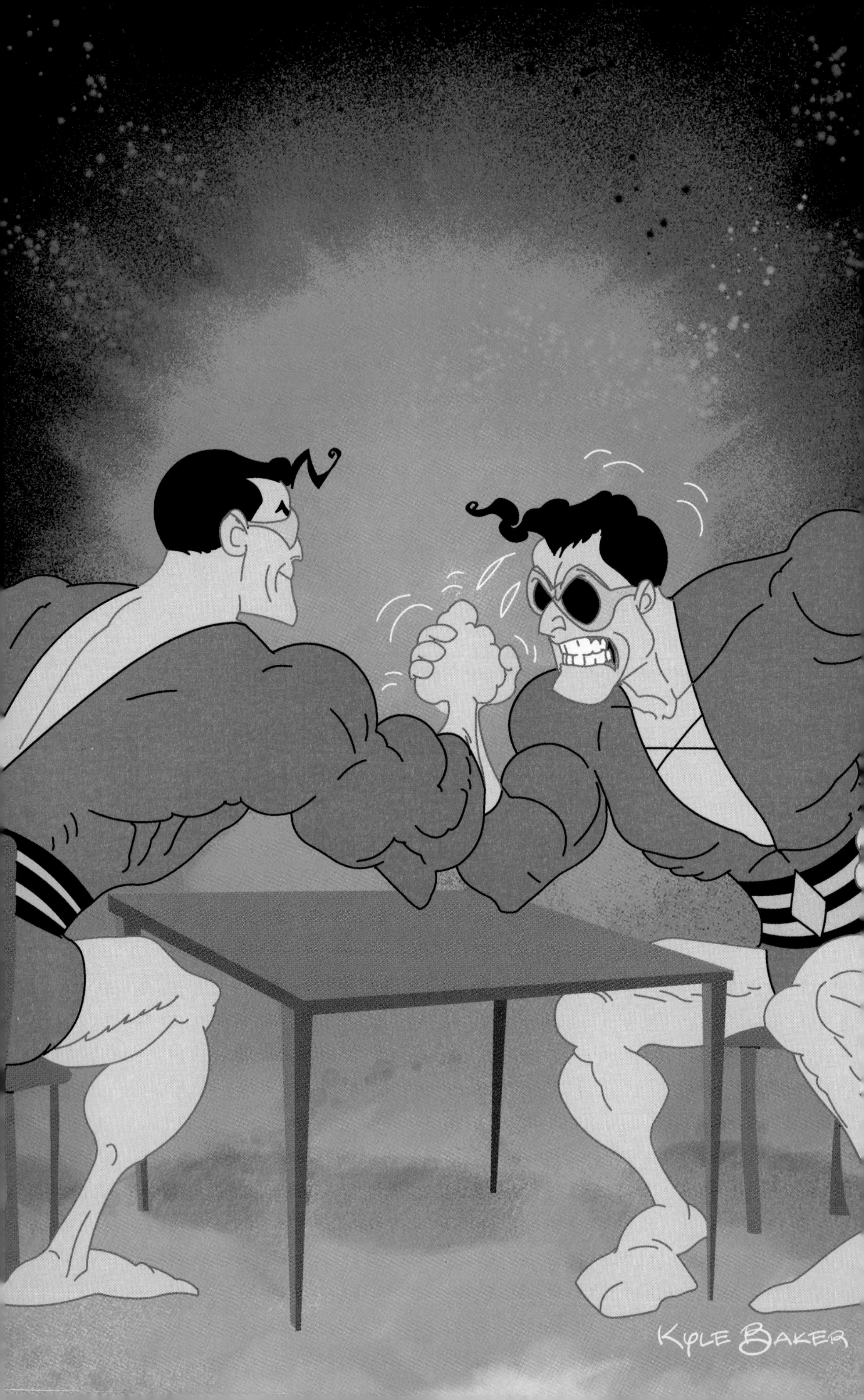
KYLE BAKER

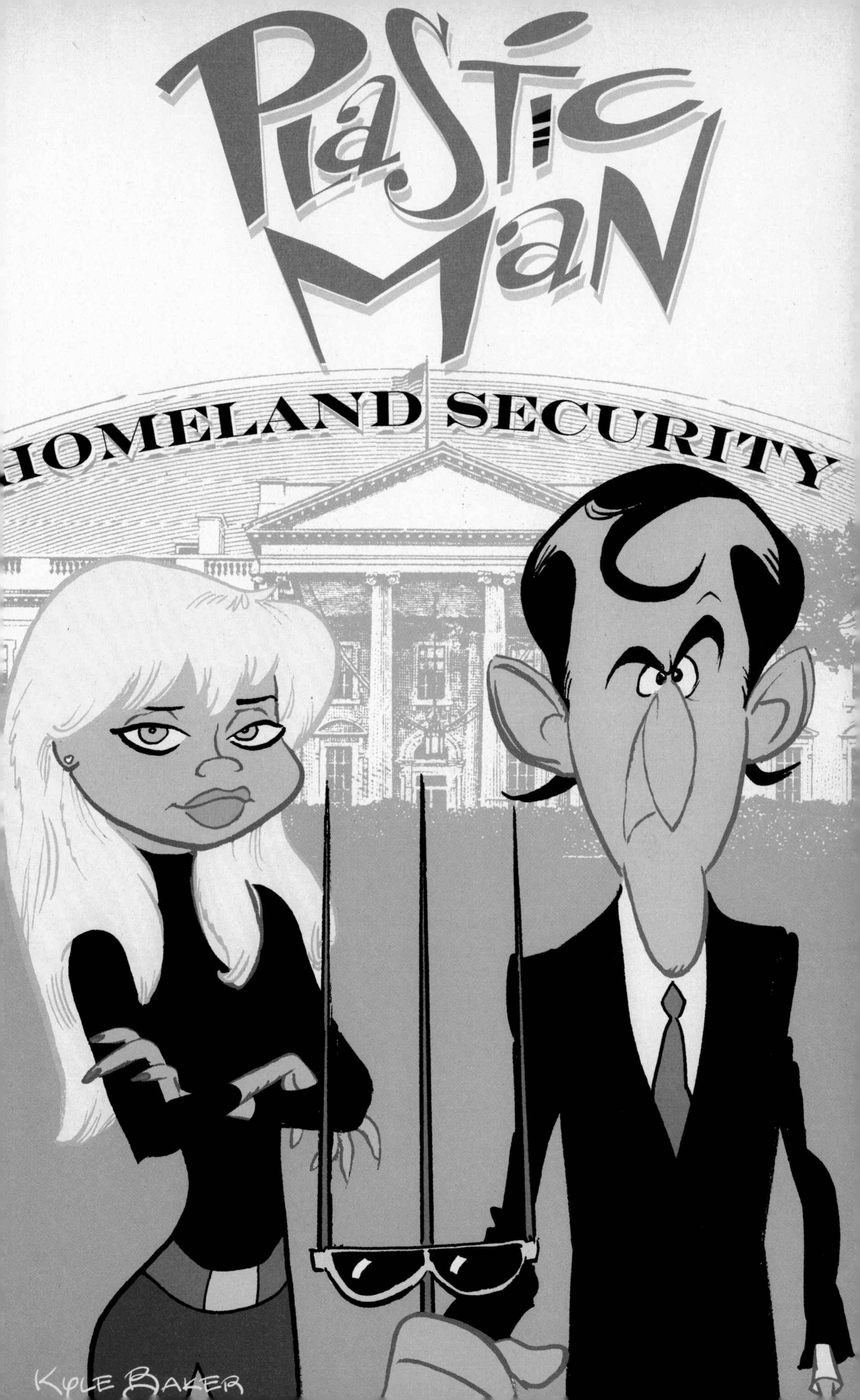

Plastic Man
HOMELAND SECURITY
KYLE BAKER

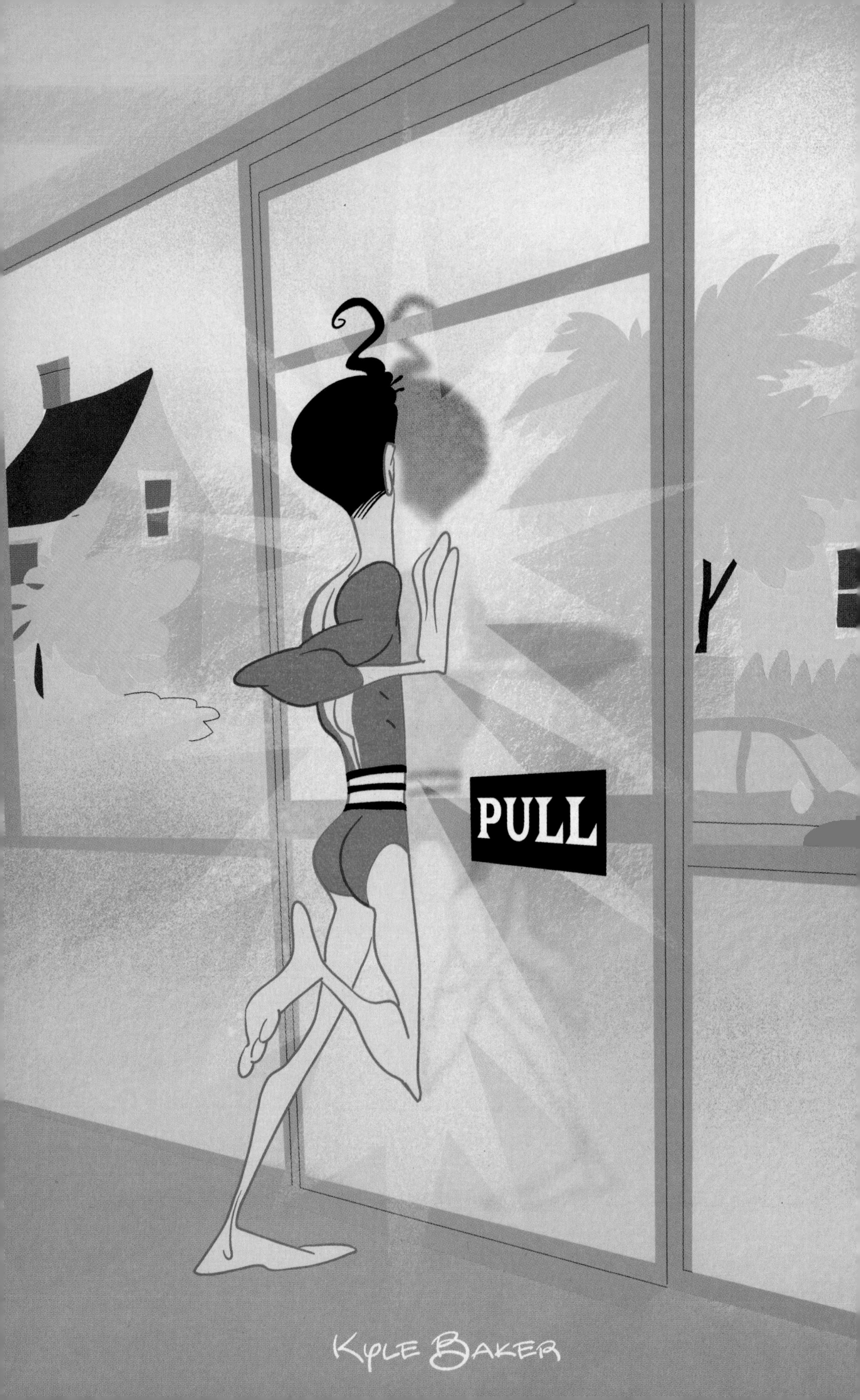
PULL
KYLE BAKER

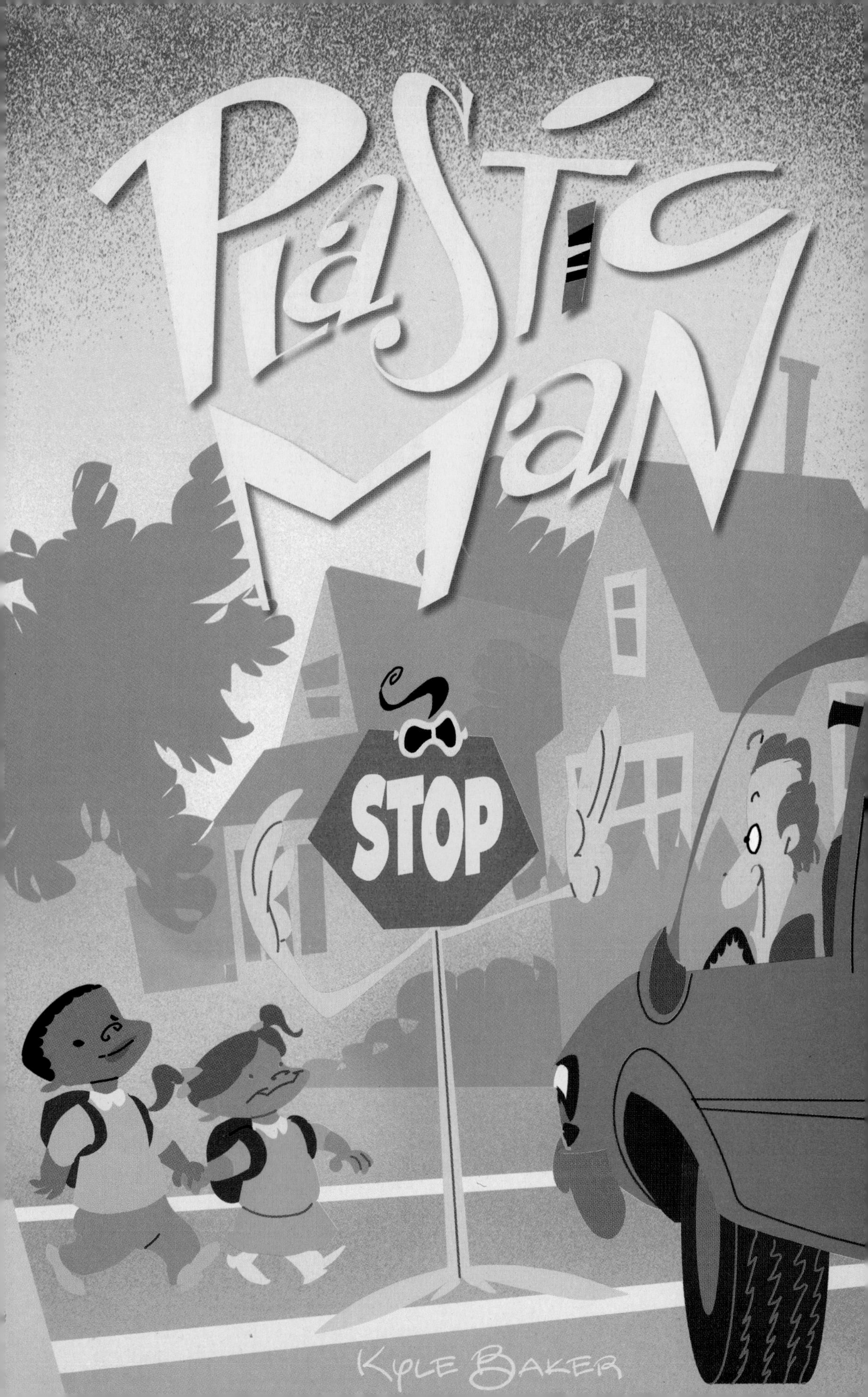
Plastic Man
STOP
Kyle Baker

THE STARS OF THE DC UNIVERSE
CAN ALSO BE FOUND IN THESE BOOKS:

ACROSS THE UNIVERSE:
THE DC UNIVERSE STORIES
OF ALAN MOORE
A. Moore/D. Gibbons/various

BATGIRL: YEAR ONE
S. Beatty/C. Dixon/M. Martin/
J. Lopez

BATMAN/SUPERMAN/
WONDER WOMAN: TRINITY
M. Wagner

BATMAN BLACK AND WHITE
Vols. 1-2
Various

BATMAN: HUSH Vols. 1-2
J. Loeb/J. Lee/S. Williams

BATMAN: YEAR ONE
F. Miller/D. Mazzuchelli

BIRDS OF PREY
C. Dixon/G. Simone/G. Land/
E. Benes/various
    BIRDS OF PREY
    OLD FRIENDS, NEW ENEMIES
    OF LIKE MINDS
    SENSEI AND STUDENT

BIZARRO COMICS
various

BIZARRO WORLD
various

CRISIS ON INFINITE EARTHS
M. Wolfman/G. Pérez/J. Ordway/
various

CRISIS ON MULTIPLE EARTHS
Vols. 1-3
G. Fox/D. O'Neil/L. Wein/
M. Sekowsky/D. Dillin/various

FALLEN ANGEL
(SUGGESTED FOR MATURE READERS)
P. David/D. Lopez/F. Blanco

THE FINAL NIGHT
K. Kesel/S. Immonen/J. Marzan/
various

THE FLASH
M. Waid/G. Johns/G. Larocque/
S. Kollins/various
    BORN TO RUN
    THE RETURN OF BARRY ALLEN
    TERMINAL VELOCITY
    DEAD HEAT
    RACE AGAINST TIME
    BLOOD WILL RUN
    ROGUES
    CROSSFIRE
    BLITZ
    IGNITION

FORMERLY KNOWN AS THE
JUSTICE LEAGUE
K. Giffen/J.M. DeMatteis/
K. Maguire/J. Rubinstein

GOTHAM CENTRAL
E. Brubaker/G. Rucka/M. Lark
Vol. 1: IN THE LINE OF DUTY

GREEN ARROW
K. Smith/B. Meltzer/J. Winick/
P. Hester/A. Parks
Vol. 1: QUIVER
Vol. 2: SOUNDS OF SILENCE
Vol. 3: ARCHER'S QUEST
Vol. 4: STRAIGHT SHOOTER
Vol. 5: CITY WALLS

GREEN LANTERN/GREEN ARROW
Vols. 1-2
D. O'Neil/N. Adams/various

GREEN LANTERN
J. Winick/G. Jones/R. Marz/
D. Banks/M.D. Bright/
D. Eaglesham/various
    EMERALD DAWN
    EMERALD DAWN II
    THE ROAD BACK
    EMERALD TWILIGHT/
    A NEW DAWN
    BAPTISM OF FIRE
    EMERALD ALLIES
    EMERALD KNIGHTS
    NEW JOURNEY, OLD PATH
    THE POWER OF ION
    BROTHER'S KEEPER
    PASSING THE TORCH

GREEN LANTERN: LEGACY —
THE LAST WILL AND TESTAMENT
OF HAL JORDAN
J. Kelly/B. Anderson/B. Sienkiewicz

GREEN LANTERN: WILLWORLD
J.M. DeMatteis/S. Fisher

HARD TIME: 50 TO LIFE
S. Gerber/B. Hurtt

HAWKMAN
G. Johns/J. Robinson/R. Morales/
M. Bair/various
Vol. 1: ENDLESS FLIGHT
Vol. 2: ALLIES AND ENEMIES

HISTORY OF THE DC UNIVERSE
M. Wolfman/G. Pérez/K. Kesel

JACK KIRBY'S FOURTH WORLD
Jack Kirby/various
    FOREVER PEOPLE
    FOURTH WORLD
    NEW GODS
    MISTER MIRACLE

JIMMY OLSEN ADVENTURES BY
JACK KIRBY Vols. 1-2
J. Kirby/V. Colletta/M, Royer

JLA
G. Morrison/M. Waid/J. Kelly/
J. Byrne/C. Claremont/H. Porter/
B. Hitch/D. Mahnke/J. Ordway/
various
Vol. 1: NEW WORLD ORDER
Vol. 2: AMERICAN DREAMS
Vol. 3: ROCK OF AGES
Vol. 4: STRENGTH IN NUMBERS
Vol. 5: JUSTICE FOR ALL
Vol. 6: WORLD WAR III
Vol. 7: TOWER OF BABEL
Vol. 8: DIVIDED WE FALL
Vol. 9: TERROR INCOGNITA
VolL. 10: GOLDEN PERFECT
Vol. 11: THE OBSIDIAN AGE
    BOOK ONE
Vol. 12: THE OBSIDIAN AGE
    BOOK TWO
Vol. 13: RULES OF ENGAGEMENT
Vol. 14: TRIAL BY FIRE
Vol. 15: THE TENTH CIRCLE
Vol. 16: PAIN OF THE GODS

JLA: EARTH 2
G. Morrison/F. Quitely

JLA/JSA: VIRTUE & VICE
D. Goyer/G. Johns/C. Pacheco/
J Meriño

JLA: ONE MILLION
G. Morrison/V. Semeiks/P. Rollins/
various

JLA/TITANS: THE TECHNIS
IMPERATIVE
D. Grayson/P. Jimenez/P. Pelletier/
various

JLA: WORLD WITHOUT
GROWN-UPS
T. Dezago/T. Nauck/H. Ramos/
M. McKone/various

JLA: YEAR ONE
M. Waid/B. Augustyn/B. Kitson/
various

JUSTICE LEAGUE:
A MIDSUMMER'S NIGHTMARE
M. Waid/F. Nicieza/J. Johnson/
D. Robertson/various

JUSTICE LEAGUE: A NEW
BEGINNING
K. Giffen/J.M. DeMatteis/
K. Maguire/various

JUSTICE LEAGUE OF AMERICA:
THE NAIL
JUSTICE LEAGUE OF AMERICA:
ANOTHER NAIL
Alan Davis/Mark Farmer

JSA
G. Johns/J. Robinson/D. Goyer/
S. Sadowski/R. Morales/L. Kirk/
various
Vol. 1: JUSTICE BE DONE
Vol. 2: DARKNESS FALLS
Vol. 3: THE RETURN OF
    HAWKMAN
Vol. 4: FAIR PLAY
Vol. 5: STEALING THUNDER
Vol. 6: SAVAGE TIMES
Vol. 7: PRINCES OF DARKNESS

JSA: ALL STARS
D. Goyer/G. Johns/S. Velluto/
various

JSA: THE GOLDEN AGE
J. Robinson/P. Smith

JSA: THE LIBERTY FILES
D. Jolley/T. Harris/various

THE JUSTICE SOCIETY RETURNS
J. Robinson/D. Goyer/various

THE KINGDOM
M. Waid/various

KINGDOM COME
M. Waid/A. Ross

LEGENDS: THE COLLECTED
EDITION
J. Ostrander/L. Wein/J. Byrne/
K. Kesel

THE LEGION: FOUNDATIONS
D. Abnett/A. Lanning/T. Harris/
T. Batista/various

MAJESTIC: STRANGE NEW
VISITOR
D. Abnett/A. Lanning/K. Kerschl

THE NEW TEEN TITANS
M. Wolfman/G. Pérez/D. Giordano/
R. Tanghal
    THE JUDAS CONTRACT
    THE TERROR OF TRIGON

OUTSIDERS
J. Winick/T. Raney/Chriscross/
various
Vol. 1: LOOKING FOR TROUBLE
Vol. 2: SUM OF ALL EVIL

PLASTIC MAN: ON THE LAM
K. Baker

THE POWER OF SHAZAM!
J. Ordway

RONIN
F. Miller

STARMAN
J. Robinson/T. Harris/P. Snejbjerg/
W. Grawbadger/various
    SINS OF THE FATHER
    NIGHT AND DAY
    INFERNAL DEVICES
    TO REACH THE STARS
    A STARRY KNIGHT
    STARS MY DESTINATION
    GRAND GUIGNOL
    SONS OF THE FATHER

SUPERGIRL: MANY HAPPY
RETURNS
P. David/E. Benes/A. Lei

SUPERMAN/BATMAN
J. Loeb/E. McGuinness/D. Vines/
M. Turner/P. Steigerwald
Vol. 1: PUBLIC ENEMIES
Vol. 2: SUPERGIRL

SUPERMAN FOR ALL SEASONS
J. Loeb/T. Sale

SUPERMAN: BIRTHRIGHT
M. Waid/L. Yu/G. Alanguilan

SUPERMAN: GODFALL
M. Turner/J. Kelly/T. Caldwell/
P. Steigerwald

SUPERMAN: RED SON
M. Millar/D. Johnson/
K. Plunkett/various

SUPERMAN: UNCONVENTIONAL
WARFARE
G. Rucka/I. Reis/various

TEEN TITANS
G. Johns/M. McKone/T. Grummett
Vol. 1: A KID'S GAME
Vol. 2: FAMILY LOST

UNDERWORLD UNLEASHED
M. Waid/H. Porter/P. Jimenez/
various

WATCHMEN
A. Moore/D. Gibbons

WONDER WOMAN (early years)
G. Pérez/L. Wein/B. Patterson
Vol. 1: GODS AND MORTALS
Vol. 2: CHALLENGE OF THE GODS

WONDER WOMAN
G. Rucka/P. Jimenez/J. Byrne/
W.M. Loebs/D. Johnson/
M. Deodato/various
    THE CONTEST
    SECOND GENESIS
    LIFELINES
    PARADISE LOST
    PARADISE FOUND
    DOWN TO EARTH
    BITTER RIVALS

WONDER WOMAN: THE HIKETEIA
G. Rucka/J.G. Jones/
W. Grawbadger

ZERO HOUR: CRISIS IN TIME
D. Jurgens/J. Ordway/various

TO FIND MORE COLLECTED EDITIONS AND MONTHLY COMIC BOOKS FROM DC COMICS,
CALL 1-888-COMIC BOOK FOR THE NEAREST COMICS SHOP OR GO TO YOUR LOCAL BOOK STORE.

DATE DUE

11/20/09			

FOLLETT